Smasher!

Smasher!

THE LIFE OF SID JAMES

by Robert Ross

BOOKS

Nighty Night
In memory of Jack Douglas 'Jackson':
This one is for you, my friend.

First published in Great Britain in 2009 by
JR Books, 10 Greenland Street, London NW1 0ND
www.jrbooks.com

Paperback edition first published in 2012 by JR Books

A catalogue record for this book is available from the British Library.

ISBN 978-1-90753-216-0

1 3 5 7 9 10 8 6 4 2

Typeset by SX Composing DTP, Rayleigh, Essex

Printed and bound by CPI Group (UK) Ltd, Croydon, CR0 4YY

Contents

Acknowledgements

BEST OF FRIENDS

After a hilarious chat with Bernard Cribbins, in connection with this book, I thanked the friend and national treasure for his memories. 'My pleasure, Robert,' he replied, 'it's been lovely to remember Sid like that.' It is a thought echoed time and time again over the years when, in the company of someone who had encountered Sid, I relentlessly and doggedly steered the conversation round to the great man.

It is no surprise to many people to discover that Sid James is my all-time favourite actor. He's also among my all-time favourite people although, alas, I never met him. He is a role model. And a hero. The most endearing of all heroes: one with feet of clay and the spirit of the common man forever coursing through his veins.

For shared stories of Sid represented in this affectionate biography, I wholeheartedly thank: Robin Askwith, Roy Ward Baker, Amanda Barrie, Kitty Black, Roy Castle OBE, Diana Coupland, Bernard Cribbins, Jim Dale MBE, Vera Day, Clive Doig, Angela Douglas, Jack Douglas, Shirley Eaton, Myfanwy Evans, Harry Fowler MBE, Liz Fraser, Hugh Futcher, Ray Galton OBE, Sally Geeson, Fred Griffiths, Carol Hawkins, Geoffrey Hutchings, Anthony Jackson, Valerie James, Dilys Laye, Olga Lowe, Keith Marsh, Bill Maynard, Norman Mitchell,

SMASHER!

Denis Norden, Milo O'Shea, Lilly Payne, Doctor Saul Pelle, Lance Percival, Vince Powell, Wendy Richard MBE, Peter Rogers, Patsy Rowlands, Francis Searle, Alan Simpson OBE, Penny Spencer, Victor Spinetti, Julie Stevens, William G. Stewart, Gerald Thomas, June Whitfield CBE and Barbara Windsor MBE.

Also, sincere thanks to the British Film Institute, both the library and, in particular, Janet Moat and the girls of the Special Materials. Rachel Lawson and Louise North at the BBC Written Archive Centre, Caversham Park, Reading. Melanie Clark for being both my Valerie and my Barbara, and Stephanie Payne for her kind words and support. As usual, Alan Coles and Henry Holland for keeping me grounded, confident and ever so slightly and delightfully unsteady in various Soho public houses. And, last but by no means least, my agent Marcella Edwards at Peters Fraser and Dunlop.

Prologue

MY HERO

Sid James was a paradox. He was the world's best-loved cockney, but in reality he was born miles from the sound of Bow Bells. Thousands of miles, in fact: in Johannesburg, South Africa.

He was one of the most recognisable comedians of his day but he never told a joke. So inept was he, that he was terrified of fellow performers straying from the script. He just couldn't ad-lib.

He was the insecure, wood-touching gambler. The Jewish chancer who felt at home in the East End and became the embodiment of West End confidence and even found himself in the ultimate celebration of British Christianity, the Millennium Dome.

He was also a lover of the fairer sex and would tirelessly pursue the latest dolly bird cast in a film, stage show or television programme he was starring in, but he was also a devoted family man who doted on his Buckinghamshire domesticity.

More than anything else, Sid remained one of the lads, with the dirtiest laugh in film history and a face etched with the joint pleasures of whisky and sex. Well, where he comes from they can't get soda! That's actually a line from *Carry On Again, Doctor*, but it sums up Sid's public persona to perfection.

He was as surprised by his successful career as every casting director was. 'I didn't think I stood much chance with a mug like mine,' he once admitted. 'A few thousand cases of gin, some boxing, late nights in my youth, hundreds of gee-gees and worry lines left by the taxman.' But that was the secret of his success.

In 1973, at the age of 60, Sid was still Britain's favourite funny man on the big screen. While Roger Moore was inheriting the mantle of James Bond, and Paul Newman and Robert Redford were leaping off a rugged cliff edge, Sid James could still hold his own.

'Nobody would believe me,' says Carry On co-star Jack Douglas, 'but Sid was a sex symbol. Hundreds of young girls would hang about outside the Victoria Palace when we came out after a performance of *Carry On London!*. They didn't want to know me. All these young girls were shouting out for Sid. They loved him!'

Here was a drinker, a gambler and a womaniser. The perfect role model for the red-blooded male. And here was a dapper, gentlemanly star that tickled the girls in just the right place. Sid James was a cliché. Men wanted to be like him, ladies wanted to know him: either as a father figure or a sugar daddy.

Reassuringly, Sid's big film release for his 60th birthday was *Carry On Girls*. He was the wrinkly romantic surrounded by the brightest dolly birds in Britain; perfectly at home on location on and around Brighton beach. The situation couldn't have been more ideal.

Sid seemed to have the spirit of the seaside within his soul. He was the embodiment of the carefree holidaymaker who would happily blow a year's savings on two weeks of candyfloss, kiss-me-quick hats and fish 'n' chips straight from the newspaper. And he had become a valuable part of the British holiday, playing Great Yarmouth, Blackpool, Torquay and Bournemouth. Peddling easy-going, trouser-dropping, 'more-tea-vicar' farce to a grateful nation.

In those heady, harmless days you could ride on the go-karts, snog behind the bandstand *and* see Sid James live on stage . . . all on the same day!

In *Carry On Girls* there is something life affirming about the sight of Sid. Dressed in a Cecil Gee three-piece suit, he exudes confidence and worldly knowledge. His physique is that of the dancer and of the boxer he had been in his youth. The strain of a lifetime of hard-working, hard-living and the aftermath of a heart attack have clearly taken their toll. But the imperishable zest of Sid James seems undimmed. He is heading towards his pension at his own pace. The hair is slightly greyed but the face is alight with boyish mischief. The eyes twinkle with myriad experience and the fun of getting away with it. He may end the film with an empty back pocket but he's energetically clutching the prize that really matters to him: Barbara Windsor.

'Sid was a smasher,' recalls his closest of Carry On colleagues. 'I was feeling about a hundred-years-old when we made *Carry On Girls*. Here was I, fast approaching forty, and still being expected to play the giggling, boob-flashing Barbara of ten years ago! I certainly didn't feel like an object of lust during that film, I can tell you. There were all these lovely girls. Seventeen and eighteen-years-old. We were all dressed in bikinis and my figure next to them was not a pretty sight. But I remember Sid telling me: "You are the only one the audience will be looking at. You have star quality!" That meant a lot.'

And Sid would know all about star quality.

He was still the uncrowned king of situation comedy. Benny Hill may have been King Leer but Sid could claim to rule Thames Television with a fist of comic iron.

Sid's television personality was more mellow, albeit slightly. He still had an eye for the ladies but he was reassuringly domesticated as the father figure of *Bless This House*. It was the easy-going Sid of old, but now he was burdened with more mundane concerns like a mortgage and bridging the generation gap with his teenage offspring. Naturally, as often as not, this was winningly done with a resigned sigh, a head-in-hands attitude and a self-indulgent pint down the Hare and Hounds. Yes, Sid James knew all about star quality.

He was fearless. Nothing was too much for the casual charm of the 60-year-old Sid. Even a stab at pop stardom! His efforts certainly were not about to give Marc Bolan or David Bowie or the Sweet any sleepless nights. Even the Goodies were safe! But 'Our House', the single Sid released in 1973, still stands up as a hilarious, often moving, faded snapshot from a London fast disappearing, even then.

In its upbeat and joyous reflection on a tumbledown home that is soon to be put to the sword by heartless developers, 'Our House' is steeped in the ethos of Dickens and Hogarth, Steptoe and Son and Pete 'n' Dud. In the slightly off-tune, hardly even sung, belting of the lyrics, Sid channels the theatrical traditions of Dan Leno and Max Miller. A working-class delight in performing for a working-class audience. The gruff, all-enveloping warmth of Sid's performance is marinated in the combined fragrance of sour beer, cockles and jellied eels. He is the comic voice of the little man standing by his meagre achievements and ramshackle abode. The result of a lifetime of hard graft and low pay. It's simply why the little man loved him and continues so to do.

Sid had been part of the British way of life for a quarter of a century. On stage, screen or radio he had always been reassuringly the same. His prolific run of bit parts and crafty cockneys in British post-war cinema may have dwindled to a trickle of star turns in an unspoken but accepted pledge of exclusivity to Carry On director Gerald Thomas. His life-changing signature role partnership with Tony Hancock may have been long gone but it was continually repeated and discussed half a decade after Sid's friend and colleague had taken his own life. And Sid himself may have faced the inevitable and thrown himself into a relentless regurgitation of the 'comic lad' persona for delighted packed houses in South Africa and Australia and New Zealand. The play was *The Mating*

Season, the latest in a line of farces scripted for him by Sam Cree. But the play was definitely not the thing. The audiences wanted to see Sid James. The crafty cockney geezer. Sid James – in the flesh. Somehow in that summer of 1973 he seemed indestructible.

1

Up the Elephant and Round the Castle

id James was born on Christmas Day, 1946. He was 33-years-old. On that fateful day, when the nation who would take Sid into their collective hearts were celebrating with plum duff and cracker pulling, an out-of-work actor desperate to act docked at Southampton in pursuit of a career that would make him, if not rich, then extremely comfortably well-off. He would spend the rest of his life reinventing and reshaping key factors from his formative years in South Africa. As with the Wild, Wild West, when faced with the truth or the legend – concerning Sid it is always more interesting to publish the legend.

Once he had established himself as every casting director's first choice for a dodgy-dealing wheeler-dealer on film and television, Sid frequently explained that he had arrived in England without a game plan. 'I honestly didn't want a job immediately,' he said. 'I wanted to look around for a bit.' Financial necessity determined that, in reality, money was the only thing on his mind. The facts were these: he had two ladies he had left behind him. An ex-wife, Toots, and a daughter, Elizabeth. He had two ladies in tow. His second wife, Meg, and their soon-to-be-born daughter, Reina. He had little left from his subsidiary. And a rented room in Queen's Gate Mews would not pay for itself.

He was unusually frank when speaking to the *Evening Standard* in 1959: 'When I blew my Service gratuity on a one-way ticket from South Africa to Britain in 1946 I was a nobody. All I had was a burning ambition to make money, and a face that I thought would be a decided disadvantage in the pursuit of that ambition.' He was so ambitious, in fact, that while his taste buds were still tingling from turkey feet and chips he set about finding gainful employment. Less than 24 hours after settling into that small but beautifully formed flat opposite the Queens Arms pub in SW7, Sid put pen to paper to two producers prominent in radio drama for the British Broadcasting Corporation: Martyn Webster and Peter Richmond.

In two separate, exactly duplicated handwritten notes, Sid set out his acting stall: 'Forgive me for writing to you like this, but it seems the simplest method of making myself known to you,' he started. 'I have just arrived from South Africa, where for a number of years I've done a great deal of broadcasting.'

Sid had indeed made an early mark in radio in his home town of Johannesburg. It was all the more ironical that, having established himself as the erudite and ever-reliable stooge of Clown Prince Tony Hancock in *Hancock's Half Hour*, he would profess himself 'a very bad radio actor'. In fact, in South Africa, he had equipped himself well in a direct transfer of a stage success, *Double Error*, and, from just before the outbreak of war, several notable dramas and light entertainment appearances for the South African Broadcasting Corporation. He proved particularly good at children's programming, often partnering future Hancock cohort, Moria Lister.

In those earnest, but borderline desperate missives scrawled out on that Boxing Day of 1946, it was serious drama that appealed to the actor. 'I specialise in dialects,' Sid explained, 'particularly American and cockney and do "tough stuff" as well as comedy.'

Interestingly, although American characterisation and 'tough stuff' would loom frequently in his subsequent career, it was the cockney accent and a leaning towards comedy that would make him a national figure.

That essence of instant cockney that hung about Sid like a trenchcoat, not yet a day in Britain, set him both apart and as part of the crowd of dependable, jobbing character actors he would join forces with.

As one of Sid's oldest and closest friends, Harry Fowler, remembers: 'He was larger than life. Exuberance personified. You can't pick your family but you can pick your friends and Sid would be my number one choice every time. The thing that really appealed to me about him was that he had this in-built working class humour. He had become a cockney practically overnight. It was an instant thing. He arrived in Britain and he was the Jewish fellow out of the East End. No one questioned it again. With Sid it was a case of the cap fitted without him having to wear it!'

He may have, once and for all, embraced the cockney idiom as his way of life but Sid the actor was still very much rooted in the ways of South Africa. And, even more importantly, intensely proud of the versatile career he had enjoyed there.

In the BBC letters of Boxing Day, 1946, he continued: 'Prior to leaving South Africa I played lead for Gwen Ffrangcon-Davies in Emlyn Williams' *Wind of Heaven*. Other experience includes George in *Of Mice and Men*, Major Joppolo in *Bell for Adano* and George Pepper in Coward's *Red Peppers*. I only mention these few to give you an idea of my type of work.'

This, indeed, was merely a handful of the vast and varied work he had enjoyed in his homeland but it is meritorious in its variety. There was emotional drama, light entertainment and human melodrama in the roles in which the actor was justly proud.

However, none were of more interest than that of George in John Steinbeck's *Of Mice and Men*. This was not a performance of horrid caricature but a fully developed portrait of despair.

Adopting a slight stoop as he scurried onstage, Sid also employed a subtle, slaughtered quality for his vocal delivery. It was a whine that spoke of hardship and helplessness. And it suited his performance of a pathetic individual perfectly.

In effect a crippling two-hander with Sydney Wilkin as the mentally damaged Lennie, the play ran for just one week in the April of 1940 but it gave Sid his first major success and, arguably, the best reviews of his career. 'It was the most powerful piece of acting Johannesburg has witnessed in a long time,' gushed one critic.

The other roles Sid selected to impress his BBC producer targets were from after his wartime experience, and, both the Williams and Coward credits, were under the aforementioned watchful auspices of the formidable Ffrancogn-Davies. Recognised as one of the great Shakespearean actresses since the early 1920s, it was Ffrancogn-Davies who had given Sid a reference for the celebrated Welsh actor and playwright Emlyn Williams. She hoped Williams would help Sid on his arrival in Britain. 'I went and saw him as soon as I got here,' Sid remembered during the recording of his *Desert Island Discs* in 1960. 'I must say he tried very hard to help me,' he diplomatically concluded. Sid did not expect blanket assistance. He hoped his work would speak for itself.

Indeed, the South African tour for Ffrancogn-Davies was the culmination of Sid's theatrical experience before arriving in Britain. It was the setting of the sun before the new dawn in the country he would forever afterwards call home. But his reputation was as an actor of method; a performer who could twist and bend and curve his body into grotesque characters for a spellbinding impact onstage, as in *Of Mice and Men*. That quality would be eroded completely. It had, after all, always been something he had had to work at rather than something that had come naturally to him.

In his heart and soul, from the top of his head to the tips of his toes, Sid was a variety performer. He hadn't quite been born in a trunk but it was the next best thing. And it was his earliest memory that he would willingly trawl out for interviewers for the rest of his life. Importantly it was a brief backstage memory that remained largely unchanged in each retelling. His parents, the vaudeville team of James and Selma, 'took me everywhere with them. I mean, almost as soon as I was born, as soon as mother was able to get up and about they were on tour again. My mother used to tell me that in India – that was just after I was born – she would have me in a skip. You know, one of those prop baskets. A costume basket right in the wings. They would be doing their song and dance act, and I used to start bawling like a calf. My mother used to say it was quite horrible. They said it was shocking. I sounded like a Bull Moose or something! And she'd just nip off into the wings quickly, give me a drop of milk, quieten me down and go back and finish the number.'

Often, during the retelling of this anecdote, Sid would insist that the number his mother was performing was 'Pretty Baby' and the storyteller would amuse the listener with a few seconds of buck and wing.

The song and dance act of his parents toured all over the world and, as soon as he was on the scene, Sid was with them. Every step of the way: 'India, Australia, all over South Africa of course, and Rhodesia.' He would also get his first taste of fame during these fledgling years. 'My father used to take me out on to the stage and show me to the public,' he recalled. 'I don't really remember that, of course, but I clearly remember round about four or five years old going on and sprinkling the sugar on the stage for them and their sand routine. And then I was dancing with them from about four-and-a-half or five.'

Sid even became a proficient musician. 'I taught myself a few things,' he remembered. 'Tenor sax, alto sax, clarinet, piano. But I didn't keep it up. I wish I had.'

The break-up of the act, the break-up of the marriage and the essential break-up of Sid's fledgling vaudeville career because of his schooling, kept him away from the greasepaint and the limelight for several years. But the pull of the music hall was too strong to resist. And despite his huge popularity in dramatic fare, it was variety where Sid's heart really lay.

At the age of 16, Sid had staged a production of *Cinderella* for the friends and family in his Johannesburg neighbourhood. Typically, he cast himself as Prince Charming. And in 1940, with several years experience with the Johannesburg Repertory Company behind him, he produced and directed a charity variety performance, *Hoopla*. Held at the Jewish Guild Memorial Hall it displayed Sid's skill for comedy and soft-shoe hoofing.

Moreover, in sharp contrast to his dramatic power in Steinbeck, during the war years he was more likely to sport the flamboyant garb of the near-the-knuckle comedian and sing rousing songs for beleaguered troops.

In March 1941, Sid joined an anti-tank regiment. 'I was in that for a couple of years. And then South Africa started up [the Defence Force] Entertainment Unit. Rather on the lines of ENSA [Entertainments National Service Entertainment] here, but fully military. You only got military pay and you came under complete military discipline. Then I was transferred to that and then finally I was producing shows for that unit.'

The unit, The Amuseliers, was quickly nicknamed the Crazy Gang but Sid's key inspiration for these performances was the Cheeky Chappie himself, Max Miller: front-cloth comedian par excellence, the Pure Gold of the Music Hall and, proudly considered, the naughtiest man in Britain. If Max could get banned by the BBC for giving the working classes what they wanted then Sid could just as easily ruffle a few military authority feathers with his self-same mixture of blue jokes and salacious dance routines. The troops stationed alongside Sid in the Middle East loved it, of course. Dancing girls and dirty humour were just what they needed to, momentarily, take their mind of the conflict and bring them a sense of home. Inevitably the scripts were brutally shaven of their more risqué lines, only for Sid to reinstate them as soon as the unit was back on the road: 'The lads liked what we were doing. And the bigwigs that cut the material wouldn't be out on the front line in any case. So back the jokes went!'

Those jokes were also to serve him very well in Britain when he would become a mainstay of the London Hippodrome variety theatre. As early as April 1947, he was endearing himself to the nation in Ralph Marshall's riotous revue, *Get In*, at the Wood Green Empire. The show was subtitled 'A Pleasure Cruise of Laughter', and billed as 'The Greatest All Male Show'. Sid opened the nautical proceedings as the Petty Officer 'On the Quayside'. His contribution may have been somewhat limited, but he worked instinctively with Lawrie Owen and His Orchestra and created celebrated moments of low comedy.

More earthy variety greeted Sid when he returned to the London Hippodrome for the musical *High Button Shoes* for Jack Hylton in 1949. It was when Harry Fowler first met Sid. 'At that time he still had this slight South African lilt in his accent. He never quite lost it, if you listen carefully. But I think he must have lost a lot of the accent during his time in the services and, in particular, when he was part of The Amuseliers. All those good-natured, pale imitations of Max Miller must have really rubbed off on him! Still, he had this natural skill and natural likeability. I liked him the moment I met him. Sid was a real man's man. The Clark Gable of light entertainment. You know, people tend to forget that he was a soft-shoe shuffle dancer. And he had plenty of opportunity to show that off in *High Button Shoes*. Even though I was more interested in Alma Cogan and a young lady in the chorus by the name of Audrey Hepburn! Sid was a great performer and the ultimate lover of life. You could read the mischief in his eyes. There was a smoothness and cleanness to Sid. He was a class act all the way.'

And, undoubtedly, his debt to Max Miller was still being paid. For, although he was now not lifting the comedian's material completely, his carefree gait and working-class bluster, both on and off the stage, were clearly cut from Miller's floral cloth. Harry Fowler said, 'Put Sid and Max in the same bracket. They were very different performers, of course. Sid was an actor. Max was a comic. But the style. Their delivery. The very down-to-earth quality was the same. The main thing, of course, was the love from the audience that they both received. Some people can rise above mere popularity. You loved Max. And you loved Sid. Whatever they were doing.'

That unconditional love was key to Sid's success. And, indeed, in both Sid and Max's case, that same love could even win over the most hardened – 'more than my job's worth' – figures of authority.

There's the famous and heart-warming tale of Max and his determination to always get his last train home to Brighton. One night, faced with a particularly adoring audience, Max arrived at Victoria Station a good 10 minutes after the final train should have been chugging pass Clapham Junction. The guard, looking at his watch, smiled and said, 'You're very late tonight, Mr Miller.' Seeing the great comedian onto the train, he blew the whistle and let it depart. Now, that's not only star clout. That's devotion.

Sid had the exact same quality. A few weeks before Christmas in 1964 he was doing some shopping on Oxford Street. In those halcyon days traffic wardens would allow you 20 minutes to park outside a line of the country's most luxuriant department stores. Preoccupied with ideas of gifts for his wife and children, Sid caught note of the time. He was seconds away from being over his allotted time limit. Mildly annoyed with himself for getting caught up in the festive cheer and even more miffed at facing a guaranteed parking ticket, he hurriedly made his way back to his vehicle in the hope that the warden had other unfortunate motorists to penalise. Sid's heart sank when, four minutes late, he returned to his car and spotted a disconcerting piece of white paper under his windscreen wiper.

Snatching it in his hand he climbed into the car, sat down and unfolded it. But it wasn't a fine. On the back of an uncompleted parking ticket the warden had written: 'Don't do it again, Sid. Happy Christmas.' Sid commented: 'I was flabbergasted, especially when the warden appeared on the corner when I drove off and gave me a broad wink.'

Both Max and Sid were lionised as true cockneys. Admittedly, Brightonian Max was born a little closer to London than Sid was. But the pinpoint playing of that character was all that mattered. Intriguingly, in 1958 Sid had been cast as Educated Evans for producer Eric Fawcett's BBC television presentation of the fast-talking bookie and expert on horseflesh created by prolific crime writer, Edgar Wallace. It had been a signature role of Max Miller's, who had played him twice on film. Both Sid and Max were fundamentally of the East End. The horses. The greyhounds. The barrows. And the boxing. Both were heroes of the public. And both screamed out London Town.

Having used the lion's share of his £100 army gratuity to get to Britain, Sid had gleefully, for all intents and purposes, bought himself a national identity. As he fondly remembered, upon his demob, 'I came straight over here as soon as I could get here.'

'Sid was part of this huge South African clan of actors and writers and producers who came over after the war and settled in Britain,' explains Harry Fowler. 'Sid was all three of them: actor, writer and producer. And good at all of them. Particularly acting. His closest pal at that time was a young bloke by the name of Larry Skikne. Now, Larry had been creating these great army shows under the auspices of Sid. In fact Sid was instrumental in changing Larry's name. I think it was atop a number 47 bus as I recall Sid telling it! Larry would become very famous, very quickly, as Laurence Harvey.'

Considering Sid's almost constant presence in British films, it is perhaps surprising that he only worked with Harvey on screen once, in 'The Silent Enemy' (1958). But still, thanks to light comedy in *Three Men in a Boat* and gritty drama in *I Am a Camera* in the Britain of the mid-1950s, Harvey subsequently conquered Hollywood and Broadway.

Harry Fowler remembers: 'The other close friend that kept Sid close to his South African roots was a chap called Gordon Mollholland. His acting career quickly petered out and died while Sid and Larry went from strength to strength, simply by exploiting their own strengths. Ironically, both Sid and Larry died young in the nineteen seventies. Gordon, as far as I know, is still with us and successfully reinvented his career. He ultimately became the Head of South African Television.'

But whether at the top or the bottom, Sid's countrymen did – albeit for a short time – seem to dominate British light entertainment. Both conductor Harry Rabinowitz and dancer Olga Lowe would find success in Britain after gaining experience in Sid's Amuseliers shows. Indeed, Rabinowitz would conduct the music for the first couple of series of radio's *Hancock's Half Hour*. While another South African, Moira Lister, would act in the shows. There must have come a time in the mid-1950s when Sid felt that his home country had taken over Broadcasting House. And Sid was certainly the unquestioned Don.

Still, that was nearly 10 years after he had arrived in Britain. With no money and an impressive list of acting credentials behind him, it was hardly surprising that Sid rounded off his Boxing Day 1946 letters with a simple request: 'I'd be grateful if you'd grant me an interview. Sincerely, Sidney James.'

The letter of reply from BBC producer Martyn C. Webster of New Year's Day, 1947, was friendly but discouraging: 'I am working on serials just now which are already cast until the end of March, so I'm afraid there is nothing I can do for you at present.' This would have done little to dishearten Sid, for the secretary to the other BBC producer he had written to, Peter Richmond, had dispatched a more positive missive on New Year's Eve. It asked whether Sid, 'would care to come to Rothwell House on Thursday 16 January at 11.30am, [where] Mr Richmond would be pleased to see you.'

Sid's radio work in Britain started with a vengeance, though he would have to wait until September 1947 to begin, when he recorded six thrilling instalments of *The Fabulous Miss Dangerfield* for producer Cleland Finn.

Now billeted in Allen House, W8, Sid wrote once more to Martyn Webster on 30 October. It is important to note that, even at this early stage, Sid already found the attention of listeners to his liking. There is a genuine interest in his question: 'What was the reaction to our Dangerfield epic?' And a genuine amazement in his comment that, 'The greatest surprise of my life was getting some fan mail, from all the kids between two months and twelve years. I'm not sure whether I ought to feel flattered or not.'

However, it was future employment that was at the front of his mind. The letter was mainly to 'congratulate [Webster] on *Lady in a Fog*. I honestly think it's the most interesting, best written and best treated serial of its type I've heard on the air.' Deeply aware of the cat-and-mouse game that he was playing with Webster and, equally, aware that Webster knew the rule book intimately, Sid frankly stated: 'Also let me hasten to assure you that this is not meant as a "sweetener" for what follows . . . I mean it sincerely. Secondly . . . I want to remind you that I do a lot of dialect stuff, mainly American and the "Akim Tamiroff" type of stuff. Any time you feel you need me, the phone number is above.'

This is simply an actor in a new country finding his feet. He is still unsure of himself. There is an insecurity and gullibility that would never quite leave him. And, endearingly, he is well aware that he has yet to find his own style or identity as an actor. Rooting himself alongside Akim Tamiroff, the burly Russian character star, already twice Oscar-nominated in Hollywood, Sid projects himself as the tough heavy. The villain of the piece.

On Bonfire Night 1947, Webster emerged from his Fog to agree: 'It is very well written and I think we have gathered a nice cast together. As you know I am not doing many productions these days, but when something does come along I shall certainly be very glad to cast you.'

And, true to his word, when Webster's December schedule began to take shape, Sid was cast as the mysterious Mr Constantine in a single episode of the serial, *Paul Temple and the Sullivan Mystery*.

Still, wireless activity was by far the least profitable part of his career. The year-long timeline that he had given himself to bed down acting roots in England had been achieved with ease. It had taken Sid a lot less than 12 months to get established in the British film industry. A little less than 12 days, in fact.

Sid explained that 'John Tore, an old friend from South Africa, took me along to his agent. She thought I looked right for a film part that was going. Then someone thought I was OK for a tough café proprietor in another film [*Black Memory*] – and since then I haven't stopped.'

From Sid's point of view, *Black Memory* was like a gift from heaven. And the string of non-stop film assignments that resulted from his casting in that very first film job was as smooth as he remembered. Tore was married to Olga Lowe who had been swimming in Sid's ken since the age of 15 when she had partnered him in his dance for *Hoopla*. She remembered Sid as 'charismatic and a gentleman . . . someone who you had to focus on once he came into a room. You were pleased to be in his company. He made you feel good.' That feel-good factor would prevail right up to Sid's final stage tour in 1976 when their paths would cross again.

John Tore's agent was Phyllis Parnell, who had been in control of the Archie Parnell Agency since her husband's death in 1942. Mr and Mrs Tore were in the frame for a tough gangster and his doe-eyed moll in a quota quickie thriller scheduled to begin shooting in early January. In the event, neither Tore nor Lowe were cast, but Parnell spotted something in Sid and suggested him to producer Gilbert Church.

Years later, Sid admitted, typically, that 'I was very lucky'. But, despite a fortunate train of events, the business demands that you make your own luck and Sid had successfully manoeuvred his way into a killer position. 'I walked into a part at Bushey in a small film, starring Michael Medwin. A picture called *Black Memory*. And Mickey liked the work and he was friendly with [producer/director] Harold Hughes who was doing a film called *Night Beat*, and I walked straight into that.' But only because his performance in *Black Memory* (1947) was so startling and compelling.

Viewed today, Sid's role is nothing more than a rather cowardly café owner in the clutches of the baby-faced, two-bit crook played by Michael Medwin. But, with hindsight, you can see why the director Oswald Mitchell was so enchanted by Sid. He gives a performance of underplayed emotional tension, always shifting, always wary, always preparing for an outbreak of violence to envelop him. Indeed, the sheer truth that Sid brings to the role is a revelation, particularly in contrast to the acting that was going on around him. Clearly the South African stage was far less stagy than the English one. And Sid's naturalistic delivery is even more measured and even more believable because of, rather than despite, the frantically over-the-top acting around him. Medwin chomps at the bit as the faux cockney tearaway. The rest of the cast, rather sweetly, behave like they are in a matinee performance for the Salisbury Rep.

Celebrated director Roy Ward Baker worked with Sid twice and remembers he had a different quality, 'an edge over those actors who had been brought up on the English stage. At that time I didn't know anything about his South African background but Sidney had a real strength of character. A real conviction in his acting.'

It was a conviction that was still being honed splendidly onstage in Britain. Experienced play translator Kitty Black always believed that Sid's first job in London was in the Jean-Paul Sartre double bill, directed by Peter Brook at the Lyric, Hammersmith. 'I called my translation *Men Without Shadows*,' she remembered, 'and when Peter saw the Angus McBean pictures he prophesied that Sid would become a film star "as his face comes off the paper".'

Brook's words were prophetic indeed, for Sid quickly became an invaluable part of the backbone of British film acting.

'Sid had this great elastic quality,' says Harry Fowler. 'He could top the bill in variety, he could shine in a good play and he would thrive in front of a film camera. He was a natural. The camera loved him.'

Roy Ward Baker saw him in the musical *High Button Shoes* at the Hippodrome: 'I remember he was very good in that. He was certainly an excellent all-rounder. He could do variety turns in that sort of musical and he could turn in a, frankly, brilliant performance in a little thriller like *Paper Orchid*.'

A taunt crime thriller released in 1949, *Paper Orchid* saw Sid playing the lead role of a troubled journalist who, Baker explains, 'ends the film by throwing himself on to the railway track. Sorry if that ruins it for anybody. No one has seen the picture for years! But Sidney was a very good straight actor. When he starred in *Paper Orchid* he was already a very accomplished actor. The script was very good: written by Val Guest (from the novel by Arthur La Bern) before he became a director. A few years later he would probably have got that job as well, but I got it that time round. In fact, the only concession the producers (William Collier and John R. Sloan) wanted was that the film should be on time and on budget. And I delivered on that. I didn't face much of a strain really. I found it easy enough. And, in particular, with an actor like Sidney James in the lead, that was plain sailing. He always knew his lines. Always hit his mark. Always looked in the right place.'

In fact, Baker's experiences with Sid stretched back even further, to 1947. 'Sidney was in the very first picture I ever directed, *The October Man*. It could only have been a matter of weeks after he had arrived in this country. I'm still very proud of it although you could hardly say I directed Sidney in it. If you watch carefully, very early on, John Mills walks away from a railway station. Out of the mist, walking in the opposite direction, is a couple. The man is Sidney James. He has no dialogue. And he's half in shadow. But it's Sidney James! I can't believe he came all the way over to Denham just for that. He was already something of a supporting figure in British films. I can only imagine that our producer, Eric Ambler, bumped into him in the bar while he was there doing another job and offered him a cash handout for the extra work. It was certainly below Sidney's standing, even then, but that's something I liked about him. He would always take on any role, however small, as long as he was available to do it. That's a true actor.'

It was a maxim that would stay with Sid throughout his life and no time more dramatically than his first decade in front of British film cameras. Sid was tireless, professional and unpretentious. With tight budgets and even tighter shooting schedules, producers and directors would call on actors who could save them time and money by delivering a quick performance. 'One-Take' James would be much in demand.

2

Little Britain

How much of a demand is certainly open to debate. Sid was the tried and tested scene-stealer. The most welcome of guest stars. And by the end of his career he estimated that he had appeared in over 250 films. As was the norm with Sid, that figure seems to be extremely ambitious but one thing is for sure, there wasn't a busier actor in British cinema during the post-war era. He was also a lucky charm for the industry. A cheeky, lecherous imp who was always just the wrong side of the law . . . even when he was playing a copper!

From that first film appearance in 1947, he carved out a seemingly endless stream of quintessential British eccentrics. He played cheery barrow boys, nervous petty criminals, rummy-eyed desk sergeants, wary pub landlords, punch-drunk boxers and far-from-discreet hotel porters. As often as not he would appear in some 10 or 12 films in a year – each one just a day or two's very well-paid employment.

He would be on continual call and directors like Val Guest or Ralph Thomas or J. Lee-Thompson – who all considered him as a valued part of their film repertory company – would bring him in for a walk-on or a comic bit of business if a film lacked that certain something. If it needed a lift in the 23rd scene, when all but the producer had fallen asleep or walked out, then that was the time when Sid was called in. He could make any film – or at least the scene he was in – unmissable by his very presence.

While researching a piece for *Everybody's* magazine, journalist Arthur W. Jacobs was privy to a typical day's filming for Sid in 1958: 'The over-ripe tomato splashed across the rugged face in the pillory. It was quickly followed by decaying oranges and pears and some elderly eggs. The face, with its complexion like a lunar landscape, was all but hidden behind the stinking mess. "Let's have one more take," said the director (Peter Maxwell). So the face of Sidney James was wiped clean again and, for our future amusement, plastered afresh with rotten fruit. Then came a close-up; for this a few tomatoes were carefully rubbed over the face by hand, so that plenty stuck on. "What some people will do for money . . ." said Mr James when it was all over. Sidney James was giving another of the performances with which he has become identified – the arch-fiddler, the Artful Dodger up to date. This time it was a costume part in a William Tell film [*Secret Death*] "I'm a phoney magician selling love-potions – useless ones, of course."'

And this was the very reason Sid became such a popular actor. He was one of us. Slightly rubbish at life. Always laughing at himself. And trying to muddle through without too much hard work. The lifestyle and glee was etched into that oh-so familiar, gnarled face. And, as a man, he was laughing all the way to the bank. His twice-weekly television fiddles and countless shady characters in British film made him a surtax-paying London suburbanite and, crucially, put him on first-name terms with the entire nation.

As Sid reflected himself: 'There's nothing "la di da" about me. Perfect strangers in the street I meet yell out "Wotcha Sid. How's it going?" I like that. I think that's real nice.'

That was Sid's secret. He played people, as often as not, from the wrong side of the tracks, and as likely to pick your pocket as look at you. But the public couldn't help but warm to him. He was the criminal cliché: a lovable rogue. As blonde bombshell and Sid's frequent co-star, Vera Day, believes: 'You couldn't help liking Sid. He was just that sort. Really down to earth. And fun. That personality lit up the screen. He always came across as the sort of bloke you could have a few drinks and a few laughs with . . . even if he was playing a seedy crook. That was Sid's magic. He had a huge likability factor.'

He had a huge popularity factor too. Sid was one of those actors who could brighten a bad film with a few minutes of cheerful cockney banter and enhance a good film with a world-weary shake of the head. Professional at all times, he was under no illusions about the business. As writer Ray Galton remembers: 'Sid was known as "One-Take" James for a very good reason. Whatever he did he always did first time. And he always did it right. But he wasn't in it for the art. He was in it for the money. I always admired his honesty. If we were all true to ourselves, the money was the main thing for all of us.'

Sid was certainly always candid about his work and why he did it. He loved what he did but he did it for one reason and one reason only. Because it paid well. Reassuringly, that attitude never changed: 'I'm not the artistic type,' he once gladly admitted. 'I do it just for the money' was his mantra. And it fitted the character he played. Even after a decade in the limelight he would tell the *Evening Standard*: 'I'm strictly a practical actor. I leave Shakespeare to Olivier and go after the money. They say I've got a cash complex. So what?'

And so what, indeed?

As soon as he had made his mark on screen in 1947, Sid was constantly in demand. He would chalk up appearances in literally dozens of films. From walk-ons in high prestige biographies to leading roles in poverty row thrillers. By the early 1950s he was making over 10 films a year. He was the archetypal East End cockney villain with a heart of gold. Most of the time.

This casting clout was an irony not lost on Arthur Mullard in his 1977 autobiography *Oh Yus, It's Arthur Mullard*: 'Now being a cockney actor, it puzzled me why I was being overlooked when cockney parts were being handed out. Sid James, a South African, was the number one cockney, and when he was not available, Sam Kydd, an Irishman, got the job. I worked with Sid many times on films and television. He used to call me Thumper. So one day we had a chat about the cockney bit and his verdict was: "Someone up there don't like you!" – and coming from Sid this made me think a bit.'

But it wasn't only true blue cockneys that Sid was relentlessly doing out of work. He would crop up as Italians, New Yorkers and Spaniards; barrow boys, cowboys and newspapermen. In fact, he was everywhere. It was no idle observation when director Ralph Thomas, who employed Sid for the first of many roles in *Venetian Bird* (1952), said, 'It wouldn't be a British picture without Sid James being in it!'

Journalists and reporters, of course, wanted the easy answer. It wasn't enough for them that the nation had taken Sid to their hearts. The real reason he was the country's most popular bit-part player was that his face seemed to have every emotion deeply etched in to it. Or, as Sid himself often put it, 'I've got the face of a diabolical fiddler. It's like a scrambled egg.' Still, he wasn't naïve about his image once the work came flowing in: 'I've got a pug ugly face, so I get pug ugly parts,' he explained. But he quickly accepted that 'my face is my fortune. I know it wouldn't win any beauty prizes, but it's never been out of work for long!'

Sid would plant his tongue firmly in his cheek and thank his ups and downs, wins and losses and human frailties. It was down to the dreaded taxman. Industrial qualities of gin. Countless lost thousands riding on the back of a horse or a dog. And, most of all, years of physical abuse in the boxing ring.

When pressed, Sid would happily string out a lengthy list of occupations that put bread on the table during his years struggling as an actor in South Africa. The most prominent of these was boxing: 'That's why my nose isn't what it was!' But it was a brutal trade that served him well: 'I used to fight in Rhodesia as a middleweight and get my nose bust in for a pound and a free feed. It was useful money in those days.'

Still, when questioned about his standing as a fighter he was harsh on his talents and qualities: 'I wasn't very good, no. I had too quick a temper.'

But the face fitted the part and film producers contemplating a boxing picture in the 1950s were almost guaranteed to turn to the services of Sid.

As he matured and established himself as a prominent figure in television and radio, he tended to lean towards the hard-bitten, established and prominent figures in the fight game. He had turned his back on its violence, corruption and day-to-day exertion. He was a moneyman now.

Intertwined almost continually in Sid's universe of the 1950s was actress Vera Day who shared several moments of what Benny Hill called the 'fingernails and aspirins' of live work. For television was live in those days. No re-takes, just blind panic with Sid on live television. 'I would say that those occasions were when Sid and I really got very close and friendly,' says Vera. 'We spent a lot of time together doing this comedy play called *The Chigwell Chicken*. It was all about a weedy boxer who makes good and both Sid and I were cast in the feature film version [*And the Same to You*] a year or so later, in 1960. We used to joke that if there was ever a film or a television play about horse racing or boxing Sid and I would be in it somewhere. Sid as a crooked bookie or promoter and me as a blonde bad girl out to nobble the favourite!'

Indeed, Sid's CV of the time is liberally littered with seedy wannabe boxing promoters desperate to make a killing. Or washed-up fighters reduced in circumstances but blissfully wallowing in memories of antiseptic rub and the smash of canvas on cheekbone. *The Extra Day* (1956), for William Fairchild at British Lion, was a typical example. One of many portmanteau melodramas which required a comic injection from Sid, here he was cast as an ex-boxer who ekes out a living as a film extra. Shades of autobiography were unavoidable, particularly in the hit-and-hope lack of talent Sid's character displays in the ring.

The Square Ring (1953), at Ealing Studios, featured him as a down-on-his-luck promotions manager continually looking over his shoulder at the big bosses he must appease. His wardrobe is second rate and shabby. The dinner jacket and bow tie are forced attempts to melt in with the upper echelons. The treasured cigar, preserved unlit. A prop to be whipped out to impress when and where the occasion arises.

There was also the influential and haunting *The Small Back Room* (1948) for Michael Powell and Emeric Pressburger. Sid seeps controlled menace as the humourless bartender with a glittering past in the boxing ring. Photographs of a muscular Sid adorn the bar and give his character an edge. A dark history. A history that is captured in a telling, extreme close-up on a dogged Sid as the situation veers towards disaster and his expression stops it in its tracks.

This prototype was repeated, almost ounce for ounce, in Compton Bennett's *Gift Horse* (1952). Again Sid is the ex-boxer reduced to running a public house populated by unsavoury types. There are the framed boxing pictures, a signed portrait of Sid in the ring and the ever-present threat that the ex-boxer might just be tempted to thump one of his military customers on the nose.

In 1953, Sid appeared in a BBC Television production of *Golden Boy* for producer Donald McWhinnie. Broadcast as part of *The Stars in Their Choices* series, it was certainly the ideal environment for Sid, being the tale of temptation, triumph and tragedy of a boxer made famous by the Hollywood film of the late 1930s that had made William Holden a star.

The very ethos of the original piece had bled into the most touching of Sid's forays into the world of boxing, *The Flanagan Boy*. Having played the fairground barker and washed-up boxer on BBC television in 1948, the part was pretty much assured for Sid when the film version came along several years later. Perhaps the closest to Sid's real experience, the pathetic chancer is reduced to dangling fivers in the faces of cynical customers as the carrot to face his boy in the booth. The morality of rich pickings and fast women of the tale of our man's young hopeful is seen for real in the expressive delivery of Sid.

That film, rather sensationally released in America as *Bad Blonde*, was one of a precious handful of films that Sid made for the fledgling Hammer Films. Produced quickly and with a skilful combination of reliable British character actors and declining Hollywood stars, they were the brainchild of producer Robert Lippert. However, reassuringly, it was homeboy Anthony Hinds who steered these energetic and entertaining little thrillers through.

The House Across the Lake (1954), or the more tempestuous *Heatwave* if you were Stateside, partnered Sid with 1940s tinseltown siren Hillary Brooke as his faithless wife. Facing Canadian beefcake (Paul Carpenter) and waspish pulp writer (Alex Nichol), it's unsurprising that Sid played his entire role with a near-permanent frown on his face. He wasn't much more cheerful in *The Glass Cage* (1955), morbidly toned down from the American title of *The Glass Tomb*. Perfectly at home in this bleak and emotive tale of fairground freaks and corruption in low places, John Ireland was the imported headline star while Sid was playing a success story for once. A seemingly embittered one, admittedly, but a success story none the less. Director Montgomery Tully tossed in every cliché that made Sid such a rounded character: there's the booze and the showgirls and the fags and the money. He's the self-made man but one who is scarred and downtrodden. He has the trappings of wealth but he has clearly worked for it. And trodden on a few friends along the way.

These films were good solid acting assignments and Sid was happy within the cosy confines of Bray Studios.

In fact, his association with Hammer spanned back even further; to the late-1940s when Anthony Hinds was profitably turning radio shows into feature films. *The Man in Black* was the big screen treatment of the 'BBC Sensation'. Produced in the autumn of 1949, *The Man in Black* is one of Sid's earliest leading roles. Hinting, momentarily, at what he had left behind on the South African stage and, at the age of 36, giving him, arguably, the most astounding film role of his career.

In fact, the convoluted plot twists and turns more than enough times to present him with two separate characterisations. The primitive, theatrical confines of Hammer's Oakley Court location is a blessing rather than a curse. The frightfully refined supporting performances run the gamut from arch camp to inexperienced ingénue and are so knowing and deliberate that the cast and crew must have been having a ball during the film's production.

Indeed, director Francis Searle recalled at least one memorable evening in which Sid was instrumental in the fun being extended well beyond the call of duty: 'It was a very cheap film to make,' Searle said. 'We had Valentine Dyall who was very famous as the host of the radio series – The Man in Black himself. But it was Sidney James who was the star of the film. He was a very professional actor. Very good. But he liked to live life to the full. We were shooting in and around Oakley Court, a beautiful house on the river and a stone's throw from Bray Studios and the Hinds Head pub in Bray! After a particularly long and gruelling night shot Sid and Betty Ann Davies [cast as his malicious spouse] and several other members of the cast [including the innocent, butter-wouldn't-melt Hazel Penwarden] took a punt out on the river. There was enough alcohol on board to sink a battleship but off they went. Early next morning, the punt docked outside Oakley Court. Sid and the girls climbed ashore. The booze had all but gone. And they were word perfect and ready for the day's filming. That was life filming *The Man in Black*!'

Within its limitations and delightfully twee boundaries, *The Man in Black* shows Sid at his very best: as the gentle, kind and thoughtful student of the unexplained. But also at his most outrageous: as the heavily whiskered, booze-soaked sea dog. The contrast between introspection and pantomime makes this one of Sid's most challenging and enjoyable film performances. And something far, far more worthwhile than its all too infrequent relegation to television's graveyard shift deserves.

Happily, Sid's most important Hammer credential is anything but uncelebrated. By the time he returned to the studio after a gap of 18 months, the place was on the verge of international success with their string of colourful Gothic horrors. In fact, Sid's performance in *Quatermass II* (1957) was the final piece of the puzzle that put Hammer Films within a whisker of immortality. This, in effect, was hour zero. And Sid was about to leave his finest Hammer contribution behind as a deposit.

In his semi-drunken, hard-boiled and committed newspaper-man, his muted performance comes to an all-too-soon and unpleasant end in the public house at Winnerden Flats. There's a grim understanding at work behind the throwaway quips of the early stages of the film. For his final scenes are underplayed and real. For once the character is sober and on the case. A situation enforced even more by the surroundings. And the presence of a cinematic signifier of jollier times, Vera Day: 'I had seen the television series and been suitably and nicely scared by it. It had been a real talking point. And it was great to be in the film. I didn't have a lot to do. I was just the chirpy barmaid who gets the dreaded alien pox on the neck. Sid was rather splendid in it but he was just the same. There were never any airs and graces with him.'

Sid and Vera would spend the better part of a decade continually cropping up against each other on both film and television. So much so, that, recalls Vera: 'We became known as the "Gruesome Twosome". Actually, that's what Sid called us. We would bump in to each other in the canteen at Shepperton or Elstree or Pinewood and he would cry: "Oh gawd, not you again! You're not in this are you? The Gruesome Twosome are back together again!" Because we seemed to be in every other film together. That was the way films were then. If you were good at playing a particular type you played it all the time.'

Their paths had first criss-crossed on *The Crowded Day* (1954): '[It] was my second film and probably Sid's one hundred and second! It was my first with Sid in the cast although I didn't really work with him on it. He was the caretaker of this big department store where all the girls worked. I was one of the salesgirls with Rachel Roberts, Joan Rice and various others. Sid was always just in the background, smoking his pipe and talking about what all the girls were getting up to! But Sid had been doing just that. Just being around in the background in British films for years. He was totally professional.'

Directed by John Guillemin, Sid is indeed the glue that keeps the portmanteau of *The Crowded Day* together. The top and tail bookend of the story, shuffling through the shadows and setting up the episodic and dramatic tale like a muffler-encased prophet. The film also prophesied the delight the ad men would have with Vera Day's name when, several years later, she joined Sid on the set of *It's A Great Day* (1955): 'That one was based on the BBC soap opera, *The Grove Family*,' remembers Vera. 'It's almost forgotten now, I suppose, and there's certainly no family like that on today's soaps but the best way to describe it was that it was the English equivalent of *The Waltons*. They were very nice and down to earth. The dad was a real pipe-and-slipper sort of man. He would come in from work ready for his tea. The wife was nice in her little pinny and little hairstyle. The daughter was very sweet and nice. Me and Sid were the only naughty people in the film! And of course with a title like that the press people had a field day. Vera Day is always great but she's never been as great as she is in *It's A Great Day* and all that. I'm convinced it's the only reason they cast me! But Sid was lovely. Again, we had absolutely nothing to do together on screen but the "Gruesome Twosome" were back! Sid was the perfect used-car salesman.'

He was also extremely useful for a cheaply made spin-off film such as this. Shot in less than four weeks and on a budget that wouldn't have covered Lord Reith's cigar bill, Sid's single scene, seemingly shot with just one camera on one afternoon, is dripping with dubious experience.

He was also the perfect East End barrow boy. Arguably the most high profile pairing of Sid and Vera Day came in Carol Reed's *A Kid for Two Farthings* (1955). A touching East End fairy tale of a small boy and his one-horned goat, the bunting of barrow boys, low-life corruption and boxing made it the perfect setting for Sid and the director: 'Carol Reed was magnificent,' remembers Vera Day. 'He was the greatest director I ever worked with, no question. And he really liked Sid. I think he used him a few times. Carol should have been an actor and I think he had been one early in his career. When he was directing he played everybody's part. He was a real actor's director. He would act out the little boy's part. Diana Dors' part. Sid's part. My part. Everyone's. Now some actors don't like to be shown what to do, they would rather be told. It's very different. But both Sid and I were what I would call natural actors. We weren't trained. We just did what came to us naturally. Carol Reed liked that quality. They certainly got on very well. Sid never had any stand-up fights with directors but underneath that lovely, happy exterior Sid could be a little bit touchy about how a scene was going. He would certainly have his say because he was a very dedicated actor. He was a natural. Sid James played Sid James. But that's a very hard discipline. To play yourself on camera at a moment's notice and to always get it right. That's not easy. He always had his eye on the ball. And was well aware if anyone was trying to upstage him. He wasn't temperamental but he was the height of professionalism.'

A *Kid for Two Farthings* was made for Alexander Korda's London Films and the boss really liked Carol Reed. However, now the Hungarian immigrant, who had single-handedly revolutionised British film in the early 1930s with the historical romp *The Private Life of Henry VIII*, was being forced to diminish his vision. Beholden to the British government, with a £3 million loan haplessly lobbed into the mix, the tone of the British film industry was set at a small and cuddly reflection of Britain itself. Carol Reed's rose-tinted vision of the East End was one thing, but, while Korda smarted at the financial loss of his late-forties efforts like the epic *Bonnie Prince Charlie* and the coy culture of *An Ideal Husband*, he was reluctantly nurturing populist filmmakers like Frank Launder and Sidney Gilliat.

Naturally, Sid was the kind of actor who could fit in with any director's vision of Britain. And certainly with the clever, witty and slapstick world of Launder and Gilliat. The partnership, having graduated from scriptwriters to producers, had tapped into ensemble comedy casts and entertaining lowbrow entertainment. And nothing fitted that bill more than the naughty schoolgirls from the vivid imagination of Ronald Searle. *The Belles of St Trinian's* (1954) was another familiar situation for Sid: seedy backhanders and wheeler-dealing within the world of horse racing. Typically, Sid's roving eye was more interested in horseflesh than gymslips, but the small supporting role perfectly illustrates that he was an essential part of this 1950s set-up. In a strange sort of way, without Sid's reassuring presence, the equation just wouldn't add up.

He had earlier dropped in to Launder and Gilliat's *Lady Godiva Rides Again*. In a minor turn as a seedy show-business promoter, Sid plays cards and uncaringly offers to take the youthful enthusiasm of beauty pageant winner Pauline Stroud down the road of nude shows. With a single throwaway remark he sums up the dark recesses of a glamorous industry. But Launder and Gilliat knew that, even with a limited amount of screen time, Sid's appearance would cut the need of back story and explanation for this character. When British film audiences saw Sid James on screen in 1951 they knew he wasn't going to be playing with a straight bat.

Even in Alexander Korda's last-ditch efforts to stage more high profile pictures with his most treasured and high profile star, Vivien Leigh, the visage of Sid creeps into shot to bring the production happily down to earth. Indeed, so minute is his appearance in Terence Rattigan's *The Deep, Blue Sea* (1955) that he must have been walking through the sound stage on his way to another job when director Anatole Litvak spotted him. Again, it is shorthand.

Sid is the chancer. The failure. The working man. The cynic who tries his luck at the porcelain beauty of Vivien Leigh and is rebuffed.

He was probably more at home in the penny-pinching world of Group Three. On a scale far smaller than that of Alexander Korda, the producers at Group Three were, in turn, churning out visions of the British way of life for the British masses. Community was important to them. As was beating authority. And Sid was often called upon for leading roles of dishonest bureaucracy and larger-than-life flamboyance.

The typical Group Three effort was *Time Gentlemen, Please!* (1952) in which Sid, reassuringly, runs a pub but also sides with the distrustful and disliked councillors personified by rotund Raymond Lovell and sneaky Thora Hird. The basic premise screamed the work ethos of Group Three; in that scruffy but lovable Irish wastrel, Eddie Byrne, is the annoying blot on the landscape. The only jobless one in the village! Adapted by Val Valentine from R.J. Minney's novel *Nothing to Lose*, the film is awash with British character actors doing British character actor things. Sydney Tafler hints at blackmailer contacts. Dora Bryan flits around with goggle-eyes on any man. And Peter Jones turns on the supercilious man from the ministry full of pomp and earnestness. All is right in the cosy world of British films for British audiences.

Group Three would embrace bigger budgets and bigger subjects as long as they fitted in with their maxim of Britishness. *John and Julie* (1955), for example, centred on two small children and their determined journey to London to see Elizabeth crowned Queen.

A colourful celebration of a colourful coronation, Sid is again the wet blanket in all the patriotic fever. Dubbing it 'mass hysteria' at one point, he grumbles and moans and belittles at every point. On the trail of his missing child, he rants at the police force, the postal service, the military and British Rail. But even this downbeat character is unable to resist being melted by the power of heart-pumping pride in the British Royal family. Sid's very last moment unleashes his inner-royalist as he screams 'Gawd bless 'er!' as the procession goes by. Sid is the common man here. He may have little money and unionist loyalties but he's British first and foremost. And if that means that no one can stop him having a good moan as he mellows into a kindly father figure, then so be it.

However, Sid certainly wasn't called upon for much parental warmth at Ealing Studios: the doyen of fun factories designed to produce British films for the British. The very term Ealing

Comedy has came to represent the cosy output of middle-England of the mid-1950s, as often as not encompassing films that weren't produced by the legendary studio. Indeed, the best Group Three efforts have an ersatz Ealing quality about them. And Ealing gratefully embraced Sid himself on several occasions. Indeed, the studio offered him, debatably, his most important film role. That of Lackery, the petty thief with a winning way, who joins Alec Guinness, Stanley Holloway and Alfie Bass to form *The Lavender Hill Mob*.

The brisk direction of Charles Crichton. The crisp dialogue of T.E.B. Clarke. The note-perfect ensemble playing. Everything came together to form the definitive Ealing Comedy: rounded, likeable characters forced to unite against authority and against the law, in order to better themselves. Crime could never actually pay in 1951, but even the audiences of the day would have willed on this particularly robust quartet of criminals.

Surprisingly, it was also Sid's first experience under the Ealing banner. Having given the actor one of the choicest parts of his career, the studio seemed happy and eligible to use and re-use him in a variety of supports, walk-ons and gag appearances. For Sid suited the mentality of the studio perfectly. Whether he let rip with a steamroller in *The Titfield Thunderbolt* (1953), mournfully flogged snacks at a racetrack in *The Rainbow Jacket* (1954) or enjoyed a quick flutter at the airport in *Out of the Clouds* (1955), Sid was a vital part of the Ealing community.

Harry Fowler, who had been a stable of the studios since he was a lad said, 'I loved that place. It was my home for so many happy years. I served my apprenticeship there. I owe a lot to Ealing. And Sid was the sort of actor that Sir Michael Balcon and the Ealing bosses would have loved. Always quick. Always on time. Always word perfect. Just what they wanted. It's funny. We were both making lots of films at that time but we didn't really work together very much. We were both always working . . . but always working

on other films. We did a few together. *Idle on Parade* (1959) with
Tony Newley. Sid was the crooked agent, of course. I was his
lackey. He came to Ealing a fair bit. And Sid was in *I Believe in You*
(1952) with me. That's the one in which I kiss a young Joan
Collins . . . and got paid for it! But he made hundreds of film and
television appearances. He wasn't one of those actors who
considered it beneath him to do a small role. If he was working on
Monday and Thursday and a last-minute role came up for
Tuesday and Wednesday he'd gladly pop down to Pinewood or
Shepperton or Riverside studios and play it. It was three lines. Sid's
attitude was "so what? I'm free, I'll do it!" He loved working. And
he loved living. Sid really came alive when he was working and in
particular in a film studio. That was his domain. He was so skilled
and confident. That quiet confidence that comes with knowing
exactly what you are doing.'

That desire to always keep working never left him. As soon as he
had finished one job he was looking for the next. His agent didn't
need to do a thing. Sid was continually on the case. Proving
himself as the king of the supporting role.

On 25 March 1952, for example, he penned a note to BBC
television producer Eric Fawcett, letting him know that he was
now having 'a "resting" period until about the 15 April when my
next movie starts. Are you still entertaining the idea of *Burlesque*
[Sid's early stage success]? Of course I won't complain if it's
anything else. Perhaps I had better remind you that really tough
stuff is my cup of tea.' Fawcett explained that unfortunately his
next production was *Pagliacci* and, try as anyone might, Sid would
have struggled to slot into that with any ease.

Alas, muted plans to broadcast a version of *Burlesque* came to
nought. That would have been some 'really tough stuff' for Sid to
sink his teeth into. In the end Fawcett cast him as the cheeky
chappie bookkeeper, Educated Evans. For Sid was forced to leave
the really tough stuff behind him. He was embracing his softer

side. His warmer side. He was a comedy actor now. The archetypal grinning fiddler. And, besides, it paid more than truthful menace.

3

Valerie

By the time *The Lavender Hill Mob* was released in 1951 to international acclaim and award-winning status – it picked up the Best Film award at BAFTA – Sid was reluctantly resigned to his fate. That one film had skilfully taken the edge off his criminal class performance. He was still the lag. The dodgy guy you would spot acting suspiciously at the dog track. But now he had a glow of humanity. A cheery wink as he sold you down the river. The villain had become a rogue.

Again, Sid was resigned to the fact that his face was his fortune: 'Poker sessions, late nights and too much gin completed the picture you see before you today. Call it an ugly mug if you like, but my wife loves it and it brings in more lolly than most of the pretty-pretty boys earn.'

Sid was extremely proud of his wife: 'My Val'. And the family man that beat at the heart of all those womanisers and western baddies and sly criminal types he played on the screen were made all the more humane because of it. Sid first met Valerie Ashton during rehearsals for the revue *Touch and Go*. It was a typical theatrical assignment for Sid in the late 1940s. Lots of cheap gags. Lots of outrageous sketches. Lots of lavish musical numbers. And lots of pretty girls.

For Sid, none was prettier than the young dancer Valerie. She would become his world. And he would become hers: 'I know he used to make gags about his face,' she says, 'but I thought he was the most handsome, attractive man I'd ever met. And what I loved about him most was that he was so masculine and protective. He really treated a woman like a woman, old-fashioned style. If a man didn't hold a door open for a woman he'd want to hit him.'

But this wasn't the love at first sight accompanied by a string quartet moment as depicted in the corniest of Hollywood musicals. This was real life. And real love. It had to be worked at. Particularly by Sid. As the ultimate man's man, he fell in lust with the attractive blonde dancer in the show, long before he fell in love. Valerie wasn't going to give in at once: 'In fact, my first impressions were that he was conceited, arrogant and irritating. Sid obviously liked me, I could tell, the way a woman can. He asked me out every day for three months and for three months I said "no". In fact I only finally and very reluctantly agreed to have a date with him to shut him up. But what a difference when we were alone and away from the theatre and talking together.'

He told her, 'You've got the biggest inferiority complex I've seen in anyone, but you're the most beautiful woman in the room,' Valerie revealed to the *Daily Mail*'s Lynda Lee-Potter in 1998. 'He gave me confidence in myself.'

Valerie remembers: 'The great Sid charm hit me right between the eyes and by the end of the evening I was happily agreeing to see him again. By the end of a fortnight I knew I was head-over-heels in love with him. Even though he was eighteen years older than me.'

Despite being double her age, Sid's relentless charm offensive paid dividends. He was a natural with the ladies and when he spotted someone he really wanted he would go out and get her. But Valerie was no wide-eyed ingénue. She knew the score. And she knew that Sid was married.

'He was really very unsettled in those days,' she explained. 'He was unhappily married and had come over from South Africa.' Despite the frantically busy nature of his career in 1951, Valerie maintains that, 'he earned little then, and times were difficult. Even so, I knew he was my man. I couldn't imagine falling in love that way with anyone else.'

The age difference was not the only concern that Valerie faced. Not from her own point of view, but from the worried stance of her family: 'I was only nineteen and I was terrified of taking him home to meet my parents. I knew they'd disapprove, because of the age difference as much as anything else. But as soon as they met him they, too, fell under his spell and they really loved him. Sid's divorce came through and we were married four days later, 21 August 1952, at Caxton Hall.' Sid was 39 and had secured himself to the rock that would support him for life.

Caxton Hall was the first choice for show-business weddings. Peter Sellers, Diana Dors, Ringo Starr and Richard Attenborough were among its celebrated clients over the years. Indeed, Sid and Valerie later attended Tommy Steele's marriage at the venue. In the newsreel footage that survives, Sid is clearly delighted to have Valerie on his arm. He points at her, smiles and mouths: 'My wife!' to the waiting photographers. He remained proud of her until the end of his days. They were true soulmates: 'She's attractive, sexy, a wonderful cook, a wonderful mother. She's everything a man could want,' he told a Pinewood Studios publicist in 1963.

'We moved into a little one-room flat and things were tough at first,' remembers Valerie. 'The flat cost five pounds a week – a fortune. We tried never to be separated. If I had a job, say, in Leeds and Sid was out of work, then he'd come with me. In those days I often played the principal boy in pantomime and Sid would sit in my dressing room mending my fishnet tights!

'After a few months I decided to give up work. I was in a show in Blackpool at this time and Sid was working in London. I said I would rather have a successful marriage than a successful career. So I made a complete break and I never worked after that, nor have I ever regretted it.

'Sid was delighted when I gave up working, although he never pressurised me into doing so.'

Besides, by this stage, Sid was earning more than enough to keep the family unit together and secure. That's all he ever wanted to do. Talking in 1958 he explained: 'I have reached the stage now where the stuff just comes in. [Although] it's not a good thing to have to rush after work and be too eager. Can't ask the same money.'

Earning money wasn't the problem. Where and how it was spent was. And, despite the blissfully happy marriage, Valerie could not have been blind to the tales of his roving eye and his infidelities. They were infidelities, after all, that informed his on-screen persona and shaped the very man he was both in public and in private.

His first marriage, to Toots Delmont, had ended when he met Meg Sergei. And even before his marriage to Meg, Sid could charm the birds out of the trees as far as the ladies were concerned. A fellow performer and friend from the Unit Entertainment days during the war, Myfanwy Evans, remembers that Sid 'possessed the most terrific sexual power. He was broad-shouldered, slim-hipped, and he moved well because he was a dancer. He just stood there, said something funny and the girls – all the girls – would fall for him like crazy. Not that he ever led the girls on, he didn't need to.'

He was married to Meg when he met Valerie. True the marriage was in tatters, but the girlfriend who replaces the wife must always think that when she herself becomes the wife there may well be another girlfriend around the corner waiting to replace her. Sid's frequent film and television co-star, Liz Fraser, experienced this.

'The love of my life was my husband, Bill Hitchcock. In fact he directed Sid once. A Christmas comedy for television [*All This – and Christmas Too!* in 1971]. But when I met Bill he was a notorious womaniser. You always think you are going to be the woman who tames them. But as soon as we were married he started up with his affairs. The scriptwriter Sid Colin told me, "What do you expect? You knew what he was like!" But you never listen.'

However, despite Sid's cavalier behaviour and healthy passion for young ladies, it wasn't so much the countless chorus girls and glamorous extras that Sid worked with that was the source of Valerie's concern. It was the horses.

As *Hancock's Half Hour* scribe Ray Galton observes: 'As far as Sid was concerned, if it wasn't horse racing, it was rubbish!' Indeed, waxing even more lyrically with his writing partner Alan Simpson in tow, the boys put the perfect words into Sid's mouth in the radio episode *The Poetry Society*: 'As long as my horses don't stagnate I don't care what happens!'

For Harry Fowler the racetrack was all part of Sid's charm: 'He certainly liked a gamble on the gee-gees,' he recalls, 'but that was Sid. He lived the part he played. And he loved life. He would certainly always buy a round of drinks when I knew him and not only for people he knew. He would meet new people and include them in the round. He was everybody's friend, was Sid.'

One of Sid's favourite scriptwriters, Dave Freeman, proclaimed: 'It always struck me that Val and his family meant a great deal to him and as far as I could see his only vice was gambling, if indeed that is a vice. To be honest, although this goes against every accepted report of him, Sid always struck me as having a puritanical streak.'

In the early days of the marriage Sid seemed to openly indulge his passions. 'He certainly wasn't on a short rein, from my experience,' says Harry Fowler. 'Sid was his own man. Very much so. As was another good friend of ours, Bonar Colleano. They both died far too young, Bonar in even more tragic circumstances, but they were very much cut from the same cloth those two. Bonar's family were celebrated wire-walkers and Sid's family were vaudevillians. It's in the blood. We all met through each other in a strange sort of way. Sid used to call us the terror of the West . . . the West End! And boy did we socialise. Sid and Bonar's attitude was exactly the same. "Oh no, it's nearly midnight. What else can we squeeze into this day to make it last longer!" They would live twenty-five hours out of twenty four those two.'

Although the actor's insecurity would always be apparent to interviewers – Sid would continually thank luck for his success and touch wood with alarming regularity – the gambling and the women were not merely there to relieve boredom and continually prove himself as a man. Both pleasures drove Sid. Relentlessly and joyously. Indeed, as Harry Fowler continues, 'It was hard for a bloke like me to keep up, he says tongue firmly in cheek! But Val knew exactly what Sid was like. She was his wife for heaven's sake. But Sid could do both. He was domestic with her and one of the lads – actually *the* lad – with us.'

The gambling became a vital part of Sid's screen image. As with boxing films, producers putting together a film with a horse-racing background would automatically call his agent to check on Sid's availability. He would crop up as a bookmaker in *The Galloping Major* (1951) and *Aunt Clara* (1954). Add a gambling edge to comic leads in *Dry Rot* (1956) and *What a Carve Up* (1961). Even hobnob with the jockeys in Ealing's *The Rainbow Jacket* (1954) – 'Probably the best racing film ever made,' according to critic C.A. Lejeune. Sid became 'Honest' Sid in whatever role he played. The blurred edges between fact and fiction vanished completely.

Many charity events would centre round the dog track or the horse track in a way to make gambling fun, profitable and tempting for higher and higher stakes in favour of a good cause. Always eager to give something back to the industry that had been so good to him, Sid was the obvious choice to gee on the gee-gee and dog businesses at these fund-raising rallies. As friend and film cohort Bernard Cribbins remembers: 'Sid was a straightforward man. You hear all these stories about his womanising and his gambling. I don't pay any attention to them. I knew Sid. I knew him very well. We were really close friends. And I'm telling you. He was a marvellous bloke. But he certainly enjoyed a flutter. He was one of the boys. And that's why the nation took him to their hearts. You can see, in almost every performance, there's that carefree quality at work. The charm. Even when he was playing the villain, there was always something likeable about Sid. In real life you could times that quality by ten. He was an extremely likeable man. We used to go to White City quite a lot, with the Variety Club and what have you. Sid would often come over to me and slip twenty quid in to my hand and say: "Here Bernie. Twenty quid on the number six dog." And he would get me to put on side bets for him. He had a limit when Val was around, of course, because he would have bet on anything if he could. But he always found allies, like me I'm rather pleased to say, who would slip on the odd side bet for him. He never won. He just loved the thrill of betting. There are a lot worse things in the world. But Val would often catch his eye when he was talking to me and he would say: "All right love, don't worry." And another twenty quid would come out to put on the nose of another dog that is probably still running to this day! But he was a generous, funny, very warm man, was Sid. I really liked him.'

Another beloved confidant was his *Two in Clover* co-star Victor Spinetti who, by the time they worked together in the late 1960s, saw the gambling become something of an obsession: 'There is no question of that. If it wasn't for Valerie he would have been flat broke. I mean, if he were in this pub having a drink with us now he'd bet you a thousand pounds on the next bloke to fart. It was that bad. I did this show about Sid a few years ago [the 1993 documentary *Seriously Seeking Sid*] and I told the producer [Jane Oliver] that they really should call the programme 'Don't Tell Val'. That was almost a catchphrase with Sid. It wasn't meant in a nasty way. It's just that he knew she would hit the roof if it got out that he had been gambling. He used to come round to my house, having told Val that he was rehearsing. We would never rehearse on a Saturday. Actually he just wanted to come and watch the racing on the television in peace! I say peace. He would be frantic. Absolutely loving it. Shouting the jockey on. He came alive when he was watching the races. I wasn't interested but I liked him. So I indulged him. Val wouldn't let him watch it at home because she knew it would make him want to gamble and she had tight reins on that. It wasn't a pleasant thing for a wife to do but she had to do it otherwise they would have had nothing. It was a tough job for her really. Little did she know, frankly. Nothing could have stopped Sid gambling. If Sid had had total freedom and access to the money he was making it would have been five thousand quid. Ten thousand quid. Twenty thousand quid on any bet going.'

So determined was Sid that, as often as not, personal appearances and promotions would glean cash payments that would go straight on the next horse race running. Even in the more restricted, agent-ruled world of film and television, Sid would get round the rigid contracts as Victor Spinetti explains: 'He would have a certain amount of his *Two in Clover* fee paid in the proper way. With invoices and agents and everything. That was his official earning for the job. And that money would be given to Val. But Sid would negotiate with producers to get a hefty percentage of his fee paid to him in cash and that would be his horse money. I mean, he used to borrow a fiver a week off me. He always gave it back. But he was always short of cash to put on a horse. That's an addiction, I'm afraid. Little else mattered to Sid. Often he would work out various ways to get off early. Rehearse through lunch or something. Just so he had time to get to the bookies and put his bets on. He would sidle over to me and whisper: "I'm just popping round the corner, Vic. Won't be long." And he would be off. But that was all part of his appeal. An appeal that remains undimmed today. He will always be one of the lads with her indoors keeping an eye on him.'

But Valerie took on the role of restrictive mediator with grim determination and, in her own heart, beat it: 'Certainly his passion for the gee-gees brought concern to me. But it never endangered our wonderful relationship. It never ever became a destructive thing between us. I was determined it never would.'

'That was one of our things – neither of us ever pressurised the other into doing anything we didn't want to do. If you have someone who says you can't do this or that, you end up wanting to do it. That's why I never tried to stop him gambling – because I knew he needed it.'

This seems to contradict Victor Spinetti's memory of snatched Saturday afternoons in front of the television but it does, in fact, reveal that even in his private life Sid was keen to be all things to all men. He couldn't hide his love of gambling completely from his wife but, clearly, he also couldn't reveal the full extent of the passion. Sid having the occasional 50 pence each way flutter was one thing. Sid putting everything he could lay his hands on on the nose of a sure thing that never romped home was quite another.

Valerie realised that gambling – in moderation or in extreme – 'was part of Sid. It was as simple as that. I'd known about his gambling from the beginning, but I dismissed it from my mind. To tell the truth, I think I loved him too much and didn't think it was important. Gambling was like breathing to Sid, second nature. Of course it worried me . . . I knew how these things can get out of hand. But the point about Sid's gambling was that it never badly affected us, his family. Perhaps that was because right from the start of our marriage, Sid asked me to look after the finances. I would pay the bills . . . and Sid would have what he used to call his "pocket money". I'll admit there were times when I got pretty scared, and I never thought it would escalate as much as it did on occasions.'

Almost as soon as he became a part of the British way of life in the 1950s, the image of Sid the actor and Sid the character, both as the hopeless gambler, was galvanised. Whenever the Grand National or the Derby came round, Sid would be asked for a quote. And he would always oblige. Always cynically. Always in character: 'I'm watching this Derby on the telly,' he told the *TV Times* in 1961. 'I'm tamed. No more of this spieling lark at racetracks. I gotta system, and it only works when you don't spend hours looking a bookie straight in his paying-out bag. Pick a horse . . . any horse. Put your money on, and forget all about it. This way you lose your bet, your shirt, you're broke, you're skint. But you don't break your head for four hours working out a system to lose your dough. This system of mine is marvellous. It can lose your money the easy way – on horses, casinos, football pools . . . anything.'

A few months earlier, in November 1960, he had lamented missing the chance of a bet because of a commitment to a newspaper interview with the *News of the World*. 'Dammit,' he muttered. 'Too late to have something on my namesake, Jamestown. Still, I reckon I've paid enough out on that nag to feed it for a year.'

Even the success or failure of his new series, *Citizen James*, was discussed in betting terminology: 'I'm what you'd call a reluctant star. I don't wanna be a star,' he explained. 'Still, I feel the time's come when I've gotta have a flutter on my career which is something I've never done before. If you can find a bookmaker who'll give you five hundred to one, you should have a nibble each way. Wiv a bit o'luck I might just might be placed!'

It became a way of life for him. The image wasn't an image. This was Sid. Compulsive gambler. 'I've got the losing gambler's walk,' he once muttered. 'Head down looking for a winning tote ticket.'

Ultimately he tried to insist to the press that he had kicked the habit. Desperately trying to lose the image of a hopeless gambler, even if only to try and fool himself: 'I've had to give up backing the gees-gees, mate. I hit such a bad patch recently, I just couldn't carry on.'

But even when his failing health dictated the excitement of the bet had to go, Sid just couldn't help himself. Talking to the *Daily Mail* in 1971, several years after his first major heart attack, he proclaimed that the major cutback on his lifestyle was: "NO HORSES".' And those words really were in capitals! 'That's the hardest bit,' he continued. 'I was taught to read with a racing sheet.'

However, he couldn't resist the temptation for long. And he was still everybody's friend. Everybody wanted to cover up for him. Even when that meant roping in his television producer for the hit situation comedy *Bless This House* and putting the emphasis of his debt on to him. William G. Stewart recalls being asked to pay off Sid's gambling debt. Sid thrust the money into his hands and Stewart went along to the betting shop. 'The man behind the counter looked dumb and tried to tell me I was in the wrong shop,' says Stewart. 'He insisted, "Sid James doesn't owe us money." In the end I slammed the money on the counter and said I was going to leave. "OK, but don't tell anyone. Sid isn't supposed to gamble".'

Even close friends, brought in to help Sid out, were in turn confronted by betting-shop employees and comparative strangers eager to protect Sid from discovery and embarrassment. It's that old age thing again. Sid was one of the people. And the people loved him. 'Sid was just a nice man,' says Stewart. 'Some people have that quality, they attract niceness in other people. You just couldn't help but like Sid.'

Even when he was asked to guest star on *Cilla* for the BBC, the show dictated that he take part in a 'dead secret new act'. However, true to type, this turned out to be a comedy sketch centred on horse racing. 'Consider me converted. I've lost too many shirts, mate,' he said. '[The sketch is] only for fun though. I used to be a ruddy maniac about horses. But I've been tamed once and for all. I didn't only lose money, I lost stones in weight. I gave too many tips. I was lousy at it into the bargain.'

But the image refused to budge. Indeed, one of Sid's last jobs was endorsing the board game 'Derby Day' for Aurora. A small part of him would have smirked to think he was getting a whole new generation hooked on gambling as early as he had been.

Through it all, Valerie was his rock of Gibraltar. 'That woman is a marvel. I go out to work. But she does the real work and worrying. And I've got the kind of children, and relationship with them, that other parents pray for.'

His domestic life was all that mattered to Sid. That was the thing he worked all his life for. It had bought him 'all the things I like. Comfortable living. Nice home for the wife. Good schools for the kids. Money to gamble a bit, I'm a born gambler.' He valued it. And treasured it. And it was always there when he returned home. *Everybody's* magazine reported in 1958 that, 'weekends find him helping his wife with the shopping and "doing the heavy work" in the garden. The tree-lined road where he lives is much too respectable for the kind of character he really isn't.'

If he really wasn't that crafty character on screen then there were certainly elements of him in the real Sid. He was an actor and a man who always wanted to please his audience. And give them exactly the sort of copy they expected of him. To this end Sid's numerous press interviews were usually conducted in a saloon bar. However, on very rare occasions he would reveal the real man behind the scams.

During his days living in Gunnersbury Avenue, Ealing, in the early 1960s, he welcomed a snapshot of his blissful home life. His son, Stephen, put his exercise book under his nose during a chat about his latest series. '"Yes, that's very good," he said. "The kid's homework," he explained. From upstairs came the cries of two-year-old Susan. "She hates having her hair washed," said James, clearly revelling in this uncharacteristic air of domesticity.'

Sid's home was open house to film folk but Peter Dacre of the *Sunday Express* found Sid to be 'a practical and unconventional type. This much is apparent immediately you enter the hall of his modernly furnished house . . . for one thing, the hall is papered in practical and unconventional black. For another, the most outstanding feature in it is a lavishly equipped bar. "I have it in the most accessible place. This house is a halfway stopping point for actors on their way to the film studios. The doorbell never stops ringing".'

Sid would say, 'excuse the mess [in the garden], we're having a conservatory built at the back here.' While being interviewed he would happily be the domestic man he was at heart. Pumping up his son, Stephen's, flat type he would survey his lawn and tell a visiting journalist: 'When I get the lolly, I'll have a swimming pool in there. A couple more pictures should do it.'

Sid's equations were perfectly natural. A film role was simply another job. A means to an end. Two pictures equalled a swimming pool. There's nothing mercenary about that. That's pure economics. And in Sid there was a man who loved his money. If there was one thing he and Valerie disagreed on, it was this: 'I like to spend it but my wife likes to save it,' he revealed. 'Let's say we're saving it without denying ourselves the good things. The big thing that matters is that the kids should have the best possible education and that I should be able to leave them something. I saw an article the other day about David Niven leaving his children nothing. He wants them to make their own way in the world. Well, that's daft. If you're a rich man and you can make things easier for your kids why the hell not?'

It was this attitude that governed his life. In a moment of lyrical rhapsody in an episode of *Hancock's Half Hour*, 'Ericson the Viking', in 1958, Sid says: 'Eat, drink, be merry, for tomorrow we snuff it.' It should have proved his epitaph.

'Sid had this wonderful quality,' enthuses Harry Fowler. 'Every morning he would wake up and make the best of the day. His attitude was to live life to the full. He always made the best of his lot in life. The world certainly didn't owe him a living. He was out to enjoy every moment. That's a very appealing quality and I'm sure Valerie saw that. You couldn't help loving Sid because he loved life. The one word I would use to describe him is affable. That's the perfect word for Sid. Actually, if you look up the word affable in the dictionary there should be a picture of Sid as the definition!'

Vera Day was another colleague who saw this fun-loving personality shine through. 'It was during the making of *A Kid for Two Farthings* (1955) that Sid and I properly met and worked together. I vividly remember sitting in the restaurant at Pinewood Studios and seeing Sid in there with Diana Dors. As usual I had my minder with me, my husband Arthur.'

Arthur Mason had himself been an actor, making a mark for himself on the West End stage opposite Tyrone Power in *Mister Roberts*. Indeed, it was down to Mason that Vera Day got into show business in the first place: 'What a life he had! He would drive me to the studio and sit around waiting for me and watching everything I did and making sure no one made a pass at me. In a way it was good because no one could accuse me of getting there via the casting couch but it was very intimidating and restricting. But because of that restriction I remember looking at Diana and Sid and thinking: "Oh, how wonderful if I could sit there. I wish I could be on that table and have fun. Be myself and have a laugh with those two!" Sid caught my eye and, bless him, he came over and said, "Hello mate!" I suppose he had taken a liking to me but that was all. And, besides, Sid liked to engage in a bit of Jewish banter with Arthur. Sid was Jewish and my husband was half Jewish so they both spoke the Yiddish. They got on very well and, of course, Arthur was quite happy with Sid because he wasn't exactly the best-looking bloke in the studios and didn't pose a threat to him! And Arthur had a reputation for violence so most people knew it made perfect sense to keep away from me! It's funny. A lot of people say Sid must have been attractive because he was a fun person and had a lovely personality. And he was all of that. But I didn't fancy him at all. I've always been very shallow and gone for the good-looking ones!

As far as Vera Day is concerned, there was certainly no unease in Sid's family life: 'There was never a cross word between Sid and Valerie. They were blissfully happy. When I was going through my problems with Arthur it would have been natural for him to say, "Well, I've got the same sort of problem . . . " But he never hinted at anything.'

There was, however, one young blonde who Sid had a liking for. 'He quite fancied Diana Dors,' chuckles Vera, 'but every man did!'

Indeed, Swindon's own Diana Fluck had become something of a national sensation. From playing bad blondes in classic British films of the late 1940s, she had escalated to a 3-D icon by the 1950s. But, as friend and co-star Vera Day remembers, 'She had the style but, bit for bit, none of Dors was that good. But the package worked. As [her husband] Dennis [Hamilton] used to say it was the AOE. The all-over effect. Sid liked her a lot. I'm not saying he had an affair with her. Not at all. As far as I was concerned, Sid always seemed so thrilled with his classy, attractive, triumph wife that no one else could have come close.'

Indeed, like Vera Day and Liz Fraser, Diana Dors became a mate rather than an object of desire. Indeed, Valerie and Diana Dors became good friends. Sid's wife even saved her life in November 1961.

'Sidney James in Rescues at Bungalow Party' screamed the

headlines and it was no sensational bit of journalism. Three people died in the incident, many of Britain's brightest stars were in attendance and Valerie and Sid James proved heroic in a crisis. It all happened in the Buckinghamshire bungalow of agent John Kennedy. As the press reported it, 'Diana Dors, the actress, narrowly escaped with her life and had to have seven stitches in a cut leg. Sidney James, the comedian, slashed his hand when breaking a window and also had stitches. Mr Kennedy, 30, who manages Tommy Steele and Sidney James, stood near the ruins of his £8,000 bungalow yesterday and spoke of the celebration that turned to tragedy. "All the fireworks were in an upturned umbrella stand in the party. I should say there was about fifty pounds' worth. We had three fires on the lawn between the bungalow and the river and I was doing the barbecue at one of them when I heard a bang from inside. I thought it was a silly thing to happen but I did not know what caused it. I heard girls screaming and I rushed inside. Perhaps a spark from one of the fires caused it. Some of the fireworks had overflowed from the stand on to the floor. I realised what was going to happen and I screamed to everyone to get out of the house. There was panic, but Sid James kept calm. He ran back into the fire at least three times to see if anyone else was there and to bring out clothing. His wife, Val, saved Diana Dors's life. She smashed a window and pushed Diana through. "We pushed the cars away from danger." Mr James said last night that fireworks were exploding sporadically as he sat eating with his wife Valerie and Diana Dors. There was an extra loud bang which he thought was a cracker. "I do not think anybody realised how bad it was until all the fireworks started going off. Rockets and whizzbangs began flying all over the room and I shouted, 'Get down.' We crawled over the floor from the lounge to the kitchen window. Then the room became one mess of smoke. We could not breathe and it was a terrifying thing. I saw Val shove Diana through the window but I could not get through and had to smash some more glass. That was when I sliced my finger. I went back a couple of times, no more than I felt was safe, to see if anyone else was inside. Then it became a holocaust. We did not know there were two people still inside but even if we had there was nothing any of us could have done about it."

'Dors added that: "I was sitting talking to Sid James and his wife in the lounge. I do not like fireworks much and thought I would be safer indoors. Suddenly, there was a bang from the big glass doorway from the lounge to the garden then two more bangs".'

Dave Freeman remembered the party and reflected that: 'Diana was pregnant at the time. This is what so annoys me about people writing nasty lies about Sid. He risked his life that night but it's an incident pretty much forgotten. Ah well, to quote Mark Antony, "The evil that men do lives after them and the good is oft interred with their bones."'

Ironically, at the time Sid was planning the home he had always dreamed of, in Buckinghamshire. And it was to make him a neighbour of the Duke of Kent: 'Not that I've met them, mate. I don't suppose I'm their cup of tea.' According to the *Daily Express*, Sid was 'ploughing his profits into 10 acres which back on to Coppins, the Kents' 22-room country house where the Duke will live after his wedding.' Sid had his utopian mansion all mapped out. He planned to 'build a six-bedroom job with a flat for staff'. Stock the River Colne 'so full of trout that they leap out and say, "Come and get me".' And, reassuringly, he would 'like to run a pipeline to the nice little local boozer'.

However, just under a year later Sid had changed his mind: 'The wife and I are having second thoughts,' he told the *Daily Mail* in May 1962. 'The children will both be at boarding school soon. So when I'm out working the wife will be alone in this big mansion. We can always flog the land and stay on in London.'

Two months later that was exactly what he was planning to do. The land would be developed for flats. And his initial investment looked likely to make him a very wealthy man indeed. Four-storey blocks of flats were planned and as the clenched *Daily Express* revealed, the 'man behind the flats plan is Sidney James, the film and TV comedian, who bought the plot of land next to Coppins. He planned 60 luxury flats in three blocks. There were to be a swimming pool, tennis courts and an underground garage for residents. He applied to Eton rural council for planning permission . . . [but] last night a letter to Mr James was posted from the council offices.' In the event he project was shelved simply because the land was in the Green Belt. So, for the James, it was back to Plan A and the building of their luxury Buckinghamshire home, Delaford Park.

Built on the site of an old manor house to Sid's own modern specifications, an indoor swimming pool was added in the 1970s, the latest electronic equipment filled the house and it remained the haven he would happily return to for the rest of his days.

'I loved him in a total way,' said Valerie, 'we had twenty-four fantastic years together. We had an unbelievable love. We were so close; Sid and I were like one skin, that's the way he used to put it. We were lost without each other.'

Vera Day, recalls: 'By the mid-1960s I had drifted out of the business but I was still invited to the Water Rats' balls and the Variety Club luncheons and those kind of events. I remember going to a Lady's Lunch at the Dorchester and I saw Sid there. I was there with George Sewell. I knew George when he was just an East End kid before he started acting and we both went to this lunch and chatted with Sid. That was like old times really. Sid was a hero to the East End. George was in awe. Sid never changed. It was always the same old jokes and the same old rapport. He always struck me as a very happy man.

'I remember I used to put Johnson's baby oil on my legs,' continues Vera, 'and I put perfume in the oil to make it smell nice. And Sid said: "I don't believe this! My Val does exactly the same thing. She uses Johnson's baby oil all over her body and she puts perfume in it to make it smell nice. I've never met anybody else who's done that." So there we go. Valerie and I had something in common. I only actually met her once or twice. As far as I remember she never came to the studio when Sid and I were working but I naturally met her at these functions and she always came across as a very nice, warm, lovely lady. And very glamorous. Just Sid's type. Very sophisticated. With great poise.'

Indeed, Sid and Valerie were the perfect team. 'What is it that makes for a happy marriage?' she posed. 'I'd say that one of the most important things is to have sexual compatibility. Secondly, it's important to like each other. *Really* like, I mean. Be true friends and have tolerance and understanding, to be lovers to the end. Sid and I were fantastically lucky because we shared both these essential ingredients. He always treated me with true respect and sensitivity.

'When he got back after filming he'd whistle for me when he came through the door. He had a special whistle and I'd be there like a shot. It was like we hadn't seen each other for days, and it was only hours. It was a very passionate marriage.'

For Sid, his Val was everything. Towards the end of his life he took a rare moment to reflect: 'I'm very lucky,' he said. 'My wife has been a sensational mother. Very understanding. I think I'm a fairly understanding father, too, but Val is the hub of the family.

'God has been good to me,' he said. 'I've been such a lucky sod. I've made people laugh and I've got a wonderful woman.'

There spoke a happy, contended, much loved gentleman.

4

The Two of Us

The next time you are downing a few pints in your local boozer and your attention is drawn to the trivia machine in the corner. Stop. And reflect. A question may appear to which the answer seems frantically obvious. 'Which actor starred in every episode of the radio series *Hancock's Half Hour*?' If you jump in with both feet and bash the button that reads 'Tony Hancock' you will, quite oddly, be wrong. The only actor to star in every episode of the series was Sid James.

This bizarre occasion in radio comedy history occurred in April 1955. Not even six months after *Hancock's Half Hour* had, rather sluggishly, kicked off on BBC Radio, the star of the show had thrown a little moody and gone absent without leave.

Still, instead of sticking on half an hour of bell music to fill the gap, the unsentimental bosses at Broadcasting House recruited a new star. If he could keep his head while all about him were losing theirs in *The Goon Show* then Welsh baritone and raspberry-blower, Harry Secombe, could plug a Hancock-shaped hole on the airwaves for a week. In the end, his plugging duties were required for three broadcasts. And, sweetly, Hancock's return for week four was remoulded into a trip down to Swansea to thank Secombe for stepping into the breach.

That's the way casting should always work.

For Sid, of course, this was all taken in his stride. He had quickly established a firm fan following opposite Hancock and, once and for all, his comic personality was set in stone.

He may have already been cast as Sid on screen, driving Miss Margaret Rutherford around in *Miss Robin Hood* (1952), but it was another Group Three effort that introduced him to fledgling variety and radio comedian Tony Hancock. 'I met him when I was on a film,' Sid recalled at the peak of their success in 1960. 'Oh, I can't remember the name of it; it was a bit of a stinker. Tony was playing a very small part and I was playing one of the leads. That was probably why it was a bit of a stinker!' The film in question was the delightfully ramshackle army farce, *Orders Are Orders* (1954). Based on a weary old 1930s stage play by Ian Hay and Anthony Armstrong, it indulged Sid with a larger-than-life turn as an American film director staging a pot-boiling alien invasion in the very stuffy world of the British military. Hancock was the rotund, shy and rather childlike military bandleader. 'We met on that,' Sid explained, 'and I kept giving him little bits of advice, about two shots, and close-ups and things like that.'

Despite being something of a flop at the box office, the film remains historically enjoyable for this first pairing of Sid and Hancock, as well as showcasing early appearances for Peter Sellers and Eric Sykes. Indeed, things happened extremely quickly for Sid after the film was released.

Still, it was his earlier triumph at Ealing Studios that was the real catalyst for his involvement in *Hancock's Half Hour*.

'The two writers got it on,' explained Sid. 'They had seen me in *The Lavender Hill Mob* and thought that I would be just the right type for the sort of format that they had for the programme of somebody to fiddle Tony. And it worked up from there.'

One of 'the two writers', Alan Simpson, recalls: 'Ray [Galton] and I came in to the cinema halfway through the film. It must have been some sort of revival because it was an old film, even then. We had the idea of the Hancock show [initially referred to as *The Tony Hancock Half Hour* in BBC correspondence] going around in our heads and we both looked at each other when Sid appeared on the screen.'

Ray Galton agrees: 'We had to sit and wait for the second showing of the film to check the name of the actor we wanted. That was Sid James.'

Although 'being a chronicle of the life and misadventures of Anthony Hancock, the celebrated waif' as the writers had it, it was Sid's relentless cheating, lying and carefree attitude that set the show alight from the outset. The East Cheam dreamer of Hancock needed that abrasive counterpoint that Sid provided. And, in terms of history, *Hancock's Half Hour* was the blueprint for the modern situation comedy. A fantasy based on reality, the writers delighted in highlighting their cast as actors. Even contemporary film appearances for Moira Lister (in *The Cruel Sea*) and Bill Kerr (in *The Dambusters*) were addressed and debunked in the show. Sid himself was allowed to send up *Joe McBeth*, a film in which he had had little faith.

But Sid had proved to be a reluctant comedy stooge. 'I didn't want to do it. I said, "No, no. I'm a lousy radio actor." I just can't be funny on radio because I'm one of those guys that has to use his face and hands. And I said, "No, I don't fancy it." But they said, "Well try." Then Dennis Main Wilson, who was producing it, said, "Well just try one." In the end I gave in. So I tried one and I tried two and I am very glad. From the start of that radio series we clicked.'

According to the writers, this mild trepidation had turned to mortal fear when, on 30 October 1954, Sid first stepped on to the stage of the Camden Theatre. 'He was really frightened,' remembers Alan Simpson. 'People would never believe us, but

Sid was terrified on radio. I remember vividly that first time we did Hancock on radio. Sid was so scared that he wore this trilby hat pulled right down over his head. He had the scripts arranged on a stand so that he could hide behind them. One day a gust of wind blew the scripts all over the studio. And then he couldn't hide. There was something he hated about doing radio in front of an audience.'

'He had been doing theatre work for years,' points out Ray Galton, 'so it wasn't the fact that there was an audience there. He was used to them. It was just radio work. It didn't suit him. We never did find out what it was. Mind you, you couldn't tell. Sid was a tremendous support to Hancock from the off.'

Indeed, Sid truly hit the floor running. On hearing that very first broadcast, more than 50 years on, it is a rather pale blueprint of the classic *Hancock's Half Hours* to come. Hancock himself is muted and weak. Bill Kerr, later the slow-witted idiot, is far too confident and streetwise. It is only Sid who delivers from his first line. Here is an East End rogue who loves birds, booze and betting. It was the first time that the nation heard Sid James playing a character called Sid James. And from that point on Sid was no longer merely an actor. He was Sid. He would only play a different Sid in two further TV situation comedies and six Carry On films, but from November 1954 at the age of 41, every part Sid played was Sid. By default. *Hancock's Half Hour* gave him the country on a plate and, for the time being, Sid loved it.

'*Hancock's Half Hour* was the best thing that happened to me,' he said later. 'It pushed my value up.'

It also gave the show that contemporary, abrasive, comic edge that it is remembered for today. And that effect was immediate from Sid.

The producer certainly had no doubt either, for it was Dennis Main Wilson himself who penned a memo to Sid's agent, Phyllis Parnell, mere weeks into the series. It was to confirm: 'We have agreed to put forward the recording time for *Hancock's Half Hour* to a midday recording on Saturdays from 18 December onwards for seven weeks, in order that Sidney James will be free to accept the part he has been offered in *Wonderful Town*. This arrangement is, of course, on the understanding that the management of *Wonderful Town* will release him from the Saturday matinees so that he will be available for our recordings.'

It was positive proof that Sid wasn't simply part of the furniture on Hancock's show, he was the vital component that fired the star comedian up. Sid was there to stay.

Both Sid and Hancock knew it was working. For two very simple reasons. They were performers at the very top of their game. And, from that very first meeting, they became firm, lasting friends. As Sid was proud to say, 'The two families hit it off.'

Valerie remembers: 'We had some crazy times with Tony and his first wife, Cicely. I remember once we were all invited to the premiere of a cowboy picture. The invitation stipulated we should all come in cowboy costume. So we dolled ourselves up in the right gear and took off for this big cinema in Leicester Square. When we got to the foyer everyone recognised us – for Tony and Sid were at the height of their fame – but nobody could understand why we were all looking as if we'd just come off the ranch. No wonder they looked at us so strangely. We'd got the date wrong and had arrived a week early!'

Sid enjoyed Hancock's company. For one thing, 'most actors want to talk about how they wowed 'em in Bedford or somewhere. We don't. We never talk shop.' As far as Sid was concerned, once the show was recorded it was done with. No post-mortems over a pint in the Hand and Racquet. Just a pint in the Hand and Racquet. And lots of laughter.

Sid instantly knew he was in the greatest of company. He considered Hancock 'a great comic. No, more than a comic. An acting comic. The two of us are dead opposites. I suppose that's why we hit it off so well. I love gambling. Tony doesn't. I keep relaxed. Tony works on his nerves.'

Sid would listen to Hancock on food and drink: two great passions. Even after the break-up he would slurp down Russian vodka with the throwaway comment: 'Tony introduced me to this.'

On occasions, their social life would extend from saloon bars and first nights. Both would play cricket. 'But,' as Hancock cheekily snorted, 'Sid will smoke in the slips. We do things better in East Cheam!'

From the moment both Sid and Hancock hit their stride together they automatically took the characters that Galton and Simpson had created for them and lived the parts for the press. This was a comic partnership of opposites built of a genuine friendship.

Sid would gleefully pose for publicity photographs picking Hancock's pocket. He would even answer to the name of Sidney Balmoral James with a shrug of the shoulders and a muttered 'that's a dead liberty as well!' Even though it was a middle name invented for him by the scriptwriters.

It was a part that Sid could live. The saddest thing about *Hancock's Half Hour* is that, while celebrated as the pioneer of British situation comedy, it is always tempered by the elements that destroyed it. The insecurities of Hancock himself. His concern over Sid's thriving career away from the show. His hatred of catchphrases. His hatred of two-dimensional comedy. His hatred of himself. But this was just the smallest of percentages of a five-year run that, on both radio and television, spread a lot of pleasure.

As Alan Simpson maintains, that 'all happened right near the end. As far as we are concerned it was the happiest show Ray and I ever worked on. Everyone got on well. And the laughter. We had four of the best laughers in the business in that show. Sid's laugh, of course, became legendary. Hancock would be laughing so much he would hurt himself. Bill Kerr would be rolling on the floor. And Kenneth Williams would be braying in the corner. It was a joy to go to work.'

As for those immortal catchphrases, the first one that the team tried out was for Sid himself. But it very quickly was seen to be anything other than immortal. His frustrated cry of 'Get out of it!' was hastily abandoned. The team was soon aware that Sid didn't need a catchphrase. Simply an attitude. A do-anything-for-money, police-shy, cheeky confidence trickster who would rub his hands in glee every time he saw Hancock coming. Whether it was enlisting him into a secret Druid society, selling him a rundown mystery-tour business, getting rid of a ticket to the Cup Final – a year out of date – or humiliating him in front of hundreds of paying punters, as he tried to reject society and go back to nature. Here was the black marketeer familiar from war-torn Britain, making his way through the 1950s by any means he could.

Or, as Sid's obituary in *The Times* summed it up: 'It was in comedy, however, that his wry, humorously disenchanted personality showed itself to best advantage . . . what really confirmed his popularity, though, was his long-lasting partnership with the late Tony Hancock in the television series *Hancock's Half Hour*. Here, he was the ideal straight man: Hancock's endless optimism about his own potentialities and the grandeur of his position in East Cheam society was constantly being deflated by Sidney James's cool realism and readiness to see any flaw in the master's logic.'

The major bone of contention between Sid and Hancock was one that was never talked about during the 1950s but has come to sum up their misinterpreted feud. In fact, there was no feud. There was a busy jobbing actor and a paranoid, troubled comic genius. While the factions could be contained there was no problem. And, indeed, during the early days of the partnership both were fully occupied separately onstage between their shared East Cheam duologues.

Sid was wowing them at the Golders Green Hippodrome in *Guys and Dolls*: 'the best role of my life. It was my life!' While Hancock was with Jimmy Edwards in *The Talk of the Town*, just about to transfer to the Adelphi.

Sid's commitment to *Wonderful Town*, agreed to by Dennis Main Wilson and the BBC, saw him nipping down from the Manchester Opera House to fulfil his broadcasting commitments. And, by the start of the second batch of programmes and the Hancock/Secombe solution in 1955, Sid was happily settled in at the Princes Theatre. Whether Sid liked it or not, he was now a star: 'I don't like this star business,' he said. 'I think, taking a long-term view, I am only a character actor and I think once you start this star business you have got to wait for star parts to come along and I just don't consider myself a star.'

But the BBC certainly did. The Hancock series was considered a natural to transfer to that new-fangled and increasingly popular medium: television. Kenneth Williams and a late arrival to the radio series, Hattie Jacques, were restricted to a mere handful of appearances on screen. Bill Kerr was dropped altogether. But, as Ray Galton explains, 'That was nothing sinister. Bill and everybody else was still in the radio series, don't forget. The two were happily running concurrently. People tend to forget that. And as for the television shows, you have to remember we were writing for a different medium. As far as Alan and I were concerned it was three and a half thousand words for a radio half hour and three and half thousand words for a television half hour. But you have less freedom on television. You can't jump about from scene to scene as easily. There has to be a bit more logic at work. It was for that simple reason that the television series, at its best, boiled down to lengthy two-handers between Sid and Tony. You could put those two in a room and have twenty minutes of material without even having to think up a plot. It was all in their interplay together.'

Alan Simpson reveals: 'It has been said of us that we write about two people talking in a room because Ray and I were two people talking in a room as the script developed. The Hancock and Sid relationship was the first time we did that. And it seemed to work.' As modest as ever, the writing of Galton and Simpson certainly did work. The Hancock shows on television became a legend in broadcasting history. Pubs would be near empty. People would bluster past each other to get home from work in time to watch it. Children would be frowned upon if they woke up during the show. If the coronation in 1953 had been the first televised event, when *Hancock's Half Hour* transferred to television in 1956 it became the first event television.

As a result, Sid would become one of the most familiar faces on screen. And what a face! 'The eyes ain't much cop,' he joked. 'All you can say about the nose is that short of breathing through, it's not worth a light. Now, take the mouth. It's not exactly a mouth you brag about. It's a beauty! That leaves the voice!'

That voice, described by the *Daily Mirror* as 'the sound of a concrete mixer grinding up brick dust and granite chips soaked in gin', could sum up the human condition. When artist Ruskin Spear painted a portrait of Sidney Balmoral James in 1962 he explained: 'I wanted to depict the twentieth-century mood: rheumatism, ban the bomb, income tax and another packet of fags. I sketched Sidney James by watching him on television. It was a pleasant piece of work. I'm a fan of his and he has a very paintable face.' Typically, when confronted with this snippet of news, Sid was comically dismissive: 'Paintable?' he laughed. 'Mate, you could have fooled me. One look at my face and you dive for cover. The chap who did the portrait must be a fan of mine or he would never have wasted the paint! It must have taken at least seven weeks and half a dozen brushes for the bloke to get round my nose. It ain't what you'd call petite. I don't know what 'Ancock will have to say about this!'

A potential place in the National Portrait Gallery notwith-standing, it perfectly sums up why Sid became as important to the nation as he did. The character was one of us. One of the down-trodden who worked hard and was always broke at the end of the week. Who lived for his smokes and his booze. Who grumbled his way from the cradle to the grave but always made the best of a bad lot.

In terms of the radio relationship becoming a television relationship, those gravelly tones perfectly suited that gravelly face. If an audience member had never seen Sid onstage or at the pictures, the moment he turned his wireless off and turned his newly acquired television on, that face and that voice were the perfect match.

Of course, television brought another element to the show. Although the radio programmes were recorded in front of a live audience, they weren't broadcast to the listening millions until a few days later. With television it was live.

Someone linked with Sid throughout the 1950s and a colleague on several live television jobs was Vera Day. 'Unlike on a film, when everything is shot out of sequence and you try and get everything done in one take, live television was like theatre. Only many, many times more nerve-racking. Instead of a couple of hundred people out front you could be playing to unseen millions. It was terrifying. All you had was this little red eye. That was like the demon. You knew that it was there and whatever you said was going out live and there's nothing you can do about it. Thankfully, I was always word perfect with my lines and movements. As was Sid. But it was a very hard acting discipline. Every scene was in different parts of the studio and you had to rush from one scene to another, jumping over people and as often as not having complicated costume changes along the way. It made you feel like a hurler! But working with someone as professional as Sid made it as good as it could be. Actually, it was terrifying but I enjoyed it. It was proper acting and Sid was the nicest person to have around to hold your hand.'

Liz Fraser also remembers the pitfalls of live television: 'It was in the very early days of Hancock on television. It was, in fact, only the second show Liz appeared in and the third episode of the first televised series.' Tony is looking for a wife and I'm one of the girls he considers. Irene Handl was playing the proprietress of this marriage agency and, typically of Irene, she insisted on having her little dogs on set with her. Now, this is live television don't forget. No retakes allowed! Sid was doing this scene with Irene and suddenly this little dog went for Sid and bit his hand. He was biting his lip and desperately trying to hold back an expletive. He managed. The professional as always. But, sadly, that show is one of many Hancock programmes that the BBC doesn't have in their archives. So Sid's supreme control under crisis has gone forever. But I'll always remember it. I can hear Sid now after the show muttering: "That bloody dog!"'

But by the end of the 1950s, the fame was beginning to become something of an intrusion: '*Hancock's Half Hour* started it all. I've become sort of one of the family in thousands of homes,' explained Sid. 'Take the other night. This geezer rings me up – it's four o'clock in the morning – and he says, "'Ello, Sid boy. How's it going?" "How's what going?" I says to him. "It's four o'clock in the morning." "Don't get shirty, Sid boy," he says, "just thought I'd ring up to see how things are going. Bye, Sid boy".' Sid rumbled with gravelly laughter: 'And the callers – girls too! I could understand them knocking at the door if I was Marty Wilde or Adam Faith. But to think they want to get a close look at *my* mug.'

The lapse into a jokey dismissal puts this mild irksomeness into perfect perspective. For Sid, the fact that his life was no longer really his own was the price you paid. As he said, 'The [local] kids wake me up outside the house when I'm trying to lie in on Sunday morning. They cost me a fortune in photographs. But I'd be worried if they didn't.'

In his mind, Sid owed it all to *Hancock's Half Hour*. He had become an even more tangible hero to children via the Hancock comic strip in *Film Fun*. With the Hancock crew in tow he had represented the cream of BBC entertainment in the London Coliseum Commonwealth Games presentation, *Welcome to London*. Having missed a telly episode he happily made a live introduction to the first repeat in order to add his voice to a link he had been absent from the first time round. He even made sure his strict gym training regime wouldn't affect his appearance for the programme: 'I do a bit of sparring . . . but we have a sort of tacit agreement, well it's not so tacit really, it's a very strong agreement that there is no punching on the face. Can you imagine me arriving . . . in front of Hancock with two shiners.'

Hancock's Half Hour meant the world to him as his letter to producer Tom Sloan of 15 January 1958 illustrated: 'Re: *Hancock's Half Hour* – I think I'd rather *die* than not be in it! Nobody knows better than I do that [it] has done me the world of good. All that remains then is to sort out the dates and the dough (formal business letter this!) and we're away.'

Valerie maintains that 'Tony and Sid were really fond of each other and both were totally dedicated to the show. Sometimes I thought they got on so well because they were both born under the same sign – Taurus. Not that Tony seemed aware of the fact, but I knew it because his birthday was only three days before Sid's. I remember telling Sid one morning that it was Tony's birthday that day and to wish him well. "Many happy returns, mate," Sid said dutifully when he saw him. Tony looked at him blankly, "What are you talking about?" "Well, it's your birthday today isn't it?" A surprised Tony replied: "Is it? I didn't know." Because they saw each other so much at work and the four of us used to go out together every week, we had an agreement that our holidays would always be taken separately. But this idea fell through one summer. One sunny morning, Sid and I were on the beach at Juan-les-Pins in France when we spotted two people waving frantically in the distance – a man in a large straw hat, and ludicrously long khaki shorts and a girl in a bikini. Sid said, "There are two people waving at us, lie still and pretend to be asleep." Moments later we heard a voice saying, "You're pretending to be asleep aren't you!" We opened our eyes – there stood Hancock and Cicely. Naturally we all fell about!'

The break-up, when it came, was unexpected and hurtful.

And ironically timed from Sid's point of view. He recorded his appearance on *Desert Island Discs* on 24 March 1960. For his eighth and final selection for the pile of gramophone records Sid selected an extract from a classic *Hancock's Half Hour*: 'Well, you need a bit of a giggle don't you and something to remind you of the old times and the old laughs and the old team. Let's have a bit of Hancock. We did one about a lazy Sunday, with nothing to do on a Sunday afternoon. Let's have a bit of that.'

Less than a fortnight later the cracks had started to appear. Having been approached by ITV with regards to a project, Sid explained: 'Tony's show comes first. We finish telerecording the present BBC Hancock series this month. Tony hasn't yet decided whether he'll do a new series. But whatever happens I'm going to do two films this summer. Too much TV can be a killer. Even the greatest people – and I'm a long way from being that – wear out their welcome on the screen.'

As far as Hancock himself was concerned the partnership with Sid was not die-cast: 'We work together when possible because we get on so well,' he said. 'But the situation has always been we work as we want.'

Both Sid and Hancock already knew the score. When the story finally broke at the start of May 1960, Sid revealed that Hancock had 'kept throwing out little hints. But I wasn't taking them. Not me. Then one night when we'd four more programmes to do, he dropped his bombshell on the way to the pub after a rehearsal. He said: "Look Sid. What say we pack it in at the end of the series?" I said, "Don't talk like a maniac, boy! How can you *think* of chucking up a cast-iron success like ours?" I argued and argued. I told him we could have made films, formed our own production company. Everything. But could I budge him? I still say it's a crying shame Tony and I had to break it up.'

Mutual friend Liz Fraser remembers: 'Sid was, understandably, very upset when Tony made that decision. Sid really couldn't believe that Tony could have done that to him. They had become great friends over the years. But Tony had simply made up his mind that he had to continue without Sid. Tony had told me that he was extremely concerned about the audience seeing Hancock and James as a double act. They weren't a double act in the strictest sense of the word but if you were out in public with Tony people would often shout out: "Hey Hancock. Where's Sid then?" That must have got to him quite badly. The problem for Tony was that Sid was an actor. Tony was very much a comedian. He had done his variety act around the country without Sid and he was eager to hold a television series together on his own as well. Up to that point Sid had been a constant fixture of the radio and television shows that had made Tony a star. Sid could go off and make a film before breakfast but all Tony had was *Hancock's Half Hour*.'

It was a bombshell for Sid. His wife remembers him saying, '"Tony doesn't want me in the show anymore, he wants to go it alone." He was absolutely shattered.'

But, typically, Sid was not bitter about his friend and cohort in the press. On 2 May 1960 he finally admitted, 'If Hancock goes back for another series after Christmas I won't be with him. The partnership is definitely off. There's been no row with Hancock.

I've never been fed up. You can't get fed up with a set-up like that. A comic as clever as Hancock and a script you always know will be a cracker. It doesn't make sense to want any more. But you can't go on and on doing the same thing, cocker. That diabolical little box has had enough of us for a while. I don't care who you are or how good you are, the public gets sick of the sight of you. But I don't blame Tony. He'll be a great success. He's still the funniest man I know.' There's a real sense of Sid putting on a brave face here. Like a love affair that has gone wrong he seems to be clutching at straws about the possibility of giving the relationship another chance. That phrase 'for a while' speaks volumes. It suggests that if Hancock had made the call Sid would have gone back to him in a heartbeat. But when really pressed about whether the old team would ever get back together again Sid wasn't sugar-coating the pill: 'I don't think so, mate,' he said.

However, the team never really disappeared. The BBC reacted to popular demand throughout the 1960s and repeated both the radio and television exploits of Hancock and Sid. Pye Records licensed extracts from the shows to release commercially. And, finally, in 1965, the two were reunited in a recording studio to record new versions of two television scripts, 'The Missing Page' and 'The Reunion Party', for Decca Records.

Graham Stark, a mutual friend and valued member of the Galton and Simpson repertory company, worked with Hancock during this period and was shocked to see him. 'I hadn't seen Hancock for years. There he was. Honestly. He looked like my father. He was grey. And fat. He just couldn't do it anymore. The timing was all gone.'

The reunion was certainly an ordeal for Sid. Less than a year later, while on set with Kenneth Williams filming *Don't Lose Your Head*, Sid allegedly warned Williams away from resurrecting the celebrated 'Test Pilot' sketch from the radio show, *The Diary*, with Hancock. The Royal Festival Hall show proved to be a disaster.

The last time Sid saw Hancock was in 1967. It was just before Sid's major heart attack and he was driving down Piccadilly when he spied the dishevelled figure of his old cohort. 'He looked dreadful,' remembered Sid. 'I tried to pull up and get over to him. I got the car parked, but by then he had disappeared. He was so full of liquor he didn't see me. I wish to God I had been able to catch him, because little things like that can change people's lives.'

Because of the bitter treatment he had borne, often away from the press, the break-up with Hancock was an emotional wound that Sid nursed for many years. No time more so than following Hancock's suicide in Australia in June 1968. Less than a year later, while Sid was starring in the Thames television series *Two in Clover*, he had a rare moment of reflection with his co-star Victor Spinetti. 'As you know, Sid was never one for looking back on his career. What was done was done and on with the next thing. But he was extremely cut up about Tony Hancock's death and kept on wondering why he had dropped him from the series all those years ago. He was very upset about that and he still couldn't understand it. That broke his heart because, he said that, at the time, he thought the two of them had had it made and that the show was going to run for years and years. Indeed, if Hancock had lived, I can't see why that partnership couldn't have continued well in to the 1970s, like Eric Sykes and Hattie Jacques did. As far as Sid was concerned they had a good thing going on and there was no need to change it. As far as I could tell Sid looked upon the Hancock years as his best years. They gave his career a real touch of class and quality. Something all those knockabout comedies and Carry On films didn't. Don't get me wrong. I love the Carry Ons. They never employed me but I still love them! But I certainly think once you had performed those marvellous Galton and Simpson scripts – something akin to mini Harold Pinter plays disguised as situation comedy – then you were spoilt for life.'

Indeed, the spectre of Tony Hancock never fully left Sid's side.

Even when his biggest personal success on television, *Bless This House*, started in 1971 its popularity was tampered by the fact that critics, fans and even Sid himself commented that it wasn't as good as the old days with Hancock.

It was a year when Sid was also forced to take a close look back at their partnership. It had been three years since the troubled genius had taken his own life and now, as the initial disbelief subsided, compilation albums and documentary retrospectives were emerging. The *BBC Presents Fifty Years of Radio Comedy* album even resurrected an extract from the celebrated Sunday afternoon episode Sid had selected during the happier times of *Desert Island Discs*. Sid himself, always balking at the thought of interviews, obliged for the memory of his fallen comrade and spoke warmly and candidly for the BBC Radio 4 programme, *What Happened to Hancock?* Sid recorded a seven-minute fifty-second interview for use in the programme when the show was being made under the rather less-sensational working title of *A Story of Our Time – Tony Hancock*.

Ironically the show was broadcast on the very day that *Bless This House* started on ITV.

Later in 1971, during the making of *Carry On Matron*, Sid – and for that matter Hattie Jacques and Kenneth Williams – were still discussing Hancock as new contracts and higher residuals were negotiated for extract fees and repeat broadcasts.

In 1973, Sid was around to see his work with Hancock hailed as a comedy classic. He was even around to accept the compliment of a suggested imitation when the BBC announced a series of remakes of the old Galton and Simpson scripts. Tragically, the actor chosen to replace Sid had himself died after just one programme was recorded. James Beck – the perennial spiv, Private Walker, in *Dad's Army* – had succumbed to pancreatitis at the age of just 44. Perhaps it was fitting that during Sid's lifetime he was irreplaceable. As was Hancock. When a handful of the shows were remade with Paul Merton in 1996 the recasting of the Sid role skilfully vied from the conventional (Sam Kelly in 'Twelve Angry Men') to the ground breaking (Caroline Quentin in 'The Missing Page').

Sid's character of the sharp-suited, fast-talking, wisecracking bloke with a never-ending line in dubious deals remains a comic convention that everyone can relate to. 'Is there nothing you wouldn't do for money?' Hancock once asked him. 'Nothing I can think of offhand!' was Sid's casual response.

Sid's last tangible connection with Hancock came in 1975 when Decca re-released the 1965 reunion recordings as *The World of Tony Hancock*. A copy of that album once appeared on the auction website eBay. It was signed. Not only by Sid James. A possibility. But also by Tony Hancock. An impossibility. I like to think that Sid had a hand in giving that item provenance!

5

Solo

B ack in 1960, the ending of his relationship with Hancock was still extremely raw. And Sid needed to pick himself up and face the uphill struggle to re-establish himself on television.

Sid and Hancock were never really a true double act. Very much like the Two Ronnies a couple of decades later, the two performers enjoyed a public life away from each other, all the more safe in the knowledge that the partnership would be renewed without much discussion or fanfare. Or at least Sid certainly did. However, for the audience and, most crucially, Hancock himself, the two had become inextricably linked as a team. Hancock had to cut the ties that bound them.

Sid, throughout his five successful years in support of Hancock, had also been notching up film, television, stage and radio credits at a rate of knots. Indeed, his constant schlepping from Pinewood, Elstree or Shepperton in order to rehearse or record with Hancock was the seed that refused to wither and die within the star comedian's consciousness. Typically of an insecure performer touched by genius, Hancock wallowed in the thought that his career had just been *Hancock's Half Hour*. He failed to ponder that his lucrative variety work and smash-hit West End revues were without the aid of Sid in any way. But, in the mind of Hancock, who always thought the grass was far, far greener on Sid's patch of land, the stage assignments counted for little. Indeed, when he considered Sid hobnobbing on film sets with the likes of Charlie Chaplin, Lana Turner, Burt Lancaster and Jack Palance, you can sort of see his point of view.

And, with the original BBC files bearing witness, the *Hancock's Half Hour* shows were often affably moulded to fit around Sid's other commitments. Even when his filming schedules were at their tightest, the BBC was desperate to solve the problem. Planning the second series of Hancock television episodes, producer Duncan Wood wrote personally to Sid on 5 February 1957: 'It goes without saying that we would very much like you to take part in the series, but, at the same time I fully understand that you cannot give us a definite answer until a decision has been reached regarding your film commitments. However, perhaps you would let me know the results as soon as you are able so that the writers can plan the scripts accordingly.'

In this instant, Galton and Simpson were forced to write Sid out of the opening two programmes but he returned for the live fortnightly broadcasts at the end of April 1957. But, Sid explained, 'I gave priority to the Hancock shows, which meant missing film work.' The major element that really tempted Sid to accept a film job was a nice location. In the spring of 1957 it was Italy that held an appeal to shoot *Interpol* with Victor Mature. Plus the extra money that came with such film assignments.

Moreover, from his agent's point of view, Sid's unavailability made him an even more valuable commodity in the eyes of the BBC. Upon his return home, Phyllis Parnell had renegotiated his fee up to 35 guineas an episode. A little less than half of Hancock's salary, but a tidy, regular sum to supplement his film income. However, it was an attractive location again, in Spain this time, which threatened to hold up the Hancock show for several months.

Producer Tom Ronald wrote to the Drama Booking Department at the BBC who, curiously, always dealt with Sid's Hancock work, in the hope of booking him to 'take part in 13 pre-recordings . . . between 1 and 30 June 1959. His agent has explained that [Sid] has a contract for a film to start in May, which will necessitate his being on location abroad for three weeks during either May or June. They are not able to give us any exact dates at the moment until they receive these from the film company. I have arranged that we shall contact the agent during next week . . . to find out if there is any further news. Apart from this, there would appear to be no snags in his taking part as he is very keen to do the series.'

In the event it was the BBC that backed down. Both the fifth television series of *Hancock's Half Hour* and the sixth radio series were broadcast from September 1959. And now the television episodes were telerecorded for the first time.

For Sid, the film that had blocked the passage of his BBC work had been a very important one, in several ways.

Reflecting his almost pop–culture standing, it partnered him with the teenage phenomenon of the time, Tommy Steele. The British rock 'n' roller may have been riding the crest of a wave but it was clear that Sid was in perfect control on the set. As co-star Bernard Cribbins can testify: 'We were in Seville making *Tommy the Toreador*. Me and Sid and Tommy were in a lot of scenes together so in-between the set-ups we would play a lot of poker on the set. Sid put a limit of twenty-five pesetas on it. I had never played poker before and Sid introduced me to it. Of course, Sid and Tommy were old hands at the game. And, more to the point, Tommy was loaded, of course. There's a lot of money in rock 'n' roll! Anyway, Tommy had obviously pulled a good hand because when Sid called the bet Tommy said: " . . . and twenty quid!"

That's a lot more than twenty-five pesetas, I can tell you. Anyway, Sid took one look at Tommy. Grabbed his hand. Grabbed my hand. Scooped up all the cards on the deck. Threw them up in the air and said: "That's it!" That was lovely of him. He was saving any financial embarrassment, particularly from my point of view.'

But even during these exotic days away from home filming, Sid's mind was still on *Hancock's Half Hour* and returning to the show he loved.

Bernard Cribbins continues: 'We were still in Seville. Sid had heard there was some amateur boxing on. "We'll have a bit of that, Bernie!" he said. So Val and Sid and myself decided to go. I can remember it vividly. Like it was yesterday. We had a lovely meal beforehand: prawns in a little cotta dish, covered in garlic. Followed by crayfish. And lots and lots, and I mean lots, of white wine. And then we had some more white wine. Val was saying, "Sidney, please!" She didn't like him getting too plastered. And he never did really. He could put it away though! I wasn't used to it at all, so I was well gone!

'Sid had booked up for the boxing and he had got us ringside seats. It was almost too close. It really was a case of having to look up and crane your neck to see the ring. But it was marvellous. A few *fundadors* [Spanish brandies] were consumed and we were slightly merry to put it mildly. Actually, when we got back home, Sid told Hancock that I had got so incensed by the boxing match that I had climbed into the ring myself to finish off the champion!'

Sid was clearly 'happy with the way things were. I enjoyed working with Hancock. I don't think he'll ever be quite as funny without me. I know I won't be as funny without him.'

Still, for the audience, Sid had already proved himself. Time and time again. In a career boost that can only be described as 'the Hancock effect', Sid's new found popularity at the BBC had upped his bankability at the cinema box office. He was no longer simply a jobbing character actor. He was a comedy star. In light of this, he happily returned to old stomping grounds with the same professional attitude but a lot more personal clout.

He had appeared as an irate Italian nightclub owner in Hammer's creaky comedy, *The Lady Craved Excitement* (1950). A decade later he was back for one final Hammer Films credit, in the caravanning romp, *A Weekend With Lulu* (1961). This time he was a disgruntled café owner. But his guest-starring billing and his familiar face were plastered all over the film's advertising.

He was welcomed back to Ealing Studios for the last time, teaming up with the elephantine Tessie O'Shea for much needed comic relief in the outback in *The Shiralee* (1957).

Sid had wandered through the race-horsing subplot of *The Belles of St Trinian's* (1954) just before finding national popularity in the Hancock shows. At the peak of their powers, in 1960, Sid re-joined the schoolgirls for their third outing, *The Pure Hell of St Trinian's*. This time he was given guest-starring billing. The majority of Sid's role simply involved him looking a little menacing and suspicious on board a ship set at Shepperton . . . while eating a banana!

He was recruited once more by director Ralph Thomas in his spirited remake of the film *The Thirty Nine Steps* (1959). 'The one thing I am afraid of is that if people think I'm a star they will stop offering me jobs,' Sid said. 'I've made a good career out of playing small parts. I've appeared in a hundred and fifty-three films since I came from South Africa fourteen years ago. I've just been offered twelve thousand pounds for this house and, mate, this house was bought on small parts. I can get as much as five hundred pounds a time for a morning's work. I don't want to risk losing that kind of lolly because producers think I'm a star. I know actors who turn down parts because they think they are below them. They'd rather starve. I don't refuse any part, providing I can do something with it . . . and the lolly's good.'

During his heyday with Hancock, Sid was in a unique position.

While gaining an audience at home, he was also raising his value in the eyes of film producers.

Some might even throw a leading role his way: it is important to remember that Sid had filmed his first film for Peter Rogers, *Carry On, Constable*, some six months before the break with Hancock. And film stardom didn't halt the flow of those valuable little parts that Sid relished so much. Not quite yet, at least.

Those aforementioned little parts were made all the more important to the film in question because of his reputation on radio and television. The roles were all Sid, of course. Or, at least, that aspect of Sid that his audience had come to love.

In *The Thirty-Nine Steps* he is a lorry driver happily helping Kenneth More on the run. But he's a lorry driver who has been around. And been inside. In *The Pure Hell of St Trininan's* he initiates a scheme to lure the saucier pupils of the school to an oil billionaire's harem. Basically, if there was a dodgy deal going down in British film comedy, Sid wouldn't have been too far away.

Hancock must have been a bit miffed at Sid's lucrative and popular double life as television star and film draw. It certainly wasn't the money. Hancock was earning twice as much from the show as Sid was. It was simply a matter of pride. If Sid could have it, why couldn't he?

Hancock became a comedian with an all-consuming passion to make it big in films. And not just in home-grown, home-consumed efforts from Group Three. He wanted to star in international successes. Tales of Sid's location filming in Spain, Italy and France must have sounded glamorous and fun. Because they *were* glamorous and fun. Hancock wanted a piece of the action.

As a result, the final nail in the partnership of Hancock and Sid was the film *The Rebel*. For all intents and purposes it was a big-screen spin-off from *Hancock's Half Hour* and writers Ray Galton and Alan Simpson were fully intending to include a Britain-based cameo for Sid. 'After all, he was far more skilled in filmmaking than any of us,' recalls Galton. 'During the early days of Hancock radio, Sid was knocking off ten or fifteen films a year in-between working on our scripts. He was a natural film actor. Coupled with the fact that the public loved him. And, more importantly, they would have expected him to be in the Hancock film somewhere along the lines. Both Alan and I felt very strongly that he should be included. Hancock disagreed. It was the start of the rot setting in, I suppose.'

For Hancock, *The Rebel* was to be an independent stand. A film starring him. And not Sid. Added to the fact that he would enjoy a lengthy location shoot in Paris. The thought of international awards and glitzy film premieres must have danced before his eyes like sugarplums. And, typically, Hancock would also use the film as a retreat away from the British press. He timed the public announcement concerning the abandonment of Sid from the television series just as filming in Paris began.

Sid, on the other hand, treated these little location luxuries as simply a perk of a well-paid job. He wasn't in the business to become a star. He was there to make money. And as much money as possible in the shortest space of time. Even more gratifying to Hancock must have been the fact that Sid was forced to lick his wounds after the break-up, filming a very British comedy film on the sound stages at Twickenham. Despite the fact that *Double Bunk* was 'the best thing I have ever done', it certainly didn't equate to colour, European cool and a co-starring spot with a 'proper' film star like George Saunders.

'It's funny,' says Alan Simpson. 'Anytime that Ray and I had some sort of block over a script we would sit in our office and throw out comments. "I wonder what George Saunders is doing now?" "He's putting ten bob on the number seven dog at White City!" And there we were, working with him.'

Sid, laudably, kept his cool. 'There was no unpleasantness over the break-up,' he said, 'but I am very upset about it. Tony told me, "You'll probably be better off." Financially I probably will.'

But Sid would miss him. 'We sparked each other off. I don't believe there was any jealousy. Tony just wants to prove to himself that he can go it alone. He felt he wasn't getting any better; that he was beginning to repeat himself. Tony is one of those people who feel they can go only so far on one line. They have to keep going off at right angles. But this means starting again. I don't see it that way. I'm not the artistic type. I do it just for the money.'

The blaze of publicity that surrounded Sid and Hancock when the break came was all consuming. Indeed, Sid would have to qualify every single hit situation comedy for the rest of his life with the fact that it was the best work he had done since the Hancock days. Even after Tony's death and Sid scored on a completely new, domestic pitch, with *Bless This House*.

It had certainly affected Sid's powers on BBC Radio when, back in the summer of 1956, he starred in *Finkel's Café* for producer Pat Dixon. Just a few months after the third radio series of *Hancock's Half Hour* had finished, Sid was back as Sid: the wheeler-dealer of East Cheam uprooted and plonked opposite Peter Sellers as the seedy manager of the café in question. Denis Norden, who wrote the series with partner Frank Muir, recalls: 'Sid was a dodgy cockney, of course. He was *the* dodgy cockney and the BBC was determined to milk his popularity. That series was a bit of a disaster really, so thank you for reminding me of it!' Norden chuckles. 'But we were asked to do it because a series in America, starring Ed Gardiner, and called *Duffy's Tavern*, had been very popular. This was our version. The banner tag for the US show was "where the elite meet to eat". Over here, we made that "where the posh squash to nosh", so you can get an idea of the quality of the thing!'

The Norden and Muir scripts were gems of invention, as always. Even the title is a delicious, sophisticated pun. But Sid on the radio without Hancock just didn't seem to appeal. The Irish bluster of Sellers' character didn't attract the same comic clout from Sid as Hancock's pretentious bluster. And the audiences picked up on it. After just six broadcasts the plug was pulled on *Finkle's Café*, with an option for three further shows not taken up.

When the split with Hancock hit the papers in May 1960, stories began to emerge about tentative steps to make the nation's favourite comic feed a star in his own right. 'In the cautious shadows of the BBC, negotiations for the *Sidney James Show* have begun,' revealed the *Daily Express*. 'Veteran producer Bill Ward, Programmes Controller of ATV, took him to lunch yesterday to sound out the chances of bagging Sid for the Val Parnell merry-go-round. He has already turned down a big offer from Associated-Rediffusion.'

But this had not been the first time Sid had flown alone on radio and television. And his track record had been none too good. That rejection of an Associated-Rediffusion project is fascinating. And very telling. For Associated-Rediffusion had been at the epicentre of Sid's first major starring series on television.

It was a series that the news-hungry journalists of May 1960 were continually mentioning in the aftermath of the split with Hancock. Unsurprisingly, for this starring vehicle for Sid had been a flop. An interesting flop, but a flop all the same.

East Side-West Side was 'Sidney James's own TV series . . . in which he played a philosophic and not too lucky dealer.' Set in Sid's domain of the Jewish East End with familiar British film people like Sydney Tafler and Alfie Bass in support, he told the *TV Times*: 'Your mob asked if I'd like to do a series. So I phoned Wolfie [playwright Wolf Mankowitz] and we got on to this. [It's] easy going stuff. Drifting in and out of situations. Gentle humour, not comedy. I'm not a comic. Wish I were. Character actor, that's me.'

Sid's comment about 'your mob' clearly highlighted the fact that he considered himself a BBC actor. And the BBC thought the same. Following the rising viewing figures during the third series of *Hancock's Half Hour*, they were less than impressed with his defection to the other side.

East End-West End was set to launch on commercial television in February 1958 but the news broke the month before. Tom Sloan, the Acting Head of Light Entertainment at BBC Television, wrote personally to Sid. 'After reading the reports in the morning newspapers, I have now learnt the actual position from [television producer] Duncan Wood and I must say I am very sorry to hear it.'

'As I understand it, you will be doing a series of six weekly programmes for Associated-Rediffusion with scripts by Wolf Mankowitz beginning 4 February. There then follows a seven-week lay-off and I believe Associated-Rediffusion have an option for a further series of 13 programmes at the end of this lay-off period. I am very sorry that we have not had a chance of doing this series on BBC but as you have made your decision my principle concern is safe-guarding the Tony Hancock series which we will be starting in October. I do hope that there are no other options in your present contract that are likely to prevent you coming into the Hancock series and I would like you to take this letter as a firm indication of our desire to have you in that series in October. I think it would help to keep the records straight if you could confirm that the situation is as I have outlined it and signify your willingness to be available for the Hancock series in the autumn.'

Sid replied to the letter, expressing his regret: 'Naturally, I'm sorry too that I didn't have the chance to do the series for the BBC. Quite frankly, I would have preferred to. But time was passing, I'm getting older and the money was *very* good!!' As usual, Sid's cheeky attitude won over any bad feelings.

It was just as well for, just over a month after *East End-West End* had premiered, the signs were not good. On 5 March 1958 Sid's agent, Phyllis Parnell, wrote to Ronald Waldman explaining that her client 'will shortly be concluding his current television series . . . and will be available for any part that he may be suitable for.' Tom Sloan responded, with perhaps a touch of glee: 'I presume this means that Associated-Rediffusion's option on his services for a further 13 programmes has not been taken up?'

This presumption was correct. *East Side-West Side* was pulled after just six shows. But it was a programme that Sid remained proud of: 'We're not playing for belly laughs,' he insisted. 'It was fairly successful with a few people, but I don't think the general public went for it. But I went into that in a hurry,' he explained. 'Next time we'll take more care.'

More care was essential for the next time. For the next time Sid's television career quite literally hung in the balance.

However, not quite yet. Interestingly, the BBC had been keen to give Sid his own starring vehicle even before the end of *Hancock's Half Hour*. Less than a year after the whole *East End-West End* debacle and during the hugely successful run of the fourth television series of *Hancock's Half Hour*, Eric Maschwitz at the BBC approached Sid's agent. She dutifully reported back on 9 January 1959, explaining: 'I had a chat with Sid and he is most interested in the suggestion and would like to do it, but at the moment it is rather difficult to commit ourselves to anything like definite dates. Can I contact you again a little later on when the several film suggestions we have at the moment have been cleared?'

Maschwitz, however, was not keen on playing the waiting game. He was also very determined to place the Sid series. 'How soon could you give me some idea as to when he would be available?' he wrote three days later. 'I have to make up my summer schedules now and would like to work Sid in before he is due to go back with Hancock.'

Over a week rolled by until Parnell came back with disappointing news: 'Regarding Sidney James and the suggestion of a situation comedy series for him in the summer. I have now had a long talk with Sidney about this, and he does feel that he would rather leave this over until some future date. As you are aware, he does not finish in the Hancock series until the end of March, and I understand it is possible that they may recommence sometime in the autumn, and Sid does feel that with an additional series in-between, he may be outstaying his television "welcome". Apart from this, we are being overwhelmed with film offers for him for this period, which naturally he would like to accept, particularly as one would mean a very nice few weeks on location in Spain. I feel sure you will appreciate how Sid feels about this, and we both hope that the suggested programmes can be arranged for some future date.'

Tommy the Toreador, of course, filled the gap very nicely. And, ironically, led to Sid decamping from the Parnell Agency and joining Tommy Steele's agent, John Kennedy.

Was Sid's reluctance to take on a starring vehicle for the BBC out of loyalty to Hancock or because the financial lure of the film for Associated British was too great? You get the impression that it's a little bit of both. 'After a particularly successful series with Tony Hancock on BBC TV, ITV gave me my own show,' Sid explained. 'They gave me a top writer like Wolf Mankowitz. But I was no good. I'm just not star quality, friend. So I went back to Hancock where I belonged. Now the BBC wants to give me my own show. But I've turned down the offer. I know my limitations. But my house and car have been paid for and that means a lot to a has-been middleweight who never drew more than fifty bob for a fight.' With that Sid paid the bar bill in cash and drove off.

Clearly he was happy to grab the money and run when British pictures offered him a nice little earner to play a crafty con man, so long as he had that reassuring Hancock job to come home to. And Sid was happier still as his image with Hancock was beginning to mellow slightly. There was a nagging doubt about always playing the rogue. 'I don't resent it,' he said, 'but . . . I'm afraid to walk along the streets sometimes. People walk on the other side, you know. "Keep your wallet away from him!" I'm trying to get away from that.' Indeed, this new attitude to avoiding the all-out rogue undoubtedly played a big part in Sid turning down the pick-a-pocket-or-two villain of Fagin in Lionel Bart's original 1960 West End staging of *Oliver!*. Fagin was a pantomime baddie, but a baddie none the less. Sid had had enough. As he continued: 'I think you will notice in the last few Hancock's that we are drifting away from that. It is played out. It is not funny anymore.'

For sure, Sid's words carry a lot of weight. He spent much of the final series of *Hancock's Half Hour* maturing and cultivating a slightly softer image. He is seen as a keep-fit expert. He enjoys a stint of babysitting with Hancock. He even falls deeply in love with a bus clippie. He was still doing crafty deals on the side, but it was a more rounded Sidney Balmoral James. Sadly, for Sid, he didn't have a chance to develop these changes.

'I'm not worrying, mate,' he told journalists when the break with Hancock came in May 1960. 'The offers have been pouring in. Films, stage, TV. There have been rumours around of a split you know, and people have jumped in with work. But to some the term "feed" still hangs like an irremovable nosebag.'

Not for the BBC, however. And not for Ray Galton and Alan Simpson.

Although his solo television and radio track record had not been good, 'Sid James is luckier than most,' reflected the *Daily Express*. 'He is an established comedy actor. He knows too well that a TV series is only as good as its material. The chances are that the men behind *Hancock's Half Hour* will go on writing shows for Sid.' And indeed they would. Speaking at the time, Ray Galton said, 'It's most likely that we shall be able to take on Sid. We've worked together a long time. We know each other so well. That's the important thing. Of course, there has always been this difficulty of taking the number two character and trying to turn him into a number one. You don't automatically get away with it. But I think

Sid is a different proposition. He is a good operator. He has a vast personal following. He can do it.'

And Sid was mightily relieved when it transpired that they were going to do it together.

But it meant jettisoning the new image. At least for the time being.

Talking to a *Daily Mail* reporter in a London saloon bar with a drink in one hand and an expensive American cigarette in the other, Sid mapped out his masterplan: 'I just go on working. Haven't stopped since I settled in England. Nice steady average of three films a year. Reckon it's been a poor year if I haven't earned ten-thousand nicker.' It 'wasn't my doing,' he muttered, when the conversation inevitably turned to Hancock. 'I'll tell you. It was Tony's entirely.'

He dismissed Hancock's worry. 'To begin with, TV was murder to do and in our case I felt we'd squeezed that East Cheam set-up dry.' He continued with a snort, 'Nuh! We could have got *years* more out of it. You could tell that from the way the public loved the repeats. Makes you laugh really, because I was the reluctant one when Alan and Ray brought us together on the radio. *Marvellous* pair of writers. Got 'em working now on my own new series.'

'At first I jibbed,' Sid went on. 'It wasn't the money mind. I turned down two or three films each time for the pleasure of playing with Tony. I even turned down my own TV series. I wouldn't have dreamed of doing this new one now if Tony and I could have gone on together. I'm not big-headed enough to think I can strike out on me Jack Jones and do better for meself without Tony. I'd rather be his stooge – all right – his support, than star in me own right. But that TV success gave me a terrific box-office boost and it'll earn me a lot more lolly than I've earned before. I've never been exactly cheap but I'll be a lot dearer now,' he chuckled. 'Talkin' of lolly,' he continued, 'I've promised to buy me wife her first mink coat this weekend. What's that? Hire it out to film starlets for premieres? Now there's an idea!'

This was Sid in full Sid mode. He was worried that his series wouldn't be a huge success. And he was swanking about his earnings. But, more importantly, he was again playing the dodgy geezer who would do anything for a few guineas. Actually, he was presenting that character as the real Sid. He had reverted back to the Sid of the radio *Hancock's Half Hour*. He was a hustler. A con artist. A wastrel. And a layabout.

Even his choice of book on *Desert Island Discs*, the *Encyclopaedia Britannica*, had 'a bit of method in my madness . . . when I'm finally rescued, I could come back and win every quiz programme you can think of!'

When Sid's solo series was finally announced as *Citizen James*, Ray Galton and Alan Simpson wrote: 'Sidney Balmoral James, the hero of the piece, is self-employed, and a man of some forty-something summers and some very hard winters. His face bears testimony to a difficult life, careworn, craggy and lined. We must point out, however, that he is not a crook. A parasite, public enemy, evil to society, yes . . .'

'In my new series,' Sid explained, 'I don't want to be regarded as the star. I'll be the leading actor. I'm not worried about branching out on my own . . . After the Hancock show, it's got to be good. I've always been happy to be a good supporter. When you're a star you have to start worrying. I'm in this business strictly for the money, mate. And a good solid prop can often have a longer life than a star.'

However, it wasn't just the money at stake here. Sid knew he had to play the confident bloke for the press but he was also candid about the show and the fact that his reputation was at stake: 'This time it's got to be right. I've insisted on the same scriptwriters and producer [Duncan Wood] as we had for *Hancock's Half Hour*. [I'm] roughly the same as I was in the Hancock show. A sort of smart boy with no particular job, who bets and is always ready to try a new way of making money, but isn't really as smart as he thinks he is.'

But, again, this was the Sid of the *Hancock's Half Hour* of the mid-1950s. He had regressed out of necessity and his new series awaited him. It was, effectively, *Hancock's Half Hour* without Hancock.

6

Mornin' Sarge

The BBC was quick to reassure Sid that his future was still with the corporation. By June 1960, producer Duncan Wood was fully committed to his new series, *Citizen James*. He wrote to Sid to thank him for 'a wonderful evening. I am sorry we didn't get around to talking an awful lot of business, but nevertheless I have had some fairly intensive thought about casting. Going through *Spotlight*, time and again, I really don't think we can do better than Daphne Anderson and Bill Kerr as the two major supports. I have been as far as investigating their availability over the period in question, and their reactions to the proposal. The answer is the same in both cases – they would be delighted at the prospect and are free over the period, and would do camera tests for us if required. Personally, I don't think we need look any further, since I have complete confidence in both of them, and I would even go so far as to sign them up for the series now. Perhaps you would let me know what you think.'

Bill Kerr was a natural shoe-in to the seedy East End world of Sid's two-bit rogue. The two had built up a firm friendship and rapport doing the radio shows with Tony Hancock, which had come to an end just a year earlier.

As for Daphne Anderson. Someone, somewhere along the line, didn't approve her casting. The role of Sid's glamorous, feisty and sharp-tongued girlfriend went to regular Hancock girl, Liz Fraser.

'I'd known Sid for years, since we appeared together in commercial television's first ever daily serial. It was called *Sixpenny Corner*. I suppose you could say we brought a touch of humour to it. It didn't last long and not many people have heard of it but it was there, right from the beginning of ITV in September 1955. We were later moved to an evening position [when the budget for morning programming was cut] and got a good year out of it. But playing Sid's girlfriend [in *Citizen James*] was a real joy. There was never a question of taking sides. We all still remained friends with Tony Hancock. This was just another job. But a really fun one.'

Citizen James was the culmination of over a decade of roles for Sid. Here he was as the definitive crafty cockney, holding centre stage. Still, Sid the actor disliked facing the responsibility: 'I am almost being forced into it,' he admitted. 'I was a good "feed" and I'm no new boy, chum. I know my limitations,' he said in November 1960.

Still, those perceived limitations were perfectly suited to the situations developed in *Citizen James*. This was the Sid of *A Kid for Two Farthings*, still trying to get rich quick with one final throw of the dice.

'There are some Sidneys who must ever remain so. But Mr James is a natural "Sid",' wrote one critic. 'When he drives through Covent Garden the porters call out: "Hello Sid, boy! What fiddle you on today?" or "Look out, here's Sid James. Hide the crates".'

'As he recalls this, his leathery face wrinkles into a grin. "Aw, photographers. They always say, 'Let's have one of you taking somebody's wallet.' Well . . . " He doesn't need to say any more. You realise that, in a way, Sidney James is like Dr Frankenstein: he created a character and now he's stuck with it and occasionally it overshadows his real self. But it's *partly* himself that he plays on screen and radio. Close your eyes and forget the comfortable pink and cream sitting room of his Ealing home, and the baby clothes drying in the garden, and the gruff, gritty voice and accent are the same. Keep your eyes closed and you can imagine he's trying to flog you a case of export Scotch instead of offering you a mid-morning cup of coffee. For the engaging thing about Sidney James is his naturalness. He has no pretensions".'

Sid had already tried out his eternal fiddler character on the big screen and in leading parts. In Mario Zampi's celebrated breakneck, black farce, *Too Many Crooks* (1959), he was teamed, once again, with Vera Day: 'That was the happiest film I ever did,' the actress remembers. 'I was just laughing all the way through. In fact, how we ever got any lines out at all is beyond me. That gang! Particularly Sid. But George Cole, Bernard Bresslaw, Joe Melia. Joe was the typical student really. It was his first film and he was having the time of his life. Playing practical jokes. Bantering with Sid. Sid was always happy. He was funny. Even when he was playing serious parts, in the military or small-time crooks or something, he was still likeable somehow. That Sid James warmth always shone through. That sense of fun. That sparkle in the eye. The audience would sit back and think, "Oh it's all right. It's Sid!" That was the quality that Sid projected on screen. He had that relaxed, carefree attitude. In a crisis it would be Sid who could be relied upon to say, "Oh, don't worry. Everything's going to be all right. Come and have a drink!" That's why people love him. And I use the present tense deliberately. Everything he did had that quality to it. The situation was safe as long as Sid was around.'

Jack Hylton, who had employed Sid in one of his earliest stage hits, *Burlesque*, was also quick to utilise his skill in front of the camera. He had played a black-hearted western baddie opposite Arthur Askey in *Ramsbottom Rides Again* (1956). And it was while back in harness with Askey, and under the auspices of Jack Hylton, in the satire on commercial television, *Make Mine a Million* (1959), that Sid's film career embraced that do-anything for a pile of cash persona to the full. Indeed, his second starring billing on the credits pictures him as a suave, cigarette-smoking pirate, surrounded by moneybags!

Bernard Cribbins remembers Sid taking it all in his stride: 'He loved playing those sorts of parts. That's how the public saw him and, as Sid always said, it pays the bills. I remember in one scene that I was to drive this army ambulance. Sid was my passenger. Anyway, it came to the scene and the director, Lance Comfort, explained what I had to do. I looked at him dumbly and said, "But I can't drive!" "You can't drive!" This seemed to be the cardinal sin on the set. All the props guys stopped what they were doing and chorused: "He can't drive!" To Sid's eternal credit he didn't join in. He knew the situation needed to be sorted out. Anyway, Lance rallied all these props men up, about fifteen I would think, and they had to push this ambulance while I steered it and Sid sat in the passenger seat. You could hear all this grumbling going on: "You bastard!" and all that. They put a railway buffer down in the place where I had to stop and they pushed me towards this. Sid and I did the whole stopping and jerking motion and that was that. But if you watch the film today, I'm not driving. There are fifteen extremely cross props men behind the ambulance pushing us!'

An earlier film, *Dry Rot* (1956), also cast Sid as a leading con man but, again, the actor was anything but tricky. Joan Sims remembered: '*Dry Rot* was a difficult film to make. There was an awful lot of rushing about and the director, Maurice Elvey, wasn't the most understanding of men. There was one scene that ran to several takes and Elvey was getting very impatient. Poor old Michael Shepley kept on forgetting his lines, or going through the wrong door or something, and it got to the stage where everybody was on tenterhooks and everybody knew that whatever could go wrong would go wrong. Well, Michael ruined another take and Elvey bellowed, "For Christ's sake, will you get this right! You've wasted twenty minutes on this already!" At that point, Sid calmly left his mark, walked over to the director, muttered "I will not go on with this scene until you have publicly apologised to the actor you have just insulted!" and walked off. Elvey was forced to apologise and we finished the scene. I thought at that first meeting that Sid was a most professional actor and most wonderful human being. That opinion didn't falter for twenty years.'

Sid may have been fun and understanding on set but he was fun and conniving on screen: pitching up his stall in the street or via illegal television links with the sole aim of promoting Bonko soap powder and making a fortune. Or frantically trying to earn a dishonest bob at the racetrack via kidnapped jockeys, police chases and swapped horses.

Even on radio he had been a rather disreputable tutor to the wooden-headed Archie Andrews. A job he had inherited, several stars removed, from Tony Hancock, it was never a particularly inviting prospect but the audience felt, through his handful of appearances, that the cheeky dummy had learnt a few useful tips on how to be streetwise.

However, by the late 1950s, Sid was equally as likely to be behind the desk in a police station rather than reporting to the law. He had been cast as policemen before, of course. Indeed, he had cropped up, briefly, on the right side of the law in Lewis Gilbert's hard-hitting street gang exposure, *Cosh Boy* (1952). However, it was director Ralph Thomas who, in the spring of 1959, gave him the leading, comic role of a friendly yet world-weary policeman in *Upstairs and Downstairs*. The plight of an upper middle-class couple in a secluded part of London and their problems in finding the right people to be their staff was certainly not tapping into the truth of life in Britain at the time. And, unsurprisingly, the film proved a rare miss for producer Betty Box. For Sid, however, it proved a revelation and gave him the unique opportunity to spend time with his daughter on set: 'Yes,' he explained, 'Susan. She was with me in *Upstairs and Downstairs*. I think she was about eighteen months then.'

The film also added variety to his spicy film work. As he gladly told the press, 'In my latest film I play a copper. But I'm back to form next month. I go to Spain with Tommy Steele for a film playing a crooked bull-fight impresario.'

The film, of course, was *Tommy the Toreador*. A pivotal one for Sid. But nowhere near as pivotal as the film that he started in November 1959. This was another kindly copper role, this time provided by Ralph Thomas's brother, Gerald. The film was *Carry On, Constable*. Although Sid's Hancock cohorts, Hattie Jacques and Kenneth Williams, had been with the Carry On series since the beginning, he grabbed the top billing position in this fourth outing of mildly blue jokes concerning the boys in blue.

As usual, Sid treated it as just another job. For, at the time, it was just another job, although he certainly enjoyed the publicity that surrounded him: he stopped traffic while on location in Ealing as he escorted the delectable Shirley Eaton across the road. 'He was perfect for those films,' she remembers. 'Whether the films were changing or Sid changed them, I don't know. But he was certainly suited to that "ho, ho, ho" and "nudge, nudge" style of comedy that came in after I left them. I didn't work with him very much on the film but he enjoyed the publicity stunts and the laughter on the Pinewood set with our fellow film "idiots". Sid quickly became the star of that set.'

Committed to the job in hand, Sid even missed the eagerly awaited Henry Cooper versus Joe Erskine fight because he and boxing favourite Freddie Mills had to be up bright and early for filming. Eric Boon, another great of the fight game, trying his hand at acting in the film, described Sid as 'everybody's friend'. And that's exactly how the nation saw him. Whether playing slightly off-centre or beleaguered authority figures in British pictures, Sid was a working-class hero. But it was television that had made him a permanent fixture in the hearts of the nation.

If the press heralded the start of *Citizen James* as a series with 'a ready-made audience', the *Daily Express* also reflected that this 'is a benefit that brings its own drawback'. It was, indeed, 'certain that it will be critically compared with *Hancock's Half Hour*. [Still] Mr James is entitled to a little time to establish himself as a solo artist. [The] intriguing, often amusing rogue, an elderly 20th century Artful Dodger who works harder than most to avoid work.'

Speaking on 24 November 1960, the day of the show's first broadcast, Sid was clearly nostalgic and not a little unsure of himself: 'I've tried to think of *Citizen James* as just another show but these last few weeks I have missed Tony as badly as I'd miss an arm,' he confided. Certainly, six months on from the break-up, Sid was still in recovery mode and under no illusions about life without Hancock. 'I reckon I know right now what people will say about my own new show tonight. "It's not the same," they'll say. But after that run of success they would say the same thing if I was working with Danny Kaye.'

'I'm not expecting to be a hit,' Sid continued. 'I shall be content with a reasonable, steady show which people might warm to. If I fail, it will be my own fault. [Ray Galton and Alan Simpson] have given me wonderful scripts.'

For Sid, the show was an all or nothing television gamble. He reflected that the BBC talked about making him a star. But that wasn't important to him. As far as he was concerned, this was work. Pure and simple. 'My future seems to have been plucked out of my hands,' he said.

As the press had it, 'Tonight is the very public trial of Citizen Sidney James.'

The morning after that very first broadcast the *Daily Express* reflected many people's reaction to *Citizen James* when they commented: 'There is now an almost monotonous note to the brash cockney humour, and the variety and subtlety which Hancock inspired are sadly missed. To hold the series together it will surely have to be developed and expanded to avoid constant repetition of setting and situation.'

While that is harsh, there is a grain of truth in the opinion.

Viewed today, the early episodes of *Citizen James* have a vibrant, gritty, down-to-earth quality. Sid, in pole position, and the crisp Galton and Simpson dialogue complement each other perfectly. But the series was indeed one that would develop over the years – through necessary scriptwriter changes and cast dissatisfaction though, rather than critical opinion or public disinterest.

However, while the nation prepared for *Hancock* the series and the great comedian's zenith, Sid was happily treading water over on the BBC Light Programme with Dennis Price and June Whitfield. Originally commissioned under the title *What's the Odds*, in several internal memos within the BBC the series was discussed as *The Sidney James Series*. Two separate pilot programmes were recorded with an audience at the Playhouse studio and, subsequently, the Paris studio. While Sid's agent, Phyllis Parnell, gamely suggested either Mark Mileham or Kaplan Kaye as the office boy, in the event, Robin Ray landed the role and joined Wallas Eaton and June Whitfield as the staff. 'Sid always seemed a bit lost on radio,' she remembers. 'He was wonderful in the role, of course. It was him, after all. But he was happiest on film and television. He had such a splendid face! It was written by the Two Ronnies,' chuckles June. 'Ronald Chesney and Ronald Wolfe, that is. I was the posh secretary in Sid's firm. I think he was a property developer of some sort. A particularly shady one, of course.'

Of course he was. Sid was, reassuringly, playing Sid once more. This time as the titular head of James Investment and Property

Undertakings Limited of Mayfair. However, in this set-up, Sid was very much the foil. The silky smooth Dennis Price was the brains of the operation. As the original publicity material explained, Sid 'was going to put in a bid for Buckingham Palace until he found out there was a sitting tenant.' Indeed, he is so naïve that he 'fondly imagines that the Green Belt is a boxing trophy for novices'.

When the series was given the green light in October 1960, Sid was happy to sign up. Producer Tom Ronald understood that 'he is prepared to start pre-recording his new series at any time at the beginning of 1961. He is willing to do thirteen programmes but will not sign an option for a further seven as he has a television series and feels that he does not want to undertake more than the original thirteen.'

It's a Deal may have been a short-lived run for Sid. But it was on his own terms and, more crucially, again pointed towards a softer, more innocent image for him.

With Ray Galton and Alan Simpson committed to Hancock, Tom Sloan was fully aware that series two of *Citizen James* would be under different management. On 31 January 1961 he wrote personally to Sid to enquire whether he was available to do a further series of programmes in October/December.

The BBC was clearly happy to commission 'as many as you can possibly manage'. In fact, the figure of 13 was mentioned. But *Citizen James* was still very much in the shadow of *Hancock*. A similar offer had been made to Sid's old cohort and, as far as the BBC was concerned, he would get priority. As well as first dibs on the writing of Galton and Simpson. It was still very much in the air whether Hancock would commit to another series for the BBC. In the event, he didn't. But *Citizen James* was still farmed out to other writers. The first in the frame being Sid's current radio scribes, Chesney and Wolfe.

But crucially, Sid was seen as instrumental in the redevelopment of *Citizen James*. 'I suggest you come and have a talk with all of us about the writing situation, and see what we can achieve,' Tom Sloan suggested. 'We would also like an opportunity of discussing with you possible changes in the format, which indeed may become inevitable if Ray and Alan are not the writers. The important thing is that I want to demonstrate to you quite clearly that the BBC is interested in a further series with you in October/December and if you are with us on this proposal, then I think we can start taking the matter a stage further.'

The watershed came in May 1961 when the BBC started broadcasting *Hancock*. Critically acclaimed, these much-anticipated shows kicked off with 25 minutes of Hancock alone. It was a triumph in terms of both acting and scriptwriting. For, while Galton and Simpson injected verve and energy into the scripts for *Citizen James*, there is no denying the comedy coasted along on well-established rails. *Hancock* was a departure. And a popular and influential one at that.

However, it was a short-lived victory for Hancock. And it was the parting of the waves with Galton and Simpson. Graham Stark recalls: 'It was the situation with Sid all over again. Hancock couldn't tell the boys that he wanted to move in. He had this mortal fear of conflict. I was out with Ray Galton for a few drinks one evening and we spotted the advertising board for the *Evening Standard*: "HANCOCK SACKS WRITERS!". Now I count myself as certainly one of the people who knew Tony best. I probably knew him best of all. We went back years and years and I dearly loved him. But he had lost his grasp of what he was doing when he abandoned Ray and Alan. They had created this character for him. But I'm convinced that it was the dropping of Sid that started it all. The series he did on his own was a huge success but Hancock, the man, needed Sid by his side. Simply to keep his grip on reality. I really liked Sid. He was a good, solid actor and didn't have one ounce of pretension about him. He loved working with Tony. Liked him and respected him. In Sid's mind it was a great acting partnership but he was in no doubt whatsoever that it was Tony's show all the way. Sid was the perfect comic foil. The second banana to end all second bananas. And he could have saved Hancock from himself.'

However, Hancock's split with his writers came too late for the *Citizen James* production team. Tom Sloan had already rejected the idea of Sid's *It's a Deal* writers, Wolfe and Chesney, as replacements. And the BBC had desperately held on to Galton and Simpson by offering them 'an opportunity we couldn't refuse. They said we could do anything,' says Ray Galton. 'Write them. Produce them. Direct them. Even star in them. That was *Comedy Playhouse*. And from that came *Steptoe and Son*.'

In the interim, Sid had starred in his own show, unimaginatively dubbed *The Sid James Show*, for producer Colin Clews over at ATV. One show was written by Dave Freeman, who 'had met Sid on an episode of *Hancock's Half Hour* [during the third television series in 1957]. He was playing the crook, of course, and I was a copper on his trail. The other policeman was Bill Fraser. Sid had pulled off a big bank robbery and we got on the same flight as him.' Freeman was, however, first and foremost a writer: 'I did little bits of acting, mainly with Benny Hill who I was chiefly writing for in those days. But ATV offered me *The Sid James Show* and I gladly took it. I was a great admirer of Sid's. He was a first-rate comedy actor. And, once I got to know him, I really liked him as a friend as well. The show was a good old-fashioned variety show with comedy sketches. I remember writing one which featured Sid as a Roman gladiator about to go into the arena.'

Tom Sloan had been in talks with Sid James, Roger Hancock and Dave Freeman, all of whom were strongly linked with Associated London Scripts and the domain of Hancock, Galton and Simpson. Sloan was planning a further 13 episodes of *Citizen James* for broadcast at the end of 1961 and wanted to commission a pilot script from Freeman for Sid James: 'If the pilot is acceptable . . . it is understood that the pilot will, therefore, become one of the projected thirteen programmes.'

In terms of fees, it was made clear early on that 'I would like your offer to Freeman to be a reasonable one, although I do not anticipate for a moment that it will be anything in the Galton and Simpson class.'

Freeman's memories of this were hazy: 'I have a vague idea I was asked to do something else for Sid around that time. And it was certainly a situation comedy. I was writing a successful series of situation comedies for Benny Hill at around that time as well. As far as I recall it was just Sid again. You know, the cockney geezer scraping through life in the East End.' And this could very well have been the problem. Freeman's vision for *Citizen James* was following the blueprint laid down by Galton and Simpson far too closely. Indeed, his scripts for *Bless This House* a decade later would continue to evoke the blokeish aspect of Sid's early career far more than other writers for that, predominantly, domestic situation comedy.'

The other edition of *The Sid James Show* for ATV had been penned by Sid Green and Dick Hills, two writers who were just on the verge of making a name for themselves with Morecambe and Wise's sketch series for commercial television.

By the end of April 1961, Tom Sloan confirmed with Sid's agent, John Kennedy, that the star was 'willing to accept these two writers for his series in the autumn'.

Indeed, only a matter of days went by before Sid himself wrote to Sloan, on 27 April 1961, enthusing: 'I am glad to know that you are all very impressed with the first script of Hills and Green. As requested in your letter, this is to give you formal confirmation that I will be willing to accept Hills and Green for the proposed autumn series. I think it might be a good idea for John Kennedy and myself to meet you as soon as possible to discuss the whole proposition.' Even before licking down the envelope, Sid realised his other commitments were too much and hastily crossed out 'and myself' from the body of the note and added: 'Sorry I can't come up too, but I'm very busy filming.'

But the die was cast. And the element that Sid most admired about the new scripts was their departure from the old character. This was still Sid James. A cockney geezer who would see you in the pub for a large one. But now he was something of a campaigner for lost causes. A diamond in the rough rather than a rough diamond.

For Peter Dacre of the *Sunday Express*, Sid 'has backed the biggest winner of his life. I refer to *Citizen James*, the TV programme, which has been one of the great successes of the TV year. This weekend sees the end of the series – but it will be back next year.' And for this particular reviewer the second series had been a breath of fresh air. 'Though he was backed by the writers from the Hancock stable,' he wrote, '[Sid] was only an also-ran in his first canter with his own series. James was presented in the well-worn mould of a Soho artful dodger – and failed to click with the fickle TV public.' According to the press, 'there was only one bright spot: his cut-and-run association with Sydney Tafler a "wide-boy" bookie who always outwitted James's petty plots.'

It was this relationship that the new writers seized upon. 'Here seemed the makings of a new comedy team. Unfortunately they were both the same type of character. After much head scratching, James and Tafler later emerged with new characters, provided by two writers who have put the verbal nosebag on many a top comic, Sid Green and Dick Hills. In the new series they were two ordinary, well-intentioned blokes far removed from the world of spivery. The humour came from the clash of two pedantic personalities in simple everyday situations. From the start, the combination clicked.'

As well it might. The two Sids had been indulging in Jewish banter and black market deals in British pictures for years. If

Sidney James was breaking into a jeweller, it was a safe bet that Sydney Tafler was keeping an eye out for the law. In the early days the actors were almost interchangeable. Indeed, it was Tafler and not Sid that made his debut in Ealing's *It Always Rains on Sunday*. And Tafler again who starred opposite Harry Fowler in *The Booby Trap*, yet another film erroneously credited to Sid. 'I'm pretty sure he wasn't in that one,' says Fowler. 'But Sid was popping up so frequently in those days he might have filmed a bit when I was having a loo break!'

Tafler, akin to Sid himself, had became rather fed up of the crooked image. But *Citizen James* was different: 'It's all been rather peculiar,' he remembered. 'It started when Sid rang me up and asked me to appear in the first series as a guest. I had been doing a lot of guest appearances and I wasn't too keen. But Sid is an old friend and I said "Yes".'

In that first series, Tafler is the bane of Sid's life. He is the bookie who gladly takes all of Sid's money. He is the spiv who aids and abets Sid's dubious attempt to launch a brand of cigarettes. And, most audacious of all, he is the cad who tries to tempt Liz Fraser away from her flighty boyfriend.

However, Tafler was even less sure about partnering Sid for the regular team in the second series reshuffle. 'I had a terrific resistance to series. I had been offered series before and turned them down.' But again it was Sid who made the approach and got Tafler on board. Clearly, Sid's clout over producers in terms of casting was already in full effect.

It was this second batch of programmes that fully captured the public imagination. Within three weeks the audience doubled from five to ten million homes. Moreover, its appreciation figure stood at a staggering 67 per cent despite being pitted in the schedules opposite ITV's already legendary *Coronation Street*.

Although this was a personal triumph for Sid, he wasn't amused at the cavalier attitude of the BBC. 'But it's a feather in your cap,' they soothed. 'I've got feathers sticking out of me all over,' groaned Sid. 'I don't want any feathers. I want an audience.'

But, at least in one respect, he was delighted: 'I've never been so thrilled in my life,' he reported as he quaffed a large gin and ginger beer. 'It's wonderful – touch wood. I've wanted to change my character for years but I could never manage it. Now, since the series started I've had five film offers, all of them sympathetic parts.'

7

Roger Roger

The film offers were, indeed, pouring in for Sid. And the vast majority of those he would accept were for the producing-directing team of Peter Rogers and Gerald Thomas. Having forged a successful working relationship since 1956, the two filmmakers had, in fact, bridged Sid's career from the dying months of *Hancock's Half Hour* to his emergence as something of a people's champion in *Citizen James*.

And, contrary to the womaniser image that many still associate with his run in the Carry Ons, Sid's early film ventures for Rogers and Thomas were, in the main, just those kind of sympathetic characters he yearned for.

As negotiations started for the third series of *Citizen James* in January 1962, Sid was filming *Carry On Cruising* at Pinewood. He was at his most sympathetic and timid here. Indeed, he even balks from sexual advances from flighty cruise liner passenger, Dilys Laye. It is far removed from his confident wisecracker of the films a decade later. But Sid's character of a down-to-earth, working-class success story certainly struck a chord with the actor. 'That a non-posh mariner became captain of a cruise liner – his role – delighted him,' recalls scriptwriter Norman Hudis. 'And it indicated to me that, notwithstanding certain relaxation of the emphases in British society, class was still a vital factor at that time.'

Sid had also been pleased with his central role in *Carry On, Constable*. This part had not been tailor-made for him, however. It was intended to make comedian Ted Ray the pivotal fixture of the series following his sterling role as the headmaster in *Carry On Teacher*. 'But,' as producer Peter Rogers remembered, 'Ted was under contract to ABC Pictures. They never used him and he was such a good artiste. But, because he was being gainfully employed in my pictures, my distributors, Anglo Amalgamated, were very embarrassed. ABC actually threatened to lean on them and scupper us completely. It was a pity but we had to find someone else.'

Sid fitted the bill. He was, according to Norman Hudis, 'the invaluable, made-to-measure, Carry On-type actor.' Sid was also delighted with the script. So much so that Hudis recalls, 'Sid asked me to his home. I expected some suggestions for radical script changes. He was more grateful for what had been written than anxious to achieve changes in it. It wasn't so much because of any sentiment accorded the character as relief and pleasure that a rough-spoken cockney had achieved senior police rank.'

For Hudis this was a once and only invite to Sid's home. 'Where he was concerned, it was a case of Sid We Hardly Knew Ye,' he admits. 'Sid's attitude about acting was very down-to-earth. It was "something you do and then go home". But I have always felt that his brief comments to me indicated that whatever his views on acting as a profession, he was very much alert to class distinction.'

Sid's delight with his roles at Pinewood was such that he eagerly became part of the Peter Rogers and Gerald Thomas repertory company and accepted any role that the team offered him – even the typically roguish part of a crafty music publisher in *Raising the Wind* (1961). In *Watch Your Stern* (1960) he was a weary chief petty officer, sporting a luxuriant prop beard. 'Sid could have grown a real beard, of course,' pointed out Peter Rogers, 'but

107

unfortunately it was only needed for about half of the film. At one point in the story he shaves it off to please a very persuasive Joan Sims. Since scenes are rarely shot in the order in which they are finally cut together, Gerald [Thomas] might have filmed one sequence two-thirds of the way through the film near the beginning of the schedule, thus requiring Sidney clean shaven. And then, the next day, he might have shot a scene from the start of the story in which Sidney would be required to sport the beard. Try growing one that quickly! Besides, I thought his beard was fine. Just the sort of typical, Jack Tar, Players cigarette-type maritime look I wanted.'

By the time of Sid's second appearance in the official series, *Carry On Regardless* (1961), scriptwriter Norman Hudis was well aware that Sid would be cast as the head of the Helping Hands Agency. As a result, it is the writer's most Sid-like characterisation. There's boxing. There's scantily-clad nurses. And there's that world-famous laugh that was fast becoming the ultimate signifier of British screen comedy. For Hudis 'he was the same character every time – Sid James of the dirty laugh. I wouldn't knock the dear man for the world but, purely personal, it always made me cringe a bit: time for the dirty laugh, here goes.'

Actually, Sid's roles in this pioneering, sentimental and heart-warming era of the Carry On series, have depth, truth and a difference about them. And that laugh was always skilfully woven into the characterisation. It was used as an underlining of a particularly good comedy moment or, even more wisely, a particularly bad comedy moment. Galton and Simpson, poetically and enchantingly, described Sid's as a 'wood-alcohol voice' in *Hancock's Half Hour*: 'The Scandal Magazine', while film critic Barry Norman commented that that laugh was like 'dirty bath water running down the plughole'.

To borrow from J.B. Priestley, it is the voice of the comic. The voice of humour. The voice of the British people.

Fred Griffiths recognised relaxed greatness in the Carry On

team. 'Having been one of the most prolific actors in the film world with about two hundred and fifty films to my credit I can speak from experience with complete confidence,' he asserted. 'The team of the Carry On films were amongst the best I have worked with. There was more fun behind the cameras than in front of them. Some of the films I worked on were bloody murder and I was pleased when my chores were finished but with the Carry Ons it was a pleasure just to be with the team. My old mates have passed on but they will be in my memories until I slip the anchor, particularly Sid James with his horses. They were a happy crowd, no bitchiness, no temperaments. We all mucked in together and did a job of work, which was to make the public laugh. We must have done a good job because the public still love them. In the neighbourhood where I live the kids call me the Carry On man. Other films that I worked on bloody hard are now down the tubes where the kids are concerned and the adults as well. They remember the Carry On epics as the apex of the films they see on the box so they have had a lasting effect on the minds of young and old.'

They would also reshape Sid's film career, to the point of domination. But, in 1962, the series was simply a good source of additional income. *Carry On Cruising*, for example, would net him £4,000 for a six-week contract, which guaranteed him 'star screen credit in first position'. In fact, in-between hands of poker and slaving over the *Daily Telegraph* crossword, Sid completed his captaincy in just 17 days.

'Sidney would do two or three films a year for us,' remembered Peter Rogers. 'He wasn't in all of them. But he was in a lot. And it was always a pleasure to have him on set. He was the Head Boy of my school.'

And he would hold the trophy cup up high and keep his equipment spick and span for, over the years, he would gain a unique position in the Carry On family. Even to the point of both holding up production in order to fulfil his other commitments and of having a friendly, hefty say in the casting of the films.

If it was to be earned at Pinewood, it was a clout that Sid felt he already deserved at the BBC. Not that you can blame him. Sid's *Citizen James* was now their flagship situation comedy. A huge ratings winner and a show that had mellowed and softened his image for the general viewing public, Sid could sense a sure thing. He had now adapted the character away from the 'middle-aged delinquent' image he had previously cultivated. And, at the age of 48, Sid explained, 'It's a good thing to get away from the artful dodger lark for a bit. I created this character and I got stuck with it.' Even the potential side benefits stalled at the first fence, he joked. Having established himself as 'Britain's favourite fiddler' he was inundated with offers of dubious business deals and countless tips on gee-gees. 'They were never any good!' he sighed, which just goes to show that you could write the gambling out of Sid's work but not out of his life.

Where the assured run of *Citizen James* was concerned, Sid's gambling instincts let him down again. He probably didn't help matters by mapping out an agenda for the production that made the powers that be at the BBC stop and think.

Friendly persuasion in coaxing reluctant mates to appear in the series was one thing. But a couple of phone calls to Sydney Tafler were as nothing compared to the, almost assumed, demands that Sid's agent, John Kennedy, detailed.

As far as Sid was concerned, the writing team of Hills and Green were set in stone and approved. For Sid had something approaching script approval. An increase in his fee per programme was also mentioned. A reasonable request one would think. But, most presumptuous of all, it was taken as read that Sid would have approval over the production team assigned to his show.

Having been in talks with producer Tom Sloan, Bush Bailey, the Assistant Head of Artist's Booking at the BBC, had to 'deal with each point separately'.

'You did not mention exclusivity but you will remember in my first discussion with you I said that we would expect total exclusivity as far as television is concerned throughout 1962.'

This clause in the proposed contract would certainly be important in light of the subsequent behaviour of Tony Hancock. Having proved himself with his own BBC series, Hancock, the star went into lucrative talks with ATV and, for January 1963, took the show, lock, stock and *sans* Galton and Simpson, to independent television.

Sid's exclusivity to the BBC didn't prove a problem. And even a gag appearance in a bowling alley item on ATV was cleared via Eric Maschwitz at the corporation: 'It being understood that this appearance is not to constitute a "performance", but will be confined to his presenting a cheque to the winner to the accompaniment of a short speech.'

With regard to the writers for *Citizen James*, Bailey wrote: 'It is certainly our intention to commission Hills and Green, all other things being equal, but obviously, we must first have discussions with Sidney James as to whether we want to make any changes in his series as far as format is concerned and I am afraid we are not prepared to make this a contractual point.'

Again, Sid was more than happy to retain the format established in series two. Why would he or the BBC want to change a winning formula anyway? But as for the ultimate control over the pro-gramme, Sid's clout would be limited: 'Obviously the scriptwriters will consult with Sidney whilst they are writing the series,' confirmed Bailey, 'but I am afraid it's quite impossible for us to agree that Sidney shall have approval of all scripts and director/producer. This latter, I am sure you will appreciate, is just impossible to promise as the commitments and indeed the personal presence of any one director cannot be stated so far in advance. No contract artiste in our experience has enjoyed this privilege and I am afraid it simply cannot be agreed in this case.'

In the event, producer Ronald Marsh would oversee the programmes, tellingly replacing Duncan Wood who had been Sid's first producer of choice since his days with Tony Hancock.

However, one thing was certainly clear. The BBC was not about to lose Sid to ITV as they would soon lose Tony Hancock. Again it was Bush Bailey who took up the argument over Sid's fee when he confirmed with Tom Sloan: 'I offered John Kennedy a series of thirteen programmes for Sidney James for 1962, with exclusivity for the year and no call on his services between January and June, at a fee of six hundred and fifty guineas inclusive. This has been flatly turned down by his agent who says he has a written offer from ITV for a similar series at a fee of one thousand pounds per programme. Although Sidney James would prefer to work for us he says he cannot possibly consider our offer under seven hundred and fifty guineas per programme, which we both agree is too high.'

There was room for consideration, however, for by the time Sid signed the contract in January 1962, he *was* on 750 guineas per programme.

John Kennedy was also keen to capitalise fully on the popularity of *Citizen James*. A much-mooted repeat series, under the title of *The Best of Sid James*, finally began at the end of April 1962 and attracted huge audiences. It must have seemed like serendipity in light of an earlier note in February from Kennedy to J.H. Davidson, Assistant Head of Light Entertainment, Radio, with regard to 'the proposed radio series for Sidney James. The series to be tentatively entitled *Citizen James*, and to be based on previous *Citizen James* television programmes. Messrs Hills and Green have agreed to write this series, subject to suitable negotiations between ourselves and them. Both Mr Sidney James and Messrs Hills and Green are available almost immediately to start.'

Although BBC Television had commissioned a third batch of episodes, a scribbled note on Kennedy's letter ponders: 'I doubt whether there is any market for this suggestion. But let's offer.' Another hand, rather harshly, enquires: 'Are we in the market for TV's *Citizen James* by Hills and Green – I hope not?' A fortnight later, a rather more polite refusal was dispatched, regretting that there was 'little prospect of our accepting this idea for future transmission in our radio programmes'.

For Sid and Kennedy, the radio series was quite simply seen as a way to make an extra bit of beer money off of the back of the television series. No lines to learn. Rehashes of past successes. And a few guineas for their trouble. The fact that it didn't come off certainly didn't threaten Sid's position at the BBC but it must have wrangled slightly. If only to prove, once and for all, that he couldn't have everything his own way at the corporation.

Sid would, however, welcome back two familiar faces to the new television episodes: Vera Day, who had last worked with Sid on the big screen boxing comedy *And the Same Too You* (1960), was recruited for an episode.

'That was fun,' she recalls. 'I had really got friendly with Sid by that time so that was a nice job to get. And Syd Tafler, of course, was another one of those people who I'd worked with loads of times over the years. There was a real closeness between Sid and Syd. They were both natural performers. Playing extended, elaborated versions of themselves. And that series was a big success. It's almost forgotten now, but Sid really was a leading light at the BBC in those days.'

Another welcome guest star in the third batch of *Citizen James* was Liz Fraser who, along with Bill Kerr, had been phased out of the line-up once Hills and Green took over as scriptwriters. 'I'm sure Sid was pleased,' says Liz. 'After all, I had joined him on the Carry On films by that stage, so we were spending a lot of time together and I was glad to go back to *Citizen James*. I'm not sure you can say it was Sid's influence. He might have had a word with the producer although it was all above board, from the BBC and through my agent. But, then again, it was Sid's show. He would have had some say in how it was going.'

Thankfully for Sid, the eternal cries of 'What fiddle you on today, Sid boy?' had gone 'because of the new . . . public-spirited character of Citizen James.' As the *Radio Times* reported in September 1962, 'He [now] finds himself being approached by earnest types eager to enlist his aid in good causes.' But, 'he takes it all in his stride. Nothing surprises Sid.'

Not even when he received 22 loaves of crusty bread in the post after an episode in which he valiantly tried to locate a loaf. Typically Sid commented: 'I wonder what would happen if I sort of let it slip in the programme that I could do with a new car!'

But, in complete conflict of his public laissez-faire attitude to acting, Sid once again showed signs of restlessness. Having remained one of the 'most sought-after character actors in the business . . . in most of which he has been cast as the kind of lovable crook no policeman would be mean enough to arrest, there lurks beneath the respectable façade of Citizen Sid a sinister ambition "to play a right villain, a really mean character". Not, he adds, that it is a case of the comedian wanting to have a crack at Hamlet: "That's the last part I want to play, unless I play the geezer at poker."'

There was plenty of time for poker on the set of his latest film and, surprisingly again, it was a Carry On that highlighted a harsher, more challenging side to his acting. *Carry On Cabby* was originally touted out as *Call Me a Cab*, the first Talbot Rothwell script that producer Peter Rogers put in to production, in March 1963.

Bert Leavy, a veteran cabbie employed as an adviser to the actors, found the hands of poker the only relief from the boredom of life on a film set. But, for Harry Fowler, Sid didn't need any coaching. He was 'the eternal cab driver'. And, for sure, throughout 1963 Sid did very little else.

He had first popped up as a somewhat disgruntled cabbie in the coy Richard Attenborough comedy *Father's Doing Fine* (1952). But in *Carry On Cabby* he was the working-class boss again. Caught up in a short-fuse marriage, financial concerns and yearnings for long-gone wartime camaraderie. This was a Carry On for the kitchen sink generation.

Associate Producer Frank Bevis was clear that Sid helped ease problems with the production when he confirmed with the Managing Director of the Maidenhead Authority that 'the picture is a first feature comedy being made at Pinewood Studios, starring Sidney James and Hattie Jacques.'

Sid's presence was also a reassuring one for actors new to the series. For Sid, starring in his fourth consecutive Carry On film, was feeling supremely confident in his position at the head of table.

Distinguished Irish actor, Milo O'Shea, was certainly glad of his presence: 'Sid was always on the money. Always prepared. And always happy. He was a very good person to have in a scene. He seemed to calm everything and everybody down. You had that sense that nothing could go wrong with Sid in the frame with you.

'Once the film was in the can we all had to go in for our dubbing sessions. That can be very tiresome but it has to be done. Anyway, I was due to get back to Dublin immediately to start rehearsing a play. My dubbing was scheduled after that of Sid's and he had booked to go away to Spain with his wife for a holiday. Somehow Sid got to hear about this, and that I was working with an actor called Jimmy O'Dea. Jimmy was an old friend of Sid's when Sid used to perform in variety. You could have bowled me over when Sid came over to me and said, "Look, why don't I postpone my holiday plans in Spain for a couple of days and you do your dubbing first so that you can get back to Dublin and start rehearsing with Jimmy." This was such a kind thing to do, but that's the sort of atmosphere that I found with the Carry On people. That atmosphere was typified by Sid's kindness, thoughtfulness and professionalism.'

And even before the Carry On assignment, Sid was preparing for a lengthy use of his practised cabbie eye. Towards the end of his run opposite Frankie Howerd in *Puss in Boots* on 28 February 1963 Sid wrote from the Hotel Leofric, Coventry, explaining to Tom Sloan that he was extremely sorry about the difficulties over the week out in July: 'As you know when we first discussed this contract I did say that it was essential that I had some time off in August and you agreed to this. As you well understand, being a family man yourself, it is most important to spend some time with your children. Particularly as Stephen is at boarding school and I see so little of him in any case. He doesn't break up until 29 July so you can see how useless that week would have been. I don't want to burden you with all this but I don't want you to think I'm being difficult! I can assure you I'll have much more peace of mind and I will *not* find it tiring to do all 13 and then have a holiday with Val and the kids at the end of it. I'm really looking forward to this series and I feel tremendously confident about it. I *would* like a get-together with you, the producer and Ted Willis as soon as I return. We get back on 3 March. If it's of any use to you I'm holding 11 March to 22 March open in case. There it is, mate. Our love to Pat. God bless. Sid James.'

The writer, Ted Willis, had made his name by creating *Dixon of Dock Green* and explained that 'the character Sid plays is a bit of an adventurer, always getting involved in other people's problems'. The producer for the new series was television pioneer Michael Mills. And the subject? Taxis of course. *Taxi!* was subtitled as 'Stories of a London Taxi Driver'. And the taxi driver in question was, naturally, Sid. 'Whenever I hear someone shout "Taxi!" my foot automatically goes for the brake!' he joked.

However, despite his casting this was not a gentle situation comedy. Elements of the natural, earthy London humour of the cabbies was in place but this was a gritty piece of drama. Corruption, prostitution and junior delinquency frequently dictated storylines and director Robin Nash was keen to film as much material as possible on location. This was no studio – bound, live television hint at London's low life. This was as close to reality as the BBC could get.

And Sid was instantly delighted with it. So much so that he put himself through vigorous training. 'My own car has an automatic transmission,' he told the *Radio Times* in July 1963. 'You just sit there and it goes on its own. But these taxis – you've really got to drive them. Believe me, you need muscles!'

One member of the press was treated to a vision as 'the cab drew up outside the BBC Television Centre in Shepherds Bush with a jolt. The driver, wearing a suede jacket, silk choker and cloth cap, could have been the cabbie from next door – but there was something familiar about his face. It looked like a squashed lemon after a drought, so it couldn't be anyone but actor Sid James.'

'"Just having a bit of a wangle, mate. That's taxi-talk for driving around in a cab to get the feel of it. We're just shooting a trailer for the series. It's all a bit of a rush because I wasn't free to start filming until last week. There's one deuce of a lot to learn. Being a cabbie isn't as simple as it looks. I'm still trying to learn their language. That's what I meant about taxi-talk. What would you make of this: A mush was going down the road with 'im and 'er when he had a set with a butter boy near the 'Loo, outside a bursting gaff, and got kited? You'd say I'd been working too hard and needed a rest? Not far wrong, mate. But what it actually means is: An owner-taxi driver was taking a man and a woman on a journey of more than six miles when he was in collision with another taxi, the driver of which had only recently passed his test, near Waterloo Station, just outside a theatre that was disgorging its patrons, and he lost his licence. Is that right, Bill?" Bill was the actual owner-driver of Sid's cab, and he said: "Yes mate, dead right."'

Sid was, indeed, dead right and had quite clearly seen his persuasive charm work on Tom Sloan who had assured him that 'it is now possible for us to close the gap in the *Taxi!* recordings . . . this means that on 28 July, and also on 23 June, we must do the programme in one day in the studio and not two as on eleven other dates. However, I am sure you will accept this in order to take your holiday from 18 August. I hope this now gives you what you want and all is well.'

But all was not well. Sid and his agent, John Kennedy, were less than happy at the planned scheduling for the series. Although the BBC had shoe-horned *Taxi!* into a much-coveted spot, the series was threatened with instability in the schedules. Tom Sloan, again, reassured Sid on 21 May 1963 that, 'after your visit to me I have gone into the whole question of the placing of your *Taxi!* series and whether or not it could be delayed in any way. I am afraid that the short answer is it cannot because it has been planned to fill the vital gap in the summer when Z-*Cars* is off the air. As you can imagine, this is regarded as a tremendously important spot to hold as far as audiences are concerned, and I think it is a measure of the importance we have placed on your series that it should have been given this vital placing – with every expectation on our part that you will hold the vast number of viewers who have became Z-*Cars* addicts. I am sure you will realise that from our point of view this is only another indication of the way in which our schedules are being designed in a very competitive and businesslike way. Your series is quite definitely the major venture that Light Entertainment Group will be embarking on in the next three months and I am sure that with all the resources we intend to put behind it, it will be a great success for yourself as well as for us – and I hope could only do your film a great deal of good at the box office.'

Carry On Cabby was indeed due to be on general release at the time of *Taxi!*'s run on BBC Television but that was of little interest to Sid. As far as he was concerned, by the end of May 1963, the filming was all but done and dusted. And the role had been forgotten about. He wasn't on a residual for the film. And never would be. So the success at the box office, while gratifying, was the producer's concern not his.

No, his main priority was to the television audience. If this gamble failed it could, again, threaten his small screen career. Having hit the age of 50, Sid was in no mood to compromise.

He was furiously protective of his image on screen. Vision mixer Clive Doig remembers Sid 'being rather tetchy on set. We weren't going out live but, in those days, you recorded television in lengthy blocks. About half an hour through an episode [of *Taxi!*] Sid just stopped in the middle of a scene, looked up to the gallery and said, "Michael. How many close-ups so far?" Michael Mills turned to me, rather bemused and said, "Clive. How many?" I had no idea. I wasn't keeping count! But a little girl – I think someone from Sid's agency – had actually been keeping count! "Forty seven," she said. Michael told Sid. He shouted back, "It should have been fifty by now!" He pointed both index fingers at his face and screamed, "This is what they want to see!" He knew his public and he thought he knew how to direct a television series.'

In Sid's defence, he *did* know about cameras. And he was under pressure from all quarters. Despite the popularity of *Citizen James* he was still in the shadow of Tony Hancock and the fond memories of *Hancock's Half Hour*. In his heart of hearts, Sid never got out of that shadow. He was never a star. That face he saw in the bathroom mirror every morning was the face of a jobbing actor. And the job had got less satisfying since the demise of the partnership with Hancock.

And, despite run-ins with the backroom boys at the BBC, Sid remained the champion of the put-upon small-part actor. Norman Mitchell remembered his episode of *Taxi!*: 'A Long Way to Go'. 'It was over-running,' he said, 'and the director [Robin Nash] came over to me and said, "I'm sorry, Norman, but we have to cut your line." It was the only line I had, so I was in effect out of the show. Anyway, Sid got wind of this, steamed over to the director, demanded my line be kept in and won the day. Sid thought the line was brilliant and wouldn't go on unless it was put back in. The line? I described Sid's face as looking like a bag of knitting. I was very grateful to him. He didn't need to put himself out for me. But I appreciated it. Few stars would have done the same. Sid was a good soul. As far as he was concerned, my one little line was good for the show. He also knew it was very good for me. And very good for him. He got the laugh when I said the line and I couldn't have been more delighted.'

Also, in his own defence, Tom Sloan had to accommodate the return of national favourite *Z-Cars* – rather unfortunately slap bang in the middle of the run of *Taxi!*.

Critically, *Taxi!* proved a hit. For, as Peter Knight wrote in the *Daily Telegraph* on 11 July 1963, in Sid, 'we have the comedian turned actor . . . adding a new depth to the already sizeable talent he has shown in the past.' Despite the fact that Sid had actually already been an actor turned comedian for many years, the reviewer was glad to see that 'there is still the brash, raw character lurking in the background but as a London taxi-driver Mr James is now more concerned with drama than raising the laughs.'

It seems, however, that Sid's audience was still much more interested in him raising the laughs than the drama.

A joyously typical film for him at this period was Gilbert Gunn's monster comedy, *What a Whopper* (1961). Incongruously, Adam Faith and Terence Longdon boosted the interest in the Loch Ness Monster by trying to fake a snapshot of the beastie. Sid is a cor-blimey, corrupted landlord in the film.

And, as *Variety* pointed out, 'The British appetite for this type of unpretentious, slapstick comedy appears to be insatiable . . . a long, reliable cast of known names and faces helps with the producers having gone wisely in for added UK b.o. [box office] insurance by making this the first film of Adam Faith, a leading pop singer with a big local following. There are some ripely funny performances by such well-tried troupers as Sidney James . . . '

And this, as the American reviewer latched on to, was what the home audience wanted. Still, Sid's need to prove himself an actor once more, a continued battle with the BBC and an ultimate rejection of his agent would take him to the brink of professional disaster. And on a journey to rediscover his roots.

8

Home to Roost

Sid was proud of where he came from. But was even prouder of where he was. Still, while he wallowed in East End familiarity, the dogs, the horses, boxing and public houses, this most natural of naturalised cockneys always wore his South African legacy on his sleeve.

It was where he had learnt the business, after all. And where he traced all those corny, bodily-function-obsessed gags back to. That oft told tale about being fed during his mother's brief interludes offstage offered the perfect interview punchline: 'Boy, did I suffer from wind!'

Sid grew up around the world, and around the world of theatres and circuses, but it was a myriad of jobs outside of show business that had contributed both to his physical appearance and mental assurance. This was the Sid James of Johannesburg of the 1920s and 1930s. A try anything sort of cove who loved money and loved women. He would stagger through pretty much any type of work in his pursuit of money. No crafty slacker was he. He realised from a very early age that hard work equalled being able to have the finer things in life. Whether it was heaving sack-loads of spuds or appearing on the South African Broadcasting Corporation, a job was simply a means to an end. He would try anything and everything during those formative years.

'Pull up your chair, mate,' he would offer, 'and pour yourself another drink, because it's quite a list.' It was. He would joke that 'there are hundreds of them boy, hundreds'. For one thing,'I was an electrician's apprentice.'

Now, depending on how much Sid was enjoying telling the tale, this short-lived profession could have been anything from 'about three days' to as little as 'just about an hour'. However long Sid stuck at it, it certainly wasn't very long and the final result, in Sid's telling, was always the same: 'At the end of it I blew the lights in a whole building. I nearly blew the building up!'

He might not have been that technically minded but Sid loved his gramophone records. As he told *Desert Island Discs*' presenter Roy Plomley in 1960: 'That's going all day.' And, at his Ealing home, Sid had the benefit of electricity and not just a wind-up instrument! 'I just love music,' he said, 'it gives me a kick. I get a lift. It does me a lot of good I think, emotionally.'

Here was a sensitivity and sentimentality that life as a touring vaudevillian had instilled in him. 'I don't know any music that makes me sad in any way,' he explained. 'I think whatever piece of music – it doesn't really matter what the music is – I get some kind of a lift out of it. If it's any good of course.'

Even the music that conjured up memories of a rather lonely life in South Africa: 'Years ago when I was a child, not a child but a youngster, I used to do a lot of diamond digging. And I would say that several times, you know, a couple of weeks, ten days to a couple of weeks [I would spend] on my own.'

Diamonds were Sid's business. He started as an apprentice in the industry before he 'finally became a diamond polisher . . . with the firm of D. Pearson in Johannesburg. That is my trade,' he confirmed. He even 'took part in the Grasfontein diamond rush, staking a claim'.

While in charge of a diamond-cutting machine he saw his newly-cut diamond drop in two pieces to the floor. The concrete floor had been broken up for relaying and, as unpolished diamonds look like bits of stone, he had to live on the premises for two days until he found the diamonds in the rubble.

A lonely, exacting professional, the diamond business was certainly more secure than his earliest experiences of show business. In tandem with his vaudevillian parents, he kept going back to South Africa. 'When I got to a school-going age, of course, I had to go to school and stay put.'

Reluctantly he studied, nursing a desire to return to the stage. However, 'I never went back to the act, the act split up.'

In a rare moment of talking candidly about his home life of the late 1920s, Sid told a journalist in 1959: 'Now, my mother runs a dress shop in Johannesburg. And my father – I don't know what happened to him. He must be dead I should think. They were divorced when I was sixteen.'

This sense of the family break-up, of a rather confused, contrite and dissatisfied teenager, split from the family and the show business world he knew and loved, must have had a profound effect on Sid.

'I could not help feeling sorry for my parents,' he continued. 'There did not seem to be any way they could win.'

Pretty much overnight the young Sid went from a typical pupil with little interest in his lessons, but with vivid flights of fancy of returning to the stage, to something of a rudderless vessel. A drifter. His focus had gone. The only constant he craved was that need for security. Be it financial or emotional.

'I never went back to the act, I just went into various dramatics and rep. things and broadcasting, put on my own shows and stuff like that. But you really couldn't make a living doing that sort of stuff only, you had to have some kind of a job.'

After his failure as an electrician's apprentice he was 'a junior clerk for about half an hour'. Again, when in a less playful mood, Sid would have lasted at that job a little longer. 'For two days', was his best estimate.

'I was a professional fisherman for a little while,' he would mention. 'A dock-hand in Durban'. And, as the *Diamond News and South African Watchmaker and Jeweller* quoted him soon after his big film break in Britain in July 1948: 'I've been a stevedore, a coal-heaver, a boxer, a wrestler . . .'

His life in the boxing ring was etched on to his face. And he put himself through the ringer in circuses and funfairs, taking on South African miners for 30 shillings a pop. As his obituary in *The Times* stated: 'He delighted later to tell colourful stories of his early days as a boxer (amateur, professional and semi-professional, or all three at the same time, in different places).'

The face of a hard-drinking, hard-done-by boxer became his calling card. It was a face that had seen life. And lived to tell the tale.

Although he professed his unsuitability for the fight game, mainly because he couldn't control his anger, it kept him fit and agile. In 1960 he explained, 'I still do exercises. Press-ups and a bit of shadow-boxing every day. Used to have a punchball until Valerie got tired of the noise and said "Either it's the punchball – or me." It was a beautiful punchball,' he said, resignedly.

As comedy cohort Tony Hancock commented in 1958: 'He also seems to have picked up barbering somewhere. After I'd been unable to find time for a haircut for several weeks, Sid said he couldn't stand it any longer. He gave me a very professional trim in the dressing room.'

Hancock wasn't the only co-star who got the benefit of Sid's handiwork with a pair of scissors. During the fourth series of his ATV situation comedy, *George and the Dragon*, in 1968, the plot dictated a trim for his boss, played by John le Mesurier. Sid's skill was even commented upon by an avid viewer of the show,

Mrs Joyce, when she penned a note to the *TV Times* inviting Sid to treat her husband to a good old-fashioned East End cut!

For, as with most things in life, Sid's barbering skills were down-to-earth, homely and conducted with precision and no fuss. But they owed nothing to the East End and everything to his mother. Following the break-up of her marriage, Reine saw that her teenage son needed a trade. And that was hairdressing. It would shape his formative years. Having been taken under the wing of his Uncle Sonnie Solomon, Sid grew in confidence. He treated the art of hairdressing as a theatrical performance. And, as a result of styling her hair, Sid met Berthe Sadie 'Toots' Delmont. The couple was married in 1936. Her father, Joseph, had been born a cockney, made a fortune in diamonds and was one of South Africa's most successful bookmakers. If opposites attract, positions don't and he and Sid never saw eye-to-eye. But the family's love of music rekindled Sid's passion for performance.

Again, he would indulge in his passion without fuss. This certainly extended to when he 'taught skating and dancing'. As with boxing, these too gave him a good physique.

'Sid was a good little mover,' says Vera Day, who shared a moment on the dance floor with him in the film *Hell Drivers* (1957). 'That marvellous dance-hall scene was great. That was just me and Sid doing our thing. It was hardly *Strictly Come Dancing* but it certainly showed Sid could do it properly. Actually, that scene ended in a fight and I remember Sid treating the dancing and the fighting as the same. Everything had to be rehearsed. Every step . . . be it dance or boxing . . . had to be right.'

As *Daily Mirror* critic Donald Zec noted in 1960, Sid used this skill with his feet and poise of movement to the best of his advantage. Particularly in comedy. He became 'the greatest counter-puncher' in the business!

Vera Day explains, 'Sid didn't like a lot of mucking about. He liked things to have a flow. To be spontaneous and simple. But he was meticulous when it came to the dancing and the fighting. Even if he had to re-learn things the wrong way in order to fit that character, there was a right way to make it look wrong, if you follow me. He never suffered fools gladly.'

Particularly the political stance of his homeland. Even when discussing music, Sid had a natural and sharp sense of humour. He also had a clear social conscience that wasn't reflected in his laid-back, self-centred screen persona He had built up this crafty cockney character that wandered through life with a carefree shrug of the shoulders, and he would bring that character out at any opportunity. Witness his second selection of record on *Desert Island Discs*: 'Sammy Davis is one of my favourites, and I think this would be dead right in the circumstances: *I Got Plenty O' Nuttin.*'

Even long after Sid had left his life in South Africa behind him, the verbal dexterity of Sammy Davis Junior would have got scant approval. Even in the more liberated America of Las Vegas nightspots and Hollywood parties, Davis found it necessary to embrace self-deprecation in order to find his place in the Pack.

For Sid, racial intolerance and segregation were the most unsavoury and abhorrent aspects of his home country. Talking to the respected film critic, Peter Noble, in the early 1960s, he explained, 'As far as the colour bar is concerned, I believe that all men are equal, black or white. I hate segregation.' And when quizzed about the possibility of returning to South Africa, Sid was adamant: 'Never. [I have] no desire to return at all.'

There had certainly been offers. As early as 1956, with advance plans for a second batch of television episodes with Tony Hancock on the table, Sid wrote to Tom Sloan: 're the Hancock series. The information therein certainly makes things a little clearer for me. I spoke to Tony on Sunday and he told me that all was more or less settled. My only problem is a probable film in South Africa beginning about March or April next. I'm sure, however, that things will sort themselves out.'

They sorted themselves out in that the film offer was not taken up.

But the fact Sid had even considered it proved completely that he would swallow his pride and go wherever the work and, more importantly, the money was. He had left behind him a split family, a split first marriage and immediate family, the happier days of a – now defunct – second marriage and second immediate family, a string of jobs, a string of affairs and the possibility of several little 'Sidneys' across the country. Settled in Britain with a new wife and a packed career, Sid was now a contented man. He could look back at his days in South Africa and cherry-pick the memories. He could discuss the outrageous political situation with candour. And he could thankfully consider himself a true cockney. He had found a place in the hearts and minds of the British people. He was secure at last.

But by 1964, Sid had grown wary of the presumed apathy of the BBC and with Tom Sloan. Sid's flagship drama series *Taxi!* had already faced competition from the corporation's assured ratings winner, *Z-Cars*, during its first series. Now, with a second batch of 13 episodes, the BBC had casually thrown the *Taxi!* episodes into the spring schedule. Unsurprisingly, Tom Sloan was faced with a disrupted schedule to play with. Thanks to Wimbledon, cricket test matches and various other high profile sporting events, Sid's programme was slotted in wherever it could go. In the end, *Taxi!* was often delayed or postponed accordingly. Much to the star's chagrin and his agent's.

John Kennedy was not impressed and asked in a letter of 22 November 1963 whether it was possible 'to give us an undertaking that the series will be presented at a regular time for the purpose of building a regular audience, and thus a constant and probably rising rating? I feel sure you will accept this in the spirit in which it is intended.'

But the BBC had no choice. *Taxi!* was a martyr to the spring sporting events. It would also prove Sid's last television series for nearly three years.

An option for a third series, set for pre-production in late 1964, was rejected by Tom Sloan at the end of 1963. 'May I say that the reason for not taking up this option is not for any lack of faith I have in *Taxi!*' he explained, 'but simply that due to the post-ponement of the second series it is unrealistic to commit ourselves to a third series at this stage.'

For Sid this was simply the straw that broke the camel's back. Angry at the treatment from the BBC of both him and his show; cynical about the reassurances of his producers and intrigued by a film offer that had already been in discussion for several months, he was ready to up-sticks, albeit temporarily.

Immediately following the broadcasts of the second and final batch of *Taxi!*, in June 1964 Sid and Valerie jetted off to South Africa. Sid had been signed up to star in a £100,000 big screen adventure called *The Tokoloshe* to be shot on location and at Lone Hill Studios. When it finally emerged in Britain, seven years later, it was entitled *Tokoloshe the Evil Spirit*.

The trip was a momentous one for Sid: it was the first time he was returning to South Africa in 18 years. For Valerie it was an exciting prospect: 'I've never been to South Africa,' she exclaimed, 'so I'll be meeting Sid's family for the first time.'

In the film Sid was partnered by a small boy, frantically on the run from his fate as a sacrificial offering to a Rain God. The boy was played by Saul Pelle.

'I came to know Sid James as a gentle and kind man with his weathered face and seemingly forever smiling eyes,' he remembers. 'In those days, one had to commit a lot of text to memory, and this was kid's stuff for him. I still remember one monologue that he acted out, cool, calm and melancholy written all over his face. We were fishing by the Jukskei river, and he recited: "Once I had eyes. I could see like a bird. That's why they used to call me Birdy. "Birdy," the skipper would say, "climb up there, and see what you can see." . . . and I could see for miles.'

In a return to the meaty and emotive acting work of his days with the Johannesburg repertory company Sid played the role of a blind man. Pelle enthuses, 'But what a blind man! He played the part so convincingly. No, more than that, he lived the part for the period of time that we were together on the set.'

Sid immediately related to the isolation and truth in his role and the script by Bob O'Keefe. Saul Pelle recalls: 'Even Peter Prowse (the director, producer, screen player) revelled in the old blind man's ability to lift the film, which at times seemed a bit disjointed. That was the time when I thoroughly enjoyed myself, voraciously reading comic strips like *Richie Rich*, *Archie*, *Little Letta*, *Little Dot*, *Popeye the Sailor Man* and others, courtesy of one of the best young actors of South Africa – Cy Sacks.'

Even for a young actor of Pelle's tender years, he was enchanted by Sid's natural ability in front of a camera. He attests that, 'while it is true that he was brilliant in most parts, when we were cast alongside each other he was not acting at all, it seemed to me. There was a very touching scene when we parted and he was going into the hospital to have his eye operation. Sid James showed his prowess in a scene with Siegfried Mynhardt when I was to be taken from him to be sent to a school in one of the townships in Johannesburg.'

It wasn't just on set that Sid impressed young Saul. 'During one of his last days in South Africa,' he remembers, 'the management at Lone Hill Film Studio threw a party for him. I was invited. Former parliamentary Speaker of the Free State province, Motlalepule Chabaku and I were the only blacks at that party for the simple reason that I had to be there to receive a present from Sid James. Mistress June as Motlalepule was called then. She had to be there because she was looking after me. After several speeches, Sid James said a few words, called me forward and then presented me with a watch, a Rotary. My very first watch. It was engraved with the words, "Thanks Saul, Sid James". I have nothing but fond, sweet memories of Sid James.'

The feeling was apparently mutual. Sid was besotted with the relaxed atmosphere of filmmaking in South Africa and vowed to return to 'make at least two films a year' there. In the event, that ambition was thwarted. He made just one more picture in South Africa.

Originally discussed under the title *Don't Shoot the Shareholders*, *Stop Exchange* was based on one of the celebrated Cora Swemmer satires by Howard Rennie.

Sid's schedule on the film was just under two days and was fitted in-between his stage commitment to Sam Cree's *Wedding Fever*. A great summer season success in Britain, Sid had been invited to bring the production to Cape Town and, then, the Johannesburg Civic Centre, in the autumn of 1970.

Victor Spinetti, who had just completed work on *Two in Clover* at the time, remembers: 'Sid would go to South Africa on jobs and what have you and come back with Val having made sure he had bought shares in gold. She was always one for keeping money invested just in case the work dried up or he decided he wanted to stop working and they would have a few pounds put aside. But Sid didn't care about that. He always lived for the here and now. He was making money and he wanted to spend it as quickly as he made it. But he enjoyed doing that. And he enjoyed going back to South Africa. That was the essence of the man. It was never home again but it was a place that made him very welcome. And he loved it.'

But there was one other country that loved him even more. Australia. When he had returned from filming *Tokoloshe the Evil Spirit* in mid-July 1964 he had but six clear rest days before embarking on filming for *Carry On Cleo*.

It would prove a pivotal moment in his film career and elevate Sid's standing across the English-speaking world.

Sid's father had been a native of Australia so there had always been a connection and British comedians had long been treated like deities down under. So, when Sid premiered another Sam Cree domestic farce, *The Mating Season*, it proved a true theatrical event. But it had been *Carry On Cleo* that finally put Sid in the top bracket of comedy attractions.

Keith Moremon, the managing director of Greater Union theatres in Australia, wrote to producer Peter Rogers on 20 July 1964 to say, 'In Sydney the previous best Carry On had a run of five weeks in the city and *Carry On Cleo* ran 12, and took more money than any Carry On before, and in fact took more than twice most of them. This is certainly a very pleasing surprise but it has just caught the imagination of the public here and pleased everyone. One exhibitor in a small country town . . . has just played it for a third time having played it between Xmas and New Year for the first time. That is what he thinks of it. In most situations *Carry On Cleo* has beaten "hard-ticket" pictures like *Lawrence of Arabia*, *El Cid* etc, that has played in the same houses but increased admission prices.'

The film's success set a trend for the success of Carry On in Australia. And, it seemed, if Sid James was in one, the box-office appeal was assured. From the end of 1967 to the start of 1975 he was in every Carry On film on general release. And little wonder.

When Sid opened in *The Mating Season* at the Melbourne Comedy theatre at the very end of September 1972 it was clear that the country not only loved him as a comedian but also offered lucrative deals and touching accolades. He was named Best Actor of the Year in 1972. The following year he toured New Zealand with the show and broke box-office records across the country. He also accepted several television deals from Network Seven in Melbourne.

Dave Freeman, who wrote much of the material, remembers: 'There was a film clip show [*Carry On Sid*] and a big variety spectacular [*The Sid James Show*] that I wrote. There were sketches I had put together for him for stage appearances and material that he really liked. One had him as Mozart agonising over the finer points of *Three Blind Mice*. There was an Australia-based sketch with him as a scruffy beachcomber. And he was a sentimental barfly in one scene that I spiced up with a couple of gags. He even sang 'One For My Baby' to his Val. It may sound rather gooey but I seem to remember that there wasn't a dry eye in the house. Sid could play sentiment without a sprinkling of saccharine.'

Indeed, so popular was he in Australia that he returned at the end of December 1974 and, yet again, the following September. Scriptwriter Vince Powell, who created three situation comedies for Sid, confirms: 'Our comedies were the tops as far as the Aussies were concerned. People like Sid were mobbed out there. The Carry Ons. *George and the Dragon. Two in Clover. Bless This House.* All of it was big news. To have Sid James starring in a play in their own neighbourhood was almost unbelievable. The power of British stars like Sid cannot be over-estimated. He was a mega-star in the eyes of the Australians.

'And besides,' continues Powell, 'there was always something of the colonial man about Sid. He fitted into that mentality perfectly. He was a man's man, not an actor. The Aussies loved that about him.'

This time the touring company was joined by Sid's leading ladies from the British presentation, Joy Stewart, Sarah Maxwell and Ann Scott-Jones.

It was a comfortable and rewarding experience for Sid. But the move would never be considered permanent. Not for a second. Sid was happy to travel around the world with the stage show, but home was always in Buckinghamshire.

Close friend, Harry Fowler 'was always surprised that he never went to America. I don't even think the thought occurred to him.

He loved this country . . . and I suppose he thought he had already made the massive journey from South Africa. Why schlep all the way to America after that? Particularly when he had it so good here. It was that cliché of the jobbing actor but he never seemed to be out of work. There was no need to go looking elsewhere. His attitude was "why bother?".'

Indeed, as far as Sid was concerned: 'I always wanted to come here [to Britain]. I didn't want to go to the States because I think there are too many blokes like me, in the States.'

For Great Britain was home to Sid. Long, long before he had made that decisive journey from South Africa to Southampton in December 1946, it had still been considered home in his heart. His mother's English influence had played a massive part and instilled a love of the English theatre and English actors that remained with Sid. He could have had little idea that one day *Daily Mirror* critic Donald Zac would describe him as 'the Olivier of the cheese and pickles school of acting', but it's a description Sid would have gratefully accepted. To be seen in the same league as the greatest living actor but, most crucially, with the proviso of British working-class values and respect, would have been the only accolade Sid would have wanted.

'I've seen most countries,' he said, 'and I'll tell you. There's nothing to touch Britain.'

9

The 10 Per Centers

Sid had been with agent John Kennedy for a little under three years when, in 1964, he decided to accept an offer from the Bernard Delfont Organisation.

John Kennedy had first swum into Sid's ken in the aftermath of his filming *Tommy the Toreador* because of the actor's sustained friendship with Kennedy's main client, Tommy Steele. Indeed, in light of that fact, Kennedy even confidently predicted a pop career for Sid himself.

'He's got a song,' he reported to the *Daily Herald* in February 1961. 'It's a novelty number called "A Punch Up the 'Ooter". It's Sid's first record. And he's got a spectacular, *The Sid James Show*, coming along. Sid is making a bid for the Big Time.'

For both agent and performer the song was treated exactly how it should have been treated, as a fun joke. 'You couldn't say I actually sing,' chuckled Sid. 'I sort of *deliver* the words in time to the music'. But it made the grade. It was big time for a comedy actor, at least.

But, somehow, this tongue-in-cheek 'big time' didn't seem big enough for Kennedy. And for Sid this do-anything-for-a-buck and a headline approach was beyond what he wanted. By 1964, Sid's very worst fear seemed to have come true. Thanks somewhat to Kennedy, he had become a star. And with stardom, came the very curse that Sid had predicted.

Sid could now command a £5,000 salary for a film role. But it was a starring film role. One that would dictate he was on call for studio work over a five- or six-week period. By his own estimate, Sid could have picked up that kind of money, a decade earlier, in just over a week, by squeezing in a film a day.

'I know Clark Gable didn't make that many,' he reflected to the *Evening Standard* in the light of the death of the king of Hollywood in November 1960, 'but he made big pictures.'

Sid was also a star on television. But wrangles with the BBC and lengthy, exhausting commitments to a headlining series, again dictated that smaller roles were denied him. While Michael Mills and Peter Rogers would always want his services, other producers tended to feel Sid had priced himself out of the market. And even the conveyor-belt efficiency of the Carry Ons was only throwing up a film a year for Sid.

'I knew that in this business, if you can't pull it off as top dog there is no going back to that cosy, safe existence in the middle of the bill,' he said. 'You either make the grade or go out and sell shoelaces.'

Now Sid's professional contentment had been dented. He didn't want to be a star: 'Stars get ulcers.'

Sid's first agent, Phyllis Parnell, had represented him since the very beginning of his British career and she suited his ambition for steady employment down to the ground. She had dutifully lined up dozens of small film roles at the behest of Sid himself. And, again, she signposted the importance of these small film roles in terms of the BBC simply in order to build up Sid's reputation with the corporation and, even more importantly, build up his fee.

A typical letter regarding Sid was dispatched to BBC producer Dennis Vance in November 1953, in which Parnell pointed out:

At the height of his film career in 1956, Sid lets the wheeler-dealer bookie mask slip for a *Dry Rot* publicity session.

Sid's wartime concert party days were recreated for Michael Relph and Basil Dearden's *Desert Mice* (1959). Here he is, joined by the stellar cast of Valerie Peters, Irene Handl, Alfred Marks, Dora Bryan, Dick Bentley, Liz Fraser, Reginald Beckwith and Joan Benham.

Sid and his wife Valerie attend the 'Artists and Models' gala opening of London's new Latin Quarter restaurant on 3 March 1958. With them is Peter Noble, the film critic.

Sid as crime reporter Freddy Evans on the Nettleford Studios set of Roy Ward Baker's *Paper Orchid* (1949).

Tony Hancock, Moira Lister and Bill Kerr join Sid for the very first radio broadcast of *Hancock's Half Hour* in 1954.

The dream team of Sid, Tony Hancock and Hattie Jacques enjoy a modest launch party for the 1960 Pye recording of *This Is Hancock* with scriptwriters Ray Galton and Alan Simpson.

Sid as Perce, the lorry driver with a past, in Ralph Thomas's 1959 remake of *The Thirty-Nine Steps*. It was one of those last small-part roles that had kept Sid busy in British cinema for over a decade.

4 May 1959 – Tommy Steele, Janet Munro and Sid embark at a London airport for location work on *Tommy the Toreador* in Seville. This would prove to be a pivotal job for Sid.

Sid and his close friend Bernard Cribbins, filming *Tommy the Toreador* in Spain (1959). Director John Paddy Carstairs encouraged the pair to sing, dance and play the fool during the day. They needed no such encouragement to wine, dine and play the fool during their time off!

A pensive Sid in 1961 reflecting on the demise of *Hancock's Half Hour*, the lukewarm reaction to *Citizen James* and the gamble of ATV's variety spectacular, *The Sid James Show*.

From the end of 1959 until the start of 1975, Sid's life and work was dominated by the sauce, smut and silliness of the *Carry On* films. Here he makes his debut in the series as Sergeant Frank Wilkins in *Carry On, Constable* . . .

. . . and bows out from the long running film franchise as Big Dick Turpin in the highwayman romp *Carry On Dick* (1974).

Sid and film co-star Jim Dale in relaxed conversation at a press screening.

Sid laughs with comedy actor giants Peter Sellers and Tony Hancock several years after their first ignoble collaboration on the film *Orders Are Orders* (1954).

By 1975 Sid frequently socialised with comedians – here he is with working men's club favourites Les Dawson and Mike Reid.

Thames Television provided Sid with his biggest personal successes. Here he clowns for the camera on the Teddington Studios set of *Bless This House* . . .

. . . and is joined by his on-screen family – Robin Stewart, Sally Geeson and Diana Coupland.

John le Mesurier, Keith Marsh, Peggy Mount and Sid share a joke during a break in rehearsals for Vince Powell and Harry Driver's ATV situation comedy, *George and the Dragon*.

'You no doubt know this very clever artiste's work and if you have a part in any of your forthcoming productions for which he might be suitable, perhaps you will consider him.'

An attached 'brief résumé of his most recent work' perfectly highlights just how prolific Sid was in 1953. Prolific and versatile. He had starred in *I Am the News* for Tempean. Released as *Escape By Night*, the multi-layered, hard-bitten Italian criminal role saw Sid give arguably his finest film performance. Parnell continued that Sid had 'the Ronald Shiner part in the film version of *Seagulls Over Sorrento*, now called *Crest of the Wave* for MGM.' A film that displayed his skill for the common man comedy. While he is 'shortly finishing his current film, in which he plays the second lead with Alec Guinness in *Father Brown*.'

That was being fairly economical with the truth. Joan Greenwood, Peter Finch, and even Cecil Parker, could have made a fairer claim to supporting Guinness in Robert Hamer's presentation of G. K. Chesterton's clerical detective. Sid's role, as a reformed lag under the father's wing, was a minor delight. But it was good agent truth for a valued client. And, besides, Sid had already proved his mettle opposite Guinness before, in both *Last Holiday* (1950) and *The Lavender Hill Mob* (1951).

The fact was that Parnell was protective of Sid as a client and as a friend. And was fully in tune with what her client wanted and that, in principle, was money.

'I'll tell you the truth,' he said. 'I like money. I want to make as much money as I possibly can in the shortest possible time,' and he added with a wink, 'By fair means or foul.'

In 1960 he estimated that he had made nearly a film a month, but it was all down to luck. 'I keep touching wood. It has been going like a bomb all the time.'

And he would even put himself through physical discomfort in order to keep the dreaded taxman at bay.

He admitted that his mortal fear was snakes. 'I hate them!' But

Dave Freeman remembers he got particularly up close and personal with a snake during the making of one of his most high profile films. And he did it, simply, for the money. 'Sid didn't talk about his films that much,' reported Freeman. 'But he did tell me tales of making *Trapeze* (1956) for Carol Reed. They filmed that over at the Cirque d'Hiver in Paris. Sid loved filming in Paris. But he didn't love snakes! The problem was that he was playing the circus snake man. He spent the entire film lugging this huge python around with him. And I mean, he had it draped over him, cuddling it, petting it, stroking it. That was true acting. He seems totally at ease if you watch it today. In reality he was terrified. Mind you, I think the snake was preferable to the leading man! Again, Sid never usually spoke badly of fellow actors but he spoke bitterly of Burt Lancaster. Lancaster abused his position as a star to bully small part players and girl extras into going to bed with him. And from the latest revelations about Lancaster, not only girls! Sid didn't like him one little bit. His attitude went against everything Sid stood for. But the money was good. So he never complained.'

Phyllis and the Archie Parnell Company had certainly served Sid well. They had established him as the leading character actor on film. Nursed him through the journey to comedy stardom opposite Tony Hancock. And even turned a willing blind eye to Sid's own company, James Arts Limited. Sid would often use this company as a go-between for BBC assignments. But this relaxed and friendly arrangement led to mild conflict as early as April 1956.

Sid's performance in BBC Radio's *Saturday Night Theatre* presentation, 'The Volunteer', was rewarded with a cheque: '£31.10.0. made payable to James Arts Ltd.' George Knapman of the Parnell Company was not impressed, requesting that 'for the services of Sidney James [we] shall be obliged if you will cancel same and issue a further cheque made payable to Archie Parnell & Company Ltd . . . we wrote to you on 6 April with the necessary authority regarding cheques for this artiste but apparently our letter did not define clearly that the cheques were to be made payable to this company.'

Basking in the fame of *Hancock's Half Hour*, Sid would continually be approached for guest spots in dozens of BBC programmes, like *In Town Tonight*, *What's My Line* and *Juke Box Jury*.

For one of Sid's appearances on the latter, producer Bill Cotton sidetracked Sid's agency and Phyllis Parnell was not amused. 'I am extremely surprised that you approached Sidney James direct regarding *Juke Box Jury*,' she wrote. 'Particularly as we have been handling this artiste for 14 years, and I thought everybody was aware of the fact. I shall be happy to deal with any enquires.'

Unfortunately for Phyllis Parnell, there wouldn't be many more enquiries concerning Sid for which she would be consulted.

In May of 1960, Parnell was in discussion with Eric Maschwitz with regards to 'the new series for Sidney James. I, too, am delighted that we have been able to fix this up with the BBC.'

For Sid, *Citizen James* was the beginning of a new chapter. Less than a fortnight later, on 24 May 1960, he wrote personally to Maschwitz. 'As you may know, I have notified Archie Parnell & Co. that I intend to terminate my sole agency agreement with them on its expiration, the end of August 1960. This being the case I am sure you will understand that I do not wish to commit myself contractually through them beyond this date. I would much prefer it, therefore, if the contract you have offered me for the Sidney James show this autumn did not include options for similar shows extending into 1961. My intentions on the termination of the Parnell contract are that my business in future should be handled by my own company, "Arts Management Services Ltd." I would of course undertake to accept your options through this company after August 1960, subject of course to discussions. I hope I have made the position clear and that you will be able to assist me in this matter. I would appreciate it even though Parnell & Co. are aware of my intentions that you keep this matter confidential for the time being.'

Clearly Parnell was not aware of the break at all.

Her last assignment for Sid was the film contract for *Carry On Regardless*. Even as late as November 1960 she was still negotiating extended filming schedules for Sid. And, indeed, the relationship would never completely vanish. The BBC repeats of *Hancock's Half Hour* that would go on well beyond Sid's death, all concerning contracts signed by Sid while being represented by Parnell, constituted a string of release forms and renewed residuals.

For Sid, it was clear that although he could avoid an agent's commission by putting all his earnings through his own company, he could make even more money with another agent who he was assured would get him the really big deals. Tommy Steele was minted. And he liked the idea of having Sid by his side with his own agent, John Kennedy.

Moreover, in a letter to Tom Sloan, Sid had almost talked his projected fee for 1961 down. 'Thank you for your letter . . . in which you state that you will perform any situation comedy programmes in 1961 which meet with our join approval at an inclusive fee of £525. As your present contract calls for a fee of 525 guineas, I would hate to see you working for less in 1961 than 1960 and therefore I am taking it for granted that the figure should be guineas and not pounds.'

Sid would have hated to do himself out of money. He needed an agent. And Tommy Steele was very persuasive. Sid wrote: 'Anything that is contracted or negotiated *after* the 24 February 1961 will be done through John Kennedy. Many thanks. Happy New Year!!'

Although the arrangement was comparatively short lived, it ushered in Sid's most radical change of image with the softened-out episodes of *Citizen James* and the hard-hitting drama of *Taxi!*.

It encompassed the tragedy of the Diana Dors fire. The rejection of *Citizen James* on radio. The lacklustre treatment of *Taxi!* by the BBC. And the subsequent disillusionment Sid nursed with regards to the corporation.

The initial excitement surrounding *Taxi!* had soured greatly. An enthused John Kennedy had mooted a long-term policy with regards to the show that would have kept Sid busy on at least 26 episodes a year until the end of 1966. When the BBC relinquished its options for the projected 1965 series, it, in turn, effectively ended Sid's relationship with Kennedy.

Before the final series of *Taxi!* was broadcast and before Sid fulfilled his commitments for the South African film, he penned an open letter 'To whom it may concern' from the Jermyn Street offices of the Bernard Delfont Agency Limited.

Dated 27 February 1964, and, 'for the purpose of your records', he wrote: 'Would you kindly note that I have placed my business in the hands of the above organisation. Would you therefore address all future enquiries and offers to Mr Michael Sullivan of this office.'

Sid would be represented by Michael Sullivan for the rest of his life. And Sullivan was quick to reiterate Sid's faith in him as an agent.

'We have great pleasure in announcing that we have been appointed exclusive agents for Sidney James, who is currently appearing on television in his own series entitled *Taxi!*,' he gushed to anyone who cared to listen. 'We shall be happy to inform you of Mr James's availability upon enquiry.'

But Sid's market value was not as strong as it had been. Indeed, Sullivan's first official action as Sid's representative was as a referee between his client and the BBC in a letter dated 26 May 1965: 'As you know, I am normally not a person to make protests, but surely it cannot be in the interests of either the BBC or in my opinion certainly not in the interests of Sidney James for the showing of *Taxi!* to be at three different times over three consecutive weeks. I do not think that this is being fair to establishing the new *Taxi!* series.'

Sullivan had lost out on the projected earnings of over £20,000 for Sid's aborted third series of *Taxi!* and found himself fighting his client's corner for the proper treatment of a series that had been negotiated by his previous agent. By the end of 1964, Sullivan's tone had taken on a note of desperation. In an attempt to recapture the small screen success of *Citizen James*, Sullivan's policy was to scupper any further plans for Sid to do drama at the BBC. He realised that Sid was at his most popular in comedy. And it was comedy that would bring in the big money. He didn't quite sling Sid the red nose and the big boots but it was near enough!

A return to past glories obviously involved scribes Dick Hills and Sid Green who reworked the East End charmer of *Citizen James* for another potential series for Sid. Sullivan wrote to Tom Sloan: 'No doubt by now you will have received the pilot script from Hills and Green, and I feel sure that your reaction will be the same as ours, which is to say that we think it is a first-class pilot.'

In the most telling phrase of the letter of 13 November 1964 Sullivan assured Sloan: 'At this stage I would like to draw to your attention that there has been a complete rehabilitation of Sidney's career in the past nine months.'

Rehabilitation is a very strong word to use. Particularly from an agent to a potential employer. It implies that Sid's career has been in the doldrums. In fact, it had been Sid who had nursed a grudge against the BBC. As a result, Sid was somewhat in the doghouse as far as the corporation was concerned. And the letter is Sullivan's last-ditch effort to build bridges.

'You will be very pleased to know that he has starred in three pictures,' Sullivan continued. 'Namely *Tokkoloshe* [sic] (Cinemascope, colour, 1st star billing), *Carry On Cleo* (1st star billing) and *One Day in London* (large screen, Technicolor, 1st star billing); he also embarks and stars in a new picture *The Great Brain Robbery* in mid-January. Now the interesting point is, Tom, that all these pictures are to be released throughout 1965 commencing in January. Furthermore, he is contracted to do three more films in 1965 and all the films mentioned above are for world distribution. Therefore, we are particularly anxious to get together with you to settle dates for the new series. I will be obliged for an early appointment to discuss same.'

Notwithstanding the delayed emergence of *Tokoloshe the Evil Spirit* in Britain, Sullivan's missive details Sid's film career impressively and, in the main, accurately. It also pointed Sid towards the girl-chasing, womanising comedian. In other words, the clichéd view of Sid that he still typifies to this day. Sid was Sid. And there was no going back.

Tokoloshe the Evil Spirit was his last dramatic role in a film. Thereafter, it would be comic cameos. Or comic leads; all of which were for director Gerald Thomas.

Carry On Cleo would cement his image forever. The rip-roaring, historical adventurer was a coward, a double-crosser and a killer. But Sid made him both lovable and threatening; and 'it is all done with enormous gusto, every joke is bludgeoned home with a leer or a nudge in elaborately splendid Roman and Alxandrine settings,' as Iain Crawford had it in his *Sunday Express* review of December 1964.

One Day in London would enjoy general release as *Three Hats for Lisa* and, although top billing would actually be allocated to pop star Joe Brown, Sid was the comic cement that held the colourful travelogue together. He was cast, once again, as a London cabbie and exercised his dancing muscles for the most impressive routine he ever committed to film: a rousing, stiff-legged blast through 'Bermondsey', a rollicking pop song steeped in music-hall tradition from songwriters Leslie Bricusse and Robin Beaumont.

Vera Day had left the business following her role in the 1963 series of *Taxi!*. 'That same year I got married,' she explains, 'and producers were bringing in French and Italian girls to play the sort of roles I had been playing so I went into cabaret.'

Indeed, for *Three Hats for Lisa* (1965), producer Jack Hanbury brought in one such Italian girl, Sophie Hardy.

The Great Brain Robbery, a heist comedy for Peter Rogers and Gerald Thomas, was also renamed before release as *The Big Job* (1965), presenting Sid with an, albeit comic, return to his roots as a crafty criminal. But being a comedy, he was no great shakes at the heavy business. And being a Talbot Rothwell script, it was heavy on glorious innuendo and borrowed ideas. The original premise, that of a criminal gang emerging from a long stretch inside to discover the hiding place of their ill-gotten gains has been built over, was already 30 years old when the film was released.

But the Carry On cast worked their usual magic. For Jim Dale, fast establishing himself as the ultimate romantic lead in the films, Sid wasn't just 'a master film actor. He was just the nicest. I never ever saw him lose his temper, be moody on set or show any interest in any actress who was hired, save the natural courtesy that defined the man.'

Joan Sims agreed: 'Sid would never tolerate any of the girls being mucked about with on the set. And that wasn't with regards to just the old friends he had on set like me. I'm talking about the lovely young things that would pop in and pop out!' she chuckled. 'Sid was a real old-fashioned gentleman. Some of the executives would come down on to the floor and try and chat up the girls. One got rather frisky and Sid went over, tapped him on the shoulder and told him to cut it out. This was an actor telling one of the bigwigs where to go. But Sid got away with it. He commanded an awful lot of respect.'

Whether this was old-fashioned charm masking jealousy, is open to debate. It is claimed that *Three Hats for Lisa* star Sophie

Hardy persistently requested attention from her male colleagues and Sid happily obliged. But, whether this and other rumours are true or not, the girl chasing was great for the image. Sid's reputation made him a nudge, nudge, wink, wink hero to millions across the country and, ultimately, across the world, but the string of affairs he allegedly had during his years of stardom in Britain seem something of a publicity push. He treated his sex appeal with joyful send-up and working class mockery: 'I've never been anywhere near a stately home before,' he said when *Don't Lose Your Head* saw him on location in some of the finest houses in Buckinghamshire in 1966. 'All they've got to make sure of is that they lock up the treasure. I'm especially partial to antiques but probably all I'll get will be a couple of chambermaids.'

It was all part of the act. And they loved him for it.

Julie Stevens says that 'during *Carry On Cleo* I was covered in this awful brown make-up and stuck in this mad fur bikini. Sid took pity on me at the end of the day and let me shower in his dressing room. I only had a chorus type room with a washbasin. Sid had a lovely shower. I was most grateful to him for the kindness he showed me. And there were no strings attached, if you get my meaning. He was the perfect gentleman with me. Nothing was ever tried on. He was just a very nice man.'

Cleo herself, Amanda Barrie, has 'a fund of happy memories of Sid. The ultimate professional. I remember I was going through all sorts of doubts during the filming. I was convinced I was fat and ugly. I wasn't, of course. But we go through these phases in life. You need reassuring. And Sid was lovely. The perfect gentleman. Charming, helpful and full of lovely, kind words. And the funniest man. I doubt whether there is a single picture of Sid and I where I'm not laughing. And that asp! We would break up with laughter all of the time. We must have wasted so much film!'

Carol Hawkins, who appeared with Sid in the 1972 films *Bless This House* and *Carry On Abroad*, remembers Sid as someone who 'just seemed to get on with what he was supposed to do. He just got on with the job. Gerald Thomas [the director] never seemed to give much direction to anyone really as it appeared everyone knew what they were supposed to be doing. Sid was a very natural actor and seemed very at ease with himself. It is one of those undefined things with actors, they just have something which is difficult to put into words.'

Wendy Richard was another glamorous young star who worked with Sid James on three Carry On romps and the film of *Bless This House*. 'He was a sweetie,' she remembered. 'Always the gent! I think the appeal of the Carry Ons was their seaside postcard type humour. All self-cleaning jokes! And Sid was such a likable man, on and off [the screen]. He was the most lovely thing about the Carry Ons, for me. He was a crook or a pirate, but he always seemed the soul of discretion.'

Dilys Laye who also worked with Sid on three Carry Ons, remembered him as 'the most charming and unselfish of actors. He was always professional. I never once saw him lose his control of what he was doing. No matter how bad the conditions – and the conditions on *Carry On Camping* have almost passed into legend – Sid never complained. He always got on with the job in hand. And he was wonderful to me. However I was feeling – and you are not at your best at 7.30 in the morning in a muddy field – Sid always made you feel beautiful.'

'Sid was certainly a gentleman,' says co-star Shirley Eaton, 'but it's the nature of the public that when they see an actor – and Sid was a very good actor – when they see an actor playing the womanising rogue all the time, they begin to think of the actor and the character as the same. Sid was a rough diamond, there's no doubting that. But he and his wife Valerie came to a party Colin [Rowe – her husband] and I hosted and he was charming, funny and lovely company.'

Sid's lifelong friend, Olga Lowe 'never saw his macho side. The part of him that loved gambling, horses and drinking. And he never talked about bad times in his love life.'

The passions of Sid's best-loved characters: the booze and the birds and the betting. These were the passions of the real Sid. But he could, and indeed, needed to have the solid family life and the solid reliability of regular work. It was hardly a double life. But it was effortless. With a joke, a smile and a kind word he could get almost anything.

It wasn't just the ladies he charmed. Sid had the ability to put even the most seasoned of theatrical pros at ease on an unfamiliar sound stage. Bill Maynard recalls: 'The absolutely marvellous team spirit on the Carry Ons was really created by the warmth and absolute generosity of Sid James. It seemed to be his show, to me. He was the star of the piece. I was a guest. With a few bits and pieces to do. But Sid made you feel very welcome and included within the gang. It was a rare gift that he had. And I know I for one greatly appreciated it.'

Jack Douglas, a fellow vaudevillian, found Sid the most welcoming of people: 'Naturally I was a little nervous about joining such an established team. Comedians can be a funny lot,' he joked. 'But Sid was marvellous. He would chat to me and make me feel very at home. I had made one or two [Carry Ons] by the time we did some lengthy scenes together in *Carry On Girls*. He was very kind. And very aware of where the camera was. It was a close two-shot and Sid pulled me to one side before the take: "Here Jackson. If you take one step closer to the reception desk they'll get a much better look at you on the screen. Otherwise it's going to be my ugly mug in the centre. It'll be better for the scene. And better for you. All right, son?" I took his advice, of course. And he was right. He usually was, was Sid!'

Jim Dale remembers: 'The nearest he ever got to losing his rag was when we were playing poker during a break and an extra kept bothering Sid with silly questions. Eventually Sid said, "Listen mate, I would love to keep talking with you, but I can't stand your breath!" No insult really, just the truth, and a very embarrassed extra slunk off muttering an apology to Sid. The same guy came up to me on set the following day and breathed straight into my face. "Colgate!" he said. "Do you think Sid will like it?" That was typical of people's reaction to Sid. Everybody loved him. Everybody wanted to be his mate. He was a pro, and pros don't need to prove anything to anybody except on screen'

For Lance Percival, a comparative novice in film who had became something of a fixture for director Gerald Thomas, Sid was the most supportive of co-stars. *The Big Job* was the last of three films they made together and it was 'six weeks of pure joy', according to Percival. 'Sid had been of tremendous help to me. I had just started and Sid had made hundreds of films. It was a rather terrifying prospect going into that big film studio for the first time but Sid calmed me right down. He was a very calming influence on set. Actually, the first thing he told me was if ever you were not happy with the way a take was going, you just had to swear to make it unusable. Back in those days, a quick "Jesus Christ" was more than enough to ruin a take and give you another crack at it. That *was* Sid's technique. Although he rarely needed a second take . . . and if he did it was usually my fault!'

While Sid was cultivating an international comic image and planning the next big heist at Pinewood Studios, agent Michael Sullivan was still pitching ideas to the BBC. Writing to comedy guru Frank Muir on 18 January 1965, he explained: 'We are agreeable for [Sid] to do a *Comedy Playhouse*, and I now look forward to discussing the proposed dates. Hills and Green would, I know, very much like to write this, and we of course would be very happy for them to do so.'

Ironically, *Comedy Playhouse* had been established in 1962 as a vehicle for writers Galton and Simpson. However, thanks to the success of *Steptoe and Son* springing from the series' loins, it was now seen as the breeding ground for other new series. In effect, a batch of pilots waiting to be commissioned. Indeed, the 1965 series would yield Johnny Speight's *Till Death Us Do Part* and introduce the comic curmudgeon Alf Garnett. Tantalisingly, Sid could have been in the running to play Garnett himself after Peter Sellers had baulked at the idea. Even more intriguingly, the Sid Green and Dick Hills script commissioned for *Comedy Playhouse* was ultimately made with Ted Ray in the lead. The man who Sid had replaced in the Carry Ons was given his first tryout here in television situation comedy. *Happy Family* didn't make the grade as a series, but its premise of a distraught domestic life was something of a blueprint for *Bless This House*. The 16-year-old daughter, Jill, was even played by Judy Geeson, actress sister of Sally Geeson who would go on to play Sid's daughter in the subsequent hit series for Thames Television. Frustrations and coincidences notwithstanding, the 1965 series of *Comedy Playhouse* marked a turning point in Sid's career. He would never again have another series on BBC Television.

But Sid's fledgling agent Michael Sullivan had some choice stage assignments lined up for the year. *The Solid Gold Cadillac* was presented by Bernard Delfont, Arthur Lewis and Tom Arnold, under the direction of the self same Arthur Lewis. Rehearsals began at the end of March 1965, and the play opened on 4 May at the Saville Theatre. A comedy set in New York and Washington, it had been a play and then a film before Sid got his hands on the manipulative part of a motor car business founder and senator. Sullivan had also negotiated top star billing for Sid alongside Margaret Rutherford. Indeed, his client had come a long way since briefly supporting Rutherford's 'armour-plated other-worldliness' in the films *Miss Robin Hood* and *Aunt Clara* in the early 1950s.

It's fair to say that the reviews for *The Solid Gold Cadillac* were mixed but even the bad ones, like that in *The Times*, celebrated a 'hard-worked Sidney James, whose blow-by-blow delivery of

"Spartacus to the Gladiators" is a prodigious example of comic energy gone to waste.' While another, from the *Daily Telegraph*, called it a 'lively satire' and highlighted praise for Rutherford 'wearing some quite wonderful clothes and the air of enjoyment of an accredited witch whose magic has worked. She has a terrific time. And Sidney James, as the tycoon, shares it with her. Indeed, at one point he achieves a temporary takeover. He delivers a recitation with a wealth of overdone illustrative gesture – a perfect burlesque of every very bad actor who ever stormed a barn.'

Regardless of the critics, the healthy audiences saw the production enjoy an extended run of six months.

During the day Sid was back at Pinewood Studios shooting his favourite Carry On romp, *Carry On Cowboy*: 'I've been a killer of the old West for years,' he said. 'The West of London!' And, moreover, he was candid about the quality of the film: 'This is the funniest of the lot,' he told *Movie-Go-Round* host Peter Haigh in a radio broadcast from March 1966. 'This *really* is funny.' As if to emphasis that, to Sid, the previous films were not!

Director Gerald Thomas thought Sid 'was a kid at heart. In *Carry On Cowboy*, I'd find him behind the scenery twirling a six-gun and trying to practise a fast draw.'

And for Jim Dale, it was the most fun on set: 'We were all like kids in the playground, running around with our new toy six-shooters. And they let me have a little time to practise my revolver tricks. You can't judge where a revolver will end up when you spin it in the air unless you practise a lot. And I did. Days of practice for a second on screen. But I think Sid appreciated that. We had a ball on that film.'

Indeed, the ABC *Film Review* journalist was 'having a word with Joan Sims when I suddenly felt a gun barrel in the region of my fifth rib. I turned round quickly to find a grinning Sid James. "That's thing's not loaded?" I gasped. "Don't know," Sid answered blithely. "I ain't pulled the trigger yet!" Sid plays . . . the fastest gun in the West . . . [and] as I watched Sid James riding off into the sunset I knew that before long you'll have the opportunity of seeing, at your local ABC, one of the funniest in the long line of Carry On comedies.'

Following the play and the Carry On, it was straight in to rehearsals for Sid's pantomime of the season. It was the most prestigious pantomime appearance of his life: opposite Kenneth Connor as the robbers in the London Palladium production of *Babes in the Wood*. Alan Curtis, who chilled the children's blood as the Huntsman, remembers: 'It was a marvellous production. And what a cast! Frank Ifield warbling away. Sid, Kenneth Connor and Roy Kinnear as the clowns of the piece. The country's best-loved dame, Arthur Askey. And me! It was a tremendous experience. And the audiences! You won't believe me but we were still running in the following May! In a pantomime. In fact, I used to go with Sid and Arthur and watch some cricket before the evening performance!'

But Sid's career was in flux. The following season would be his last spent in pantomime. His stage roles were from henceforward tailor-made for him by Sam Cree.

His film roles would be for Peter Rogers and Gerald Thomas, almost to the point of exclusivity.

And his starring television career would be put in the hands of commercial television.

If agent Michael Sullivan had a game plan it was to make money. And that suited Sid.

Jack Douglas, who shared the same agent, remembered Sullivan 'as a real go-getter. I liked him. And he did wonders for my career. I never stopped working. Sid would throw these big parties at his home in Iver Heath and Mike would always be there. He was like part of the family. And Sid was earning good money during his time with Mike. Still, Sid being Sid, he was always careful with it. I remember Sid invited me to a party but I was in the theatre until late in the evening. I arrived at Sid's house after midnight and was made most welcome. "What you drinking, Jackson?" he asked me. "Champagne please, mate." "Sorry, mate," he said, "it's all gone!" I actually discovered later that Sid had ordered several crates of the stuff and two were left unopened but he had decided that no more would be opened after midnight. So that was that. He was serving his friends Cutty Sark whisky which he endorsed . . . and which he had by the crate, for free, in his cellar. He saw me drinking this and wandered over to me. "Here Jackson. Follow me." He took me down to the cellar and pulled out this dusty old bottle of brandy. "Have some of the good stuff." If Sid really liked you, money was no object. That's what comes with having a great agent.'

But Sullivan may not have been playing by the same rules as his client: his memoirs, *Confesssions of a Show Business Agent*, were published after Sid's death and focused on several lurid tales. 'I liked Sid,' said writer Dave Freeman. 'Everyone liked Sid. The people who denigrated him after his death were on the whole an unsavoury lot. His former agent Michael Sullivan wrote his own autobiography and revealed himself as a seedy individual, a wartime deserter and womaniser of the first degree. How he had the cheek to slag off Sid who had earned him a good living I don't know.'

But for Sid in the mid-1960s, Sullivan skilfully steered his career in the most profitable direction. The actor may not have been particularly challenged by the roles on offer but the compulsive earner in him was happy: 'I can't complain' said Sid. 'I've not been unemployed – and I'm booked up for the next two years. I did have thoughts of giving up comedy and going in for the heavy roles, but my wife, Valerie, being the very sensible girl she is, said, "That will be nice. Which newspaper pitch are you going to work on?"'

10

Get Well Soon

Sid treated bad health and injury with the rich, withering disdain they deserve. Throughout his career he would bounce back from illness with a determined growl. His was the boxer's mentality. If you had been knocked out by some unseen force you simply mopped yourself down and climbed back into the ring. Indeed, during the all-important opening night of the West End run of *Wonderful Town* in May 1955, Sid threw himself into the energetic 'Pass the Football' number and cracked his cranium. As the *Daily Telegraph* reported the following day the show's 'leading man . . . tripped . . . and hit his head . . . He was knocked unconscious.' The stage management quickly ushered on Sid's understudy, Michael Kent, who took up the reigns of the show until the interval. Amazingly, after the 15 minutes of chit-chat and gin 'n' tonics in the theatre bar, the audience was greeted by a, seemingly, fit and eager Sid who completed the rest of the performance. One can imagine the approving looks and buoyant reaction to the comedy hero from film and radio, reappearing to the delight of the paying audience.

As that other seasoned professional, Jack Douglas, observed: 'It's called Doctor Show-Biz. I've worked with these wonderful old music-hall performers, well into their eighties, who would be hobbling around backstage. Once they heard their overture and set foot on that stage, they suddenly dropped sixty years. Sid had that spirit in spades. The audience meant an awful lot to him. I can imagine him sitting in his dressing room as the show went on without him, thinking as soon as the curtain goes down on that first half I'm preparing to get right back out there and give them the show they have paid for. Sid really cared about the people.'

And again typically of an old boxer, he was determined to keep himself trim. But not just by visits to the gym and a home shadow-boxing regime. He would enjoy a game of cricket. Even more if he could play with pals from show business. Tony Hancock for one. And a very inexperienced Bernard Cribbins for another.

'Sid was a mate,' Cribbins says. 'We got on extremely well from the first time we worked together. We got on very well offstage as well. It was Sid who got me into cricket. I had never played at school. As a "girl" I was too busy throwing a rugby ball around. But Sid was involved with the Lord's Taverners and asked me to play in some sort of charity match. We were living in Chelsea at the time and he came to pick me up in his Ford Consul. Open top. Very flash. Very Sid! Anyway, he drove me down to the Sussex County Ground, someone lent me some whites and away we went. I was enjoying the day. Enjoying the sunshine. But I had no idea what I was doing.'

'Anyway, Sid, typically, was the nominal captain of our team and he came over to me and said, "Right, it's your turn to bowl!" I protested that I didn't know how and he breezily said, "Oh come on, Bernie." So, I took the ball and did it. With my first ball the guy in bat got two runs. The second he hit for four. But the third ball, I bowled him middle-stump. Of course, I went berserk. Leaping about. Celebrating. Overacting as usual. Sid quietly came over to me and said, "Calm down, Bernie. He's an Ice-Hockey player!" The poor bloke I had bowled out had less idea of what he was doing then I did!'

The Lord's Taverners meant a lot to Sid and he was very vocal in campaigning for them. Indeed, the BBC's Eric Maschwitz called on 'my dear Sid' in May 1960, because 'we are at long last able to televise the Lord's Taverners show which has, as you possibly know, hung fire for two years owing to our inability to find a format capable of introducing as many famous Taverners as possible. The present script consists of a Victorian cricket melo-drama entitled *Upgreen and At 'Em* or *A Maiden Nearly Over*, with twenty-six speaking parts in sixty minutes so that you will realise no great burden is to be put upon any of our actors. It would give us the greatest pleasure if you yourself would be able to appear in this, taking the part of an honest gardener-cum-groundsman. I do hope you may be able to do this. The show will be recorded in the Television Theatre on Sunday evening . . . and there will need to be a limited number of short rehearsals towards the end of the previous week, which I am sure can be arranged to suit your convenience. The BBC has agreed to make the Lord's Taverners a donation of two and a half thousand pounds, less the cost of artistes' fees, which it has been suggested should consist in each case of a nominal ten guineas in order that the donation available for the NPFA may be as large as possible. I do hope you will feel able to agree to this.'

But cricket and a regime befitting a boxer and a dancer was one thing. Sid's body was anything but a temple as he often gleefully admitted. He would conduct interviews with the press in a bar, over large drinks and big meals, while puffing his way through several cigarettes and dragging the chat away from work and back to the next race at Chepstow. He was an actor. And that's what actors did. It's also how they got parts. 'I would often see Sid in the BBC bar,' remembered seasoned player of small parts, Norman Mitchell. 'That's probably how I got the bit on *Taxi!*. We would all be down there. Working. Not working. The casting blokes would be down there too. They would stop me and say: "What are you doing tomorrow, Norman?" "Nothing!" "Right. I've got this copper part. Just a few lines. Be in studio so and so at such and such." That was what the business was like in those days. Marvellous it was!'

Bernard Cribbins was another friend who whiled away an hour or so with Sid in the bar. 'We were down in Elstree doing the studio stuff for *Tommy the Toreador*,' he remembers. 'Now Sid never ate in the studio canteen. He would always go to a little pub across the way. He would often say to me, "Come on Bernie." And, contrary to what some people say about him and some would practise, Sid would always stand a round. "What you having, Bern?" he would say. You see, Sid was the leader, really. The governor. You always wanted to follow him. So I said, stupidly, "What are you having?" Anyway, he always had gin and lemonade. Well, this huge glass of gin and lemonade turned up. At lunchtime! It was all too much for Bernard. But Sid managed to put them away without ever affecting his performance. One day Trevor Howard walked in. He had also been making a film out in Spain, with Dorothy Dandridge [*Malaga*]. Like us, he had been savouring the old *fesaors* a bit too much during his time over there and he walked into the pub a little worse for wear. To this day it remains one of my proudest achievements. I think I remain the only man to have ever bought Trevor Howard a non-alcoholic drink! Sid used to laugh about that a lot.'

Even Valerie accepted that when Sid arrived home from work 'he'd give me a huge hug . . . [and say] "Come on, darling . . . where's the gin and tonic?"' But, while 'he loved a drink . . . never in thirty years did I see him drunk.' He could handle it.

But, at the age of 53, could Sid handle the workload as well?

'There's one good thing,' he told the *Sunday Express* in November 1966, 'I don't feel my age. I've kept myself in good physical shape. Every now and then I get a surprise when I realise how old I am. I also have a capacity for enjoying life, but like everybody else in this business, I do get depressed at times. I would like to have enough money to pack it all in – and then go and lie in the sun and fish. But I've just got to keep working. I want some security for Valerie and the kids. Thank God, I feel I can keep working. I feel good enough for, well, I don't want to say how many years – He might be listening. But I feel fit enough for another several hundred cases of gin!'

Less than six months later Sid had his first major heart attack.

The year 1966 had started well for him. His rip-roaring Western baddie for the Saturday matinee audience in *Carry On Cowboy* was his best film performance for many years. Sid's agent, Michael Sullivan, wrote to producer Peter Rogers in the February to say: 'I have never seen Sidney better in any picture.'

The relationship between Sullivan and Rogers wouldn't be as cordial for the rest of the year, however. Both men, clearly, saw the long-lasting potential in making these same sort of films with the same cast of actors. Sullivan had Sid on his books as well as familiar Carry On faces Charles Hawtrey, Jim Dale and Kenneth Connor; the latter currently on a sabbatical from the series. With them, Sullivan bid fair to control the core team and hold Rogers over a barrel with regards to higher contractual fees and a percentage of the subsequent box-office receipts. During discussions about fees for his artistes on Peter Rogers's new film, *Don't Lose Your Head*, Sullivan casually mentioned the fact that he guessed Kenneth Williams and Joan Sims were also being cast. Sullivan was currently trying to charm the two Carry On stalwarts from their agent, Peter Eade.

This was the perfect opportunity to act, for Rogers was in a fairly precarious position with regards to his comedy empire. He had just accepted a distribution offer from the Rank Organisation and his previous distributor, Anglo Amalgamated, were threatening to retain the Carry On title. Rank already had cold feet over being closely associated with a successful series that the industry had linked with Anglo for almost a decade. Thus, if Sullivan had succeeded, he could have had an 'official' Carry On production team on his books. And, over at Anglo, a new team were planning to put together a Carry On without Peter Rogers. The producer was at Rank. And he was making just another comedy film. A bidding war to use the Carry On team could have resulted.

In the end, it didn't, of course. Williams and Sims remained loyal to Peter Eade. And Rogers had legal and moral right on his side. But *Don't Lose Your Head* was a jittery project for him. It was only once the film had gone into post-production that he freely requested that it should be seen as the 13th Carry On.

His headaches had started as early as July 1966 when legal bod Michael Horniman, of A.P. Watt & Son, expressed concern regarding copyright issues. Rogers' response was swift and adamant: 'Some time last year, just before Peter Watt died, he told me that he'd seen a report of an interview given by Sidney James in which he said he was playing the part of the Scarlet Pimpernel in my comedy about the French Revolution. Peter advised me in his usual kind way that the Baroness Orczy stories were still in copyright – a piece of information which was very useful. However, in spite of the fact that Sidney James had no right to make such a statement and in spite of the fact that his statement was not the truth, yet another story has appeared in the Press and I enclose this for your information. It is true, of course, that I am making a film called *Don't Lose Your Head* and that it is about an English aristocrat rescuing aristos from the guillotine but I assure you that it is not in any way based on *The Scarlet Pimpernel*.'

It *was* a parody of *The Scarlet Pimpernel*, of course, and Sid was well aware of the fact: as soon as he had read the script. And as soon as he saw his costumes. And there were a lot of those.

'I get to play everything but the Hunchback of Notre Dame,' he told press agent Ian McAsh. He also had to play a scene in drag, which he was less keen about. But a job was a job was a job. And he 'did it wonderfully and professionally', remembers Jim Dale. 'We didn't dare laugh at him though,' Dale continues, 'we just laughed with him. After the scene was shot.'

Both Sid and Jim Dale were first called on set in mid-September and were wrapped by the start of November 1966. For Michael Sullivan it had been a tricky time. His client, Sid, had never been busier and film, stage and television commitments were converging alarmingly quickly. Rogers had even threatened to recast the role if Sullivan's demands became too relentless.

In the end, Sid fulfilled all his commitments. Just.

During the making of the film at Pinewood, Sid was also travelling back and forth to the Pier theatre in Bournemouth where he was starring in *Wedding Fever*. It was an energetic role and Sid was called on to give up to two performances a day. And this was after a long, exhausting day on set. 'At the end of those hectic four weeks my face was even more crumpled than any piece of corduroy ever woven,' he joked.

Even his costume fitting was slotted in around the show. Costume designer Emma Selby-Walker noted that Sid was to be at Bermans 'for a costume fitting at 9.30am on Monday 22 August and will be returning to Bournemouth before lunch so we will have to fit in clothes and wigs during that morning.'

Although Sullivan had requested Sid's release from the filming by 28 October, the all important rehearsals for his new television series also had to fit around Sid's last few days on set for the Peter Rogers film.

It was the only way. For the television series was of crucial importance. It was his first situation comedy for ATV: *George and the Dragon*, written for him by Vince Powell and Harry Driver.

Sid was cast as George of the title; the randy handyman cum chauffeur. It was hardly a stretch for the actor. It was good, knockabout farce. He drank lots of scotch. He chased lots of girls. And he battled figures of authority, although he had a touching sense of duty to his befuddled employer. The setting was simple: the plush London abode of an English gentleman. Sid was, reassuringly, downstairs.

'I don't think I've been as funny as I was with Hancock – until now,' Sid said in 1966. 'Ever since Tony and I split I have been looking for the right partner. I think I've found it with Peggy [Mount].'

Mount was already something of a comedy legend. With her booming voice and harridan attitude she had played the farce *Sailors Beware* both onstage and on film. As a result, she was the epitome of the battleaxe. Hattie Jacques on a bad day. And Sid knew the combination would be a winner. 'I've had a hunch about this show. But that doesn't mean anything!' he admitted. 'I've been a gambler all my life and every time I've had a hunch about a horse it's got beat. I've had to give up backing the gee-gees except for the odd flutter. If I bet on a race with only one runner, it would fall at the first fence. So I'm making no predictions. The only things that count are the audience ratings as the weeks go by.'

The figures were very good. And the company excellent. Keith Marsh, who was cast as the rather fragrant gardener, remembers: 'Working with Sid on *George and the Dragon* was a joy. He was most professional and at the same time very friendly and kind. Alas, one wasn't able to really get to know him. We always seemed to be behind with the schedule. And it seemed that as soon as we had recorded one, it was being broadcast. It was a very quick turnaround. But Sid always appeared to be very laid back and easygoing. Nothing seemed to phase him.'

In fact, Sid was frantic about the series. It was pointed out to him that this was something of a comeback. It had, after all, been three years since *Taxi!* had quietly faded away from view. While it can hardly be said that Sid had been idle in those three years, television is a very fickle master. If you're not on it, the industry and, more importantly, the audience can think of you as finished. For Sid, he was happy with the break. He explained that by 1963,

'I got to the "Oh, my Gawd!" stage. "Oh my Gawd, it's him again. Switch off!" So I decided to lay off television for a while.'

But Sid never wanted to go back to the situation he had faced immediately after the split with Hancock. He didn't want another *Citizen James* series one. 'It's a terrifying responsibility shouldering a show by yourself,' he explained. 'I tried it and I made up my mind never to do another television series with Sid James above the title and nothing else. It's not a matter of cowardice. It's a matter of knowing myself. I have found that with the kind of work I do, I can only dance well with a good partner. Look at it another way. If you play tennis with a rabbit you'll play as badly as he does. Peggy [Mount], now, she can return any service you throw at her. You can't ace this girl. The funny thing is that we both have the same accountant and he kept saying to us, "Why don't you two get together?" At first I thought it was a great idea – but then I kept thinking we were both positive characters which might not work.'

It did, of course. And as soon as the ratings were in Sid could revert to his casual attitude to acting. Modestly he greeted plaudits with: 'I don't find it hard to imagine being somebody's handyman!'

Peggy Mount was delighted with the prospect: 'Sid has the one thing all good comedians have,' she told the *TV Times*, 'he is lovable. Even if he is picking someone's pocket you have the feeling that it is the right thing to do!' The two had both worked on the 1956 film *Dry Rot* but, as Peggy said, 'Then, our paths didn't really cross,' but, 'playing with Sid' was one of the main 'reasons why I'm so excited over this series.'

The first series, culminating with a seasonal special on Christmas Eve 1966, proved one of ITV's big hits of the year. A second series was rushed into production. But Sid was feeling the pressure. And, for once, it erupted on set.

'I was surprised,' says Keith Marsh, 'simply because Sid had always been so cool about everything. He was in control of the show. He liked who he was working with. It was a big hit. I only ever saw him lose his temper on one occasion. But when he lost it, it was quite a shock. On a recording day, a certain prop was missing and at each run-through Sid repeatedly and politely asked for it to be there next time. On the final dress-run it still wasn't there and he suddenly lost his temper and screamed at a poor unfortunate floor manager: "Do I have to behave like Charlie Drake in order to get anything done around here!" Of course, [diminutive comedian and star of *The Worker*] Charlie Drake was notorious for throwing tantrums if he didn't get his own way. In everything! So Sid was trying to make light of it. But he wasn't happy. I think the strain of the show was getting to him.'

If the show wasn't going quite according to plan, Sid's domestic life, however, was blissfully happy. Valerie was pregnant with their third child. But then, sadly, she miscarried.

'I was rushed to hospital and Sid was left at home with Steve and Sue [son and daughter]. Sue told me later that when the news that I had lost the baby came through, Sid broke down and wept. "It was the only time I'd ever seen dad cry, mum," she told me, "and I'll never forget it."'

Carry On film co-star, Angela Douglas, recalls: 'Sid was absolutely devastated, naturally. I remember him being on the phone to my husband [Kenneth More] and I for a very long time after he lost the baby. He was distraught. I had never known him so emotional. We tried to comfort him but he was totally broken up by it.'

However, for his wife, Sid was still the consummate professional. 'He was all smiles when he came to visit me,' Valerie said. 'He was always such a good actor when it came to hiding his own heartbreak. That night as he was leaving the hospital, he bumped into Ringo Starr who was there visiting his wife – she'd just had her first baby. "Hello, Sid mate," he said, "become a daddy again?" Sid told him the news and Ringo was bitterly disappointed for us. I'd never met him before, but the next day he came in to see me and he was really sweet. I was lying there crying when he came to my room and he tried so hard to cheer me up.

'After that I lived in hope that I'd become pregnant again, but it was not to be. People say things happen for the best and maybe that's right because within a year Sid was ill.'

Sid had been an anxious father-to-be at the best of times. 'Shortly after I gave up work on the stage our son Stephen was born [in 1954],' recalled Valerie. 'Sid insisted on me having the baby in the expensive London Clinic. We couldn't afford it – but he wanted only the best for me. On the day Stephen was born Sid was with me, running around like a panicky hen. When my labour started he drove me down to the clinic from our Hampstead flat in our dilapidated Ford Zephyr. He was in such a state, he lost the way. I sat beside him perfectly calm while he drove round and round Regent's Park, getting more and more nervous. Finally, he had to stop a police car and ask the way. The police recognised him immediately. "Don't worry, Sid," they said, "calm down and follow us." So we arrived at the clinic in great style, with a police escort. Poor Sid. He was in a cold sweat and thoroughly exhausted and I was far more worried about him than I was about myself and the baby.'

But, 13 years later in 1967, with Stephen now at school and Sid working harder than ever to keep all his employers happy, something had to give. Ultimately it was his health. For this was the time of his first heart attack.

As Keith Marsh remembers: 'It was during a rehearsal for *George and the Dragon* when Sid had his first heart attack; only mild. The director [Shaun O'Riordan] wanted to take him home, but Sid insisted on driving himself. A floor manager was dispatched to follow him in order to see that no mishap occurred on the journey.'

'At first we didn't know what the pain in his chest was,' said Valerie. 'Sid put it down to indigestion. On the quiet, I rang our doctor and told him the symptoms. He said Sid should have a cardiograph at once. I felt sick when I heard this – that surely meant he must be having a heart attack. I begged Sid to go to the doctor but he refused. "I'll see him after the show's recorded," he said. He was determined to go through with it.'

And the schedule was a hard one. Despite Sid's clout with ATV that saw him secure precious time off, particularly for old co-star and friend John le Mesurier, the team was often behind and, occasionally forced to record two episodes at a single recording session.

True to his commitment, Sid completed the second series: 'Against all my nagging,' recalled Valerie. 'He completed the show and made me promise not to tell anyone he was not well. It was hard going, for by now the pain was really taking hold. After the recording, we raced home. In fact we went so fast that the police caught us for speeding. "Hello Sid," they said peering through the car window when we stopped. "You were over the speed limit, you know." "Please bear with me," Sid said, "I'm in the middle of a heart attack. I've got to get home as soon as I can."

The police let him go. He was Sid James, after all. Everybody's friend. And he was in trouble. A cardiograph confirmed the worse.

On 14 May 1967, less than a week after his 54th birthday, it was announced to the press that Sid had been admitted to the Royal Free Hospital in London: 'An official there said yesterday that Mr James was "in need of rest" and had been working too hard.' On 19 May it was confirmed that Sid was forced to pull out of his run in *Wedding Fever* at the Grand theatre, Blackpool. He was replaced by comedian Freddie Frinton. And Sid was worried.

Despite the second batch of *George and the Dragon* starting its run on ITV the following day, Sid was fearful that his career could be over.

'I'll never forget how worried he was in case the news of his heart attack got into the newspapers,' remembered Valerie. 'When it did, he thought he wouldn't get anymore work. He really did have quite a hang-up about this. I don't think he ever realised how popular he was. He thought his luck could run out at any time.'

This was the deep-rooted insecurity of Sid. The reason he would touch wood countless times during an interview and thank his lucky stars for his career. Why he relentlessly chased the latest bit of skirt or the oldest horse in the race. Why he would work and work and work, and panic if he felt he was letting anyone down. He was an actor. And it was typical. Regardless of how big a star Sid had became, in his own heart and mind he was still the jobbing actor that could be replaced and, ultimately, forgotten. Every new job was a new audition. A new performance that he desperately wanted his audience to like. He was convinced that the bubble of popularity could burst at any moment. And a severe heart attack could be just the catalyst to topple him from the top of the light-entertainment tree.

'In spite of the fact that he liked to joke to his friends about his heart, I knew that underneath he was worried,' said Valerie.

But the industry wasn't going to turn its back on Sid. And even an estranged friend was urged to make a rare contact. 'It was the time when Sid was ill with his first heart attack,' says Valerie. 'One morning the phone rang and when I lifted the receiver I heard that familiar deep voice of Tony Hancock. "How is he then?" No hello, no conventional greeting. Just: "How is he then?" "Oh, Tony," I cried, recognising his voice at once, almost weeping with delight, "Sid will be *so* pleased to know you've phoned." And he was. When I told him later in hospital, his face lit up. He was absolutely thrilled. To most people a phone call like that would mean nothing. But Tony was a strange man. A law unto himself. He just wasn't the sort of person to ring up and ask how someone was. I knew this and Sid knew it, too. It really did mean something.'

But old friends making phone calls wouldn't put bread on the table or dosh on the nose of a dog at White City. As with his entire life, Sid was determined to present the public face that was expected of him and to be everything to everybody. And in September 1967 that meant proving to the nation, and fooling himself, that this heart attack was nothing. Certainly not enough to put him on his back and out of work for any longer than was necessary.

'I hated being in hospital,' Sid admitted to the *Sunday Express*, 'but it was a great emotional experience to receive hundreds of "get well" letters and cards. There were flowers and fruit, often from people who obviously didn't have much money. Even though you are on the films and TV you don't think about being well known. Then something like this happens and you're amazed that people should bother. You find yourself near to tears.'

Just over a year later, talking to Peter Oakes of the *People* in January 1969, Sid still reflected on his hospital experience. 'It was a lovely rest,' he said. And an alarm call. But everything was fine now. Honestly. It was just the sort of tonic and warning he needed. Returning home, he gave up cigarettes completely: 'I used to smoke sixty cigarettes a day,' he admitted. 'I didn't smoke them – I ate them. Now I don't smoke any cigarettes at all!'

He drank only tonic water. 'I used to drink a bit,' he chuckled. 'Honestly. Well, everyone knows about Sid James and booze. To say I was a drinker would be putting it mildly. I'm not to touch beer now. Mind you, I never was a beer man, more one for the shorts.'

He was a fit man . . . who liked a gurgle. As he said himself, 'Sid James has the best pair of legs in show business, topped with a bottle which has a large cork stuffed into the neck.'

The 'hardest part' of the health regime, however, was that Sid starved himself of watching the racing.

'You don't think I'd give up all the good things in life just like that, do you?' Sid reasoned. 'It's quack's orders, mate. He told me, all right: "Pack up fags, booze and starch or you'll be a gonner." Well, when you get it that straight it's silly not to do as you're told. At fifty-five you've got to go steady. I spent nine weeks in dock without being able to get out of bed. I decided then that I'd do exactly what the doctor told me. I'd learned my lesson.'

But Sid couldn't sit still for long. He chose to return to work as soon as he physically could and he announced his 'comeback' in September 1967, just over three months since the attack. By the 20th of the month he was on set at Pinewood Studios . . . in pyjamas in a hospital bed.

For this was *Carry On Doctor* and he had accepted the relatively relaxed role of a patient. 'But look what the buggers made him do,' comments co-star Jim Dale. 'They gave him the part of a patient who smokes in bed all day long. Poor Sid, he was nearly choking to death half the time. But he did it. And he never complained.'

Sid, as ever, was the first to joke about it: 'They wrote a special part for me – as a bloody patient so as I wouldn't have to get out of bed. Honest!'

'Sid was a unique actor and a very fine artiste,' says producer Peter Rogers. 'He loved doing the Carry Ons and didn't care if he played big parts or small parts. He was always the same – always wonderful to have on the set. Sid was determined to get back to work as soon as possible and that's why I gave him the comparatively small role in *Carry On Doctor*. Needless to say, Sid was excellent – and it's down to his unique ability to draw you in that you fail to realise that, firstly, he is not in much of the film and, secondly, he plays most of his part in bed!'

Sid was on set for just 13 days of the shoot and, rather harshly, earned half his usual fee: £2,500. But Jim Dale testifies: 'Sid always had fun on the Carry Ons. It was laughter from the moment you arrived at the studio to the moment you went home. And if laughter is indeed the best medicine, then Sid doing *Carry On Doctor* must have done him the world of good. There was something special about them. It may sound a bit corny but we really were one big happy family. Even when Sid was unavailable, like on *Follow That Camel*, his stand-in [Tony Mulcany] would still get work. [Director] Gerry Thomas gave him the part of one of the Arabs. The fact that Sid wasn't on the film didn't mean his stand-in didn't work. I thought that was lovely of them, actually.'

As well as the Carry Ons, Sid was also determined to keep up commitments for his television series. He returned to Elstree for a third batch of *George and the Dragon* programmes to warm applause from the cast and crew. Keith Marsh remembers: 'After his major heart attack he agreed to do another series and he was told to be careful. So, in order not to put too much strain on him we agreed to rehearse only in the morning. Later, we discovered that he had not told his wife this and she assumed that he was with us all day. In view of what has been made public in recent years we can guess where he was!'

But Sid was taking it a little more easily. At least for the time being. 'My illness was a blessing in disguise,' he said. 'I had been working too hard and drinking and smoking too much. I don't intend to work so hard in future.'

Sid tried to keep fit, without ever overdoing it. And rigorously followed medical advice. 'Listen mate,' he confided, 'there's nothing like a heart attack for helping a man get his priorities right. [It's] bloody marvellous just being alive. I could drink the best part of a bottle of vodka, lose the worst part of five hundred pounds and get through sixty cigarettes all in one day.'

But not any more. Mind you, Sid being Sid couldn't become a complete saint. Thank heavens. He revealed that his diet contained 'no stodgy foods, I just don't eat any starch or animal fat' and that he allowed himself 'three pipes of tobacco a day . . . [and] two scotches in the evening. A couple of vodka and tonics and that's me lot.'

Sid took it easy over the Christmas period of 1967. In fact, he would never return to the pantomime circuit. But by April 1968 he was once again with the Carry On team, going up the Khyber and up on location to North Wales.

Because of his heart attack, the film's insurers could offer 'accident only' cover for Sid. Peter Rogers was assured: 'We are trying to negotiate additional cover but in any event there is no doubt that an exclusion will have to be accepted for any increased costs resulting from "cardio vascular" condition.'

But Sid proved fit and well during the fairly hectic filming schedule of *Carry On . . . Up the Khyber* and would remain working on and starring in the film series until 1974. If anything, those first five Carry On films that marked Sid as back to full strength from the spring of 1968 to the spring of 1970 are the ones that define him.

He cheerfully works his way through an infidel's collection of wives without a qualm simply because of his sheer Britishness (witness *Carry On . . . Up the Khyber*). He is the cheeky plumber who eyes up bathing schoolgirls during his holiday (*Carry On Camping*). He is the womanising, hard-drinking lech (*Carry On Again, Doctor*), secretes away vast qualities of booze (*Carry On Up the Jungle*) and cheerfully clings on to his little black book during a long-term courtship (*Carry On Loving*).

It is definitive Sid. One almost gets the impression that because he had had to cut down on the finer things of life in real life, that the Carry On team allowed him to live the dream on the big screen.

One thing is for sure though. Here is a leaner, slightly diminished Sid. It was the result of his strict diet. And that meant 'no cream – not even a drop of cream – and only two eggs a week. Can't have any of the old steamed puds I used to sink into. I miss rice pud as well. I used to eat masses of it. I have lost not only the weight – I wasn't carrying a lot of fat – but muscle.' Indeed, in these films you can see the aftermath of the heart attack. Those boxing muscles have gone forever.

Actually he lost 28 pounds during his rest from the business. 'None of my clothes would fit me,' he explained. 'I had to throw everything out. About a dozen suits, dozens of shirts – everything right down to my underclothes. It's just as well they don't make ties in sizes or they would have gone as well!'

But, as with everything in Sid's life, he treated it as a joke when faced with the press: just in case anyone who might be thinking about giving him a job was reading. He gave them a sideways glance, winked and said that his family had a new nickname for him: 'Now they call me "Snake-hips"!'

11

The Green, Green Grass

At the end of the 1960s Sid was the key player in the Carry
Ons. He had starred in 11 of the films over the decade with
another one in the can. And at the end of 1969 there was
the television invasion with *Carry On Christmas* and the gang's
take on *A Christmas Carol*.

The franchise had grown up over those 10 years of swinging
liberty by getting more immature. More smutty. And much more
successful.

'Sid was a multi-talented man,' asserts Harry Fowler. 'For me,
the Carry Ons never really showed him at his greatest or really
stretched him very much but he always gave them his very best. I
think he kept on doing them because of the money. You know
everyone involved with them now complains about the lack of
money and the poor pay but don't forget that back then that was
regular work and £5,000 or £6,000 for six weeks graft wasn't to be
sniffed at in those days. Particularly if you were doing theatre work
as well. And television. And, of course, he must have enjoyed
doing them. Who couldn't? He gelled so well with Kenneth

Williams. They were totally different actors, of course. Sid was this natural, calm performer. Kenny Williams with his wonderfully mobile face and outrageous behaviour was the flamboyant performer. But together they worked perfectly. And again, even when he was delivering those terrible, corny, hilarious Carry On lines he did something with them. He made those characters and those lines come alive. It was real. He was that good an actor. He could make those films reek with quality. That's why they kept asking him back. They tried and tried, while Sid was alive and after he died, but they could never find anyone quite like him. Sid had this unique quality that the Carry Ons needed. He gave them class and they gave him a regular income.'

Television co-star, Victor Spinetti, is in no doubt why the production team took Sid to their hearts: Nothing was wasted with Sid,' he explains. 'That's why the Carry On people loved him so much. One take. Two if he was having a particularly bad day. And that was it. Pure comedy gold in the can. Done. Thank you very much. He was that good.'

For Sid, as usual, he needed a good partner to work off to give of his best, and with the regular Carry On actors he was blessed by the finest comedy repertory company ever assembled.

Talking in 1967, Sid commented: 'I think if you had a lot of bad performers in this type of comedy the vulgarity could be pretty crude. And I think that it is not. I think the performers carry it and raise the standard so much that it is enjoyable, without being objectionable. There are artistes like Kenny Williams and Charlie Hawtrey and Jim Dale who are very professional artistes. I think the comedy is so beautifully done that it's not really vulgar.'

Jim Dale fondly remembers the 'very last time I worked with Sid. It was on the film *Carry On Again, Doctor* and we had some lovely scenes together in that. Some real two-handers. It was a joy. And Sid was so giving as a film actor. I was so proud on that particular film in that Sid actually cracked up and ruined a take or two because he was laughing at something I was doing. I was chuffed to bits. Because I was cracking up ten times more every time I did a scene with him. But, for me, to corpse a pro like Sid was a thrill. That film has some very happy memories for me.'

For his own part, Sid was happy to play down his talent as an actor and, indeed, the artistic pretence of the Carry Ons in particular.

During the making of *Carry On Henry*, Sid was reminded of the many great actors who had had a go at playing the much-married monarch, Henry VIII. But, as Sid countered, 'I'm *really* having a go at him!' And so he did. Despite the grandeur of the actors who had previously donned the crown, from Charles Laughton to Richard Burton, Sid embraced the limitations of the Carry Ons and his own perceived limitations as an actor. He celebrated these limitations. Besides, this was fun. It wasn't really acting. He could put his own unique mark on every role he played, simply by being himself. As he remarked during the filming of *Carry On Up the Jungle* in 1969: 'They are all me but with different hats on!'

Indeed, his obituary in *The Times* noted: 'In all these roles his personality retained its own enjoyably astringent flavour; he was a real comic original.' And this, tellingly, was a more prospective variation on Sid's comments.

For every Carry On role *was* essentially Sid in a different hat but, then again, every role was slightly different. Even in the three stages of Sid's Carry On development, there are variations on the theme. His authority figure in *Carry On Cruising* very much wears his working-class angst on his sleeve. He has something to prove. In *Carry On, Constable* he is a grumpy authority figure. Working class certainly, but keen to bond with his lopsided group of wet-behind-the-ear law enforcers.

In Sid's Carry Ons of the late 1960s, where birds and booze are foremost in his mind, he can switch from the calculating twister playing the primitive race card to achieve his goal in *Carry On*

Again, Doctor, to the wiliness of a plumber on the razz in *Carry On Camping*. Both are thirsty, randy characters, but there is a complexity at work in the medical romp. In *Carry On Camping* Sid was happy to take his foot off the pedal and let the lines get the laughs.

He was certainly delighted with the script, in fact, penning a rare note to producer Peter Rogers on 2 September 1968 to tell him so. 'Many thanks for the script. Very funny!' And Sid really did underline that 'very' not once but twice!

'I drove Val potty laughing aloud,' he continued. 'That doesn't often happen when one reads! There are some wonderful moments. So clean too??? Our love to you both. Many thanks again. God bless. Sid.'

For the director, Gerald Thomas, Sid was the rock of the Carry Ons: 'He never resorted to any tricks at all, and he never upstaged anyone,' he said.

A newcomer to the cast was Roy Castle who confirmed that. 'Sid was marvellous on *Carry On . . . Up the Khyber*. I'd only made a handful of films. He'd made a skipful! He was kind and sweet and put everyone at ease. Even when he lost his temper he did it in a kind and sweet way! We were filming the now very famous dining-room scene when we all had to continue eating and chatting completely oblivious of the explosions going on all around us. The food was real – boiled potatoes and ham. As the place slowly disintegrated and debris fell into our food, we pushed it around our plates and tried to avoid actually "eating" any. The scene continued for what seemed an eternity, and this being a filming technique where the actors never actually played *to* the camera, no one had noticed the crew's practical joke. We carried on pushing the food around which now included Fuller's earth powder (not harmful but equally not appetising). Eventually we *had* to put some of the revolting concoction in our mouths. This made our serene acting even more difficult! Finally, Sid James broke the silence by emitting one word – "BASTARDS!"

'The director had given the cameramen and crew the wink. They had stopped the cameras but no one had said "cut". They all quietly sneaked away and left us to it!!!'

But filming was secondary to Sid's greatest passion. Gambling. And this passion fundamentally made Sid who he was. Even on the set of the Carry Ons. 'He always liked to gamble,' said Gerald Thomas. 'He would run a sweepstake every day based on how many minutes of film we'd shoot.'

And not just that. Actor Hugh Futcher, who first worked with Sid on the film *Don't Lose Your Head*, remembers in '*Carry On Again, Doctor* when I was playing a cab driver with that Sid James in the back of my cab! Other actors would watch Sid and wonder what he was doing. He was always so quiet and so in control of the situation. Often he would sit and do his crossword. Other times the paper would be turned to the gee-gees page. But by that time the man had been doing the Carry Ons so long that he had an eye for what was and what wasn't right for those films. He would purposely take notice of us supporting actors. It was just before we shot the taxi scene that Sid told me, "You know, I could actually run a book and I could put a price on every actor's head. Some I know Gerald won't have back. They behave in a way that he won't tolerate." I was very proud to know that I was one of the ones he had down as an odds-on favourite to return. "I knew you would be back!" he said.'

Sid was, at least in his own mind, back to full strength and full fitness. He was happily doing two films a year for Peter Rogers. He had recorded the fourth and final series of *George and the Dragon* for ATV before shooting started on *Carry On Camping*. And, again before the Carry On romp, he had returned to live theatre, resurrecting his lead position in *Wedding Fever* at the Torquay Pavilion for the 1968 summer season.

Six months later he was risking an attempt at doing all three at once.

His new television series was once again produced and directed by Alan Tarrant and written by Vince Powell and Harry Driver. Sid was reassuringly untaxed. Sid was playing Sid again. For this was the definitive image of the cheeky lad reheated for the small screen. He was rather work shy. Liked a drink. Preferably served by a tasty barmaid. And, in his mind at least, always seemed to get his way. But not always. Not in the show, at least. The production, however, was plain sailing for Sid.

True to his situation comedy requirements he was partnered by an actor who would, metaphorically, return Sid's comic service with gusto: Victor Spinetti. 'To be honest,' says Spinetti, 'I never felt I was up to Sid's standard. He had a knockabout quality. A real sense of truth. Even when playing farcical situation comedy. You just believed him. And liked him. It was as simple as that. I never watch myself. But I felt I was forcing it a bit.

'Sid had that magic touch as an actor. He was the common man. The working-class hero. Call it what you will, Sid had it in spades. The public adored him. They didn't just like him. They adored him.'

And so did the bosses at commercial television. Made by the newly inaugurated Thames Television, *Two in Clover* proved an instant success when it was first broadcast in February 1969. The premise is simple. And pre-dates *The Good Life* by five years. Sid and Vic, two workmates, give up the rat race and go back to nature. They buy a farm in the middle of nowhere and attempt to run it . . . with hilarious consequences.

Critics considered the obvious situations and obvious jokes unworthy of Sid. Several still lamented the long lost days of *Hancock's Half Hour*; rather unsurprisingly in light of Hancock's death less than a year earlier.

But for Sid, *Two in Clover* was a vehicle that suited him, although he was under no illusions about it. It certainly wasn't pushing the boundaries of comedy. 'I think it's virtually impossible to do anything different unless you're Marty Feldman,' he observed with a clear understanding of television humour and the pioneers at work in it. 'There's nothing new in this series except that it's in the fresh air. And it's about two fellers instead of a feller and a bird. You never know what's going to work. You may think a show's going to be a bomb and it just falls flat. Or you may think it's going to be no good and it turns out a hit.'

Two in Clover was a hit. It leapt to the top of the London audiences' top 10 in its very first week of broadcast. That, as the Thames publicity department had it, is 'what you get for teaming up big names like Sid James and Victor Spinetti with top writers like Vince Powell and Harry Driver.'

For Spinetti, the success was all down to Sid: 'The chaps who wrote and created the show actually wanted me to play my character as very broad Welsh. I maintained that there was enough Welsh in my voice. And Sid, certainly, didn't want me to play it broad Welsh. Next to his natural, laid-back performance, I would have come across as a caricature. I was nervous enough as it was. Here was an actor vastly experienced in situation comedy. And here was I in my first one. My confidence was dented slightly when [co-writer] Harry Driver said, "I don't know. When I read this out having written it, it sounds funny. It doesn't sound funny when you do it!" Thank heaven for Sid. He was a very reassuring presence on that show for me.'

Spinetti was, indeed, a virgin where television situation comedy was concerned, but he had fast established himself as a powerful stage presence. 'I had just finished doing *The Odd Couple* with Jack Klugman at the time and I think Sid saw me as the "actor" on the play, you know. He was very sweet. There was no side to him at all. He never threw a wobbly. Never used the "I'm Sid James and we're doing it this way" sort of thing. I did a few scenes with Tommy Cooper once and, after a take, he said: "Ah Vic. You make me look good." Sid had that same sense of humility. He was a massive star but never behaved like one.

'As an actor Sid was very light on his feet. He was a dancer, of course. And a boxer. He could move. Joan Littlewood [the theatre producer] always said: "You don't act a play. You dance a play. And you act a ballet." And Sid was that sort of an actor. He danced the play with such fluidity and grace. He was very good on his feet. And that laugh, of course. Which became so much a part of who he was, in terms of the public.'

However, when Sid was "off" he wasn't quite the man Victor Spinetti expected: 'It's interesting really,' he muses, 'because I always thought that with Sid, what you saw was what you got. But he was subtly different from his public image. He would turn up for rehearsals every morning, beautifully dressed. Always sporting a matching outfit that obviously Val had picked out for him. And every day it was different. I wouldn't be surprised if I turned up every day and every day I was the same! I was a jobbing actor. You turned up to rehearse in whatever you first put your hand on, on the bedroom floor. But Sid was very dapper. Totally debonair. He would wear this purple, open-necked T-shirt and over that would be a Kashmir sweater. Very stylish.'

Sid was now in a comfortable financial position. He wasn't an actor who had an all-consuming desire to behave like an actor. He loved what he did. But he did it purely to provide for a good quality of life. Fine clothes. Fine food. Fine company. If another batch of corny innuendo, flat-footed farm-based farce and a barrel-load of fruity guffaws could pay for a heated swimming pool and an extended holiday in Majorca, then Sid was a happy man. He hated fuss. He was a natural actor, for sure. But he also wanted to get the job done as quickly as possible. Fundamentally so he could get on to the next job and the next pay packet.

For Victor Spinetti that was 'another lovely thing about Sid. He didn't like to rehearse too long. I liked that. You learnt your lines and you went in and did it. He was very professional. Some comic talents can get away without knowing [the dialogue]. I did a few sketches with the lovely Kenny Everett and I remember saying to him, "Good little bit this, isn't it?" and he said, "I haven't read it yet!" and we were just about to do it! He read his stuff and I had learnt mine.

'Sid was never like that. He would have considered that both unprofessional and a discourtesy. Sid was a lovely guy. Always knew his lines and expected you to know yours!'

This was the crux of Sid as an actor. He treated it as a job. But a job you must respect and do well. The audience have invested in the work. Be it time or money. Sid appreciated that. While he gave his audience the slap-dash, girl-chasing, beer-drinking character they loved, it took a lot of talent and a lot of control to deliver the goods.

'You look at Sid from the outside and there's this carefree, laid-back person,' reflects Victor Spinetti. 'But at work he wasn't like that. He was a total professional. He wouldn't come to rehearsals all bleary-eyed from a party the night before muttering, "Where are we then? What page are we on?" That's the casual way the man in the street would think Sid would behave. He was the rapscallion. One of the boys. But in reality he knew exactly what he was doing. He was always ready for work. As tight as Noel Coward and as disciplined as Ronnie Barker. Now I've put Sid in some very illustrious company there but he deserved to be there. He was a master. There was nothing, absolutely nothing, left to chance.'

Even when the script was considered below par by the experienced team of Carry On actors ploughing through it, Sid would always deliver. With *Carry On Up the Jungle* having scored high in the box-office ratings, Sid confided, 'We all thought it was dreadful while we were making it – it stank.' Rarely this candid about his work, he certainly wouldn't be drawn on negative comments about the one he was working on at the time or the following film or the one after that: good box-office receipts kept the series going and he wouldn't scupper a piece of work until after it had done the business. But, despite the quality of the work, Sid was philosophical: 'The kids go to a good school,' he said. Still, in October 1970 he sighed, 'You'd think the public would tire of them.'

But not in Sid's lifetime.

Nor did they tire of him, despite his continual concerns about over-exposure and changes in public taste. Money was still the vital part of any job and saving money on things he considered unnecessary became a way of life.

Unsurprisingly, *Two in Clover* was commissioned for a second series. This was scheduled to be broadcast in early 1970. 'During the rehearsal period we would often go to the pub afterwards,' recalls Victor Spinetti. 'We would have a few drinks there. Sid rarely had enough money to buy a round though. He would borrow it. Then buy a round. I mean, all his spare money went on the horses. We all knew that. And we all accepted it.'

Despite earning more money for each film or television assignment there were simply less little jobs than there had been during his halcyon days of the 1950s. Bigger, initial payments meant bigger stakes at the horse or the dog track. And if he blew a film fee on one race there wasn't another small part film backhander coming up in a day or two. This was the major concern. As he became more and more famous, his regular support of petty cash jobs dried up. Bizarrely, as he became more comfortable and settled, Sid also became more frustrated and desolate. Despite his heart attack of two years earlier Sid fully reverted to the workaholic schedule for one reason: to pack as many paid jobs in as possible.

'When we were actually filming *Two in Clover* you never really had a lot of time to socialise,' remembers Victor Spinetti. 'Sid was always working. I mean, filming during the day and working in the theatre during the evening. We filmed on location up near Blackpool and at that time Sid coincided the filming with his summer season [in *Wedding Fever*].'

'He would play twice-daily farce at the Grand Theatre having been filming all day. That's not good for the heart that sort of behaviour. And the thing that always amazed me about Sid was that he had no great star attitude. He had no dresser. No one to make the tea. He didn't even have a phone in his dressing room. You see, that would cost. He was always so careful not to waste his horse money on things he didn't consider necessary. I've worked that theatre a lot and, in the days before mobiles, you wanted a telephone in your dressing room. Otherwise you would have to go all the way downstairs to make your telephone calls and all the way back up to your dressing room.'

Even these minor sacrifices would both provide Sid a little more pin money for the horses and chip away at his quality of life on location. For Victor Spinetti, his television co-star and over 20 years Sid's junior, this was inspiring, if foolhardy. 'We were taping a show up in Blackpool,' he remembers. 'John Inman joined the cast [for the very last broadcast episode of *Two in Clover*]. At that same time John was appearing onstage with Sid twice daily. I went to see the first house. The audiences were so appreciative. And vocal. There was a real sense of love and friendship when he came onstage.'

Indeed, following the first-night performance on 19 June 1969, the *Blackpool Evening Gazette* reported that Sid took the curtain call and thanked the packed audience. 'You really have been a sensational lot tonight,' he said. 'I've heard about Blackpool audiences, but blimey!' The show proved another sure-fire hit for theatrical impresarios Bernard Delfont and Leslie Grade. But it was a strain for Sid. The lion's share of the action was firmly on his shoulders.

Victor Spinetti recalls: 'Afterwards, I was sat in the dressing room chatting with Sid and he went down to phone Val. When he came back he said, "Can you have dinner with us after the show? It's Val's birthday." So I had to hang around for the rest of the evening, until Sid had played the second house. I didn't mind. I liked Sid a lot and I liked spending time with him. But, as a result, I was completely knackered the next day on the set. And I hadn't done anything! Just because I hadn't rested as I would usually, I really felt it the next day. Sid had carried two performances of breakneck speed farce. And he had suffered a heart attack a mere year or so before. But he was there on set. Bright and early. And word perfect. He was an incredible man.'

Mere weeks after the last of *Two in Clover* hit the screen in March 1970, Sid was hard at work at Pinewood Studios breathing life into *Carry On Loving*. The rest of the British film industry was on something of a life-support system as well. Pinewood Studios was empty, save for the Carry On. The pro was that the team wallowed in the best dressing rooms the studio could offer. The con was that the script seemed even more workmanlike and listless than the previous one.

But Talbot Rothwell wasn't writing art. He was writing Carry On. He was certain that 'the success of the series is that, whether it is films or television, they are undemanding. These days, comedies have become more and more satirical and when people go to the cinema to get a good laugh, they find a much more thoughtful set-up. There are more sniggers than old-fashioned belly laughs. With a Carry On film, they know exactly what they're going to get. We've sort of replaced music hall.'

The team accepted it. Even the most leaden of gags could be polished and enjoyed if the performance was true and committed. That was Sid's attitude and, besides, he said, 'We're all mates together. We have a laugh together but I like to think we're all professionals and we very, very rarely fall behind on filming schedules.'

Although another year had gone by since Sid's recorded amazement at how the public still loved them, the release of *Carry On Loving* at the end of 1970 proved the biggest, instant home grown box-office return the series ever achieved. There was no fuss. No historical costumes. No plot, to speak off. Just Sid and Hattie Jacques running a marriage guidance office . . . with hilarious consequences! That was enough. Throw in a sweater-stretching Imogen Hassell and a few flared Kenneth Williams nostrils and what more did the family cinema-going public need for Christmas entertainment?

Apart from Sid mugging and arahhhing his way through the piracy of *Carry On Again Christmas* on the goggle box, of course.

Writer Dave Freeman had lost touch with Sid since the days of the ATV special, *The Sid James Show*, in 1961. 'I didn't see much of him after that until Thames did the second of their *Carry On Christmas* shows,' he remembered. 'Sid Colin, who was first commissioned, went down with flu and Peter Eton, the producer, rang me up in desperation about three days before it was due to go into rehearsal. All they had was the outline. I worked half the night to finish it, so it was a lash-up job. It was a send-up of *Treasure Island*. Barbara Windsor had the treasure map tattooed on her bum and most of the action consisted of people by various devices trying to get a look at it. The plot has since been used extensively but I think this was the original version.'

Despite a revert to black and white – thanks to a technician's strike at ITV – the Christmas special was another ratings winner. But its popularity was dwarfed by *Carry On Loving*. Seemingly the series had reached a peak of nudge, nudge acceptability and bankability. Still, although it would go on to become one of the most successful in the long-running series, the press boys at Pinewood Studios were not being complacent. Indeed, they were already sharpening their pencils for a major promotional push for the film scheduled for production at the end of 1970.

Although the subject was still undecided, it was to be the 21st Carry On film. The series of bawdy romps that the whole world was laughing at had come of age. And Sid almost missed the party.

The idea of Henry VIII had been kicking around since 1966. 'We want Harry Secombe to play Henry,' producer Peter Rogers said. 'One of the ideas we have is that he writes madrigals which he hopes will get to the top of the Hit Parade. When he finishes up fifth in the charts he has the top four artists beheaded!'

That idea was dropped when Talbot Rothwell returned to the subject in light of the television series *The Six Wives of Henry VIII* (1970) starring Keith Michell and the Richard Burton film *Anne of a Thousand Days* (1969). The Carry On, as so often in the past, would be the cheeky comedy winking at the more sedate, high profile and, ultimately, less commercial dramas. Sid would, in fact, don the very same regal cloak wore by Burton. And, typically, one of Rothwell's original scripted ribald sub-headings for *Carry On Henry* would be 'Anne of a Thousand Lays'. It was that kind of film!

'When we heard that we were going to do a Henry VIII film we were all quite excited,' recalled Joan Sims, already earmarked for a prominent role as the King's garlic-obsessed wife. 'Sid never ever spoke about work really. He certainly wouldn't go on about his past successes like a lot of actors would. He preferred to talk about his family, or horses or the news or whatever. However, he was very much taken with the idea of playing Henry VIII. I remember he said that it would be like going back to the serious stuff he enjoyed playing in South Africa.'

Ironically, it was a serious commitment to a stage run in Johannesburg that was at the centre of the *Carry On Henry* crisis.

Having scored a huge hit with *Wedding Fever* in Great Yarmouth for the 1970 summer season, it was decided that Sid should take the play to South Africa. A run in Cape Town was to be followed by a newsworthy homecoming to the Johannesburg Civic Centre from the 23 September.

Carry On director Gerald Thomas was aware of the stage commitment but had, as far as he was concerned, been assured that Sid would be free to honour the film role. He had already offered Sid £5,000 for the part: £4,000 for his contracted six-week work on the film and an additional £1,000 in a side letter that would, as usual, be paid in cash.

Moreover, Thomas had taken it upon himself to reply to a request to have both Sid and Valerie James attend the Bexleyhealth and District Club for the Disabled. The charity wanted the star to open their annual bazaar on Saturday 7 November from 11 in the morning. Although the Carry On unit never worked over weekends, the director informed the charity's representative that his star actor would in fact be busy filming that day.

Things really came to a head when Gerald Thomas casually mentioned to Sid's agent, Michael Sullivan, that Sid would be required on set from the first day of filming.

In a frantic letter to Gerald Thomas dated 24 August 1970, Sullivan explained: 'After our discussion today, I naturally am most concerned with the date problem and at the present time I can see no way of resolving it. I did believe that you were able to, not conveniently, shoot without Sidney until the second week.

'Sidney's contracted commitment with South Africa is final and definite. Moreover, artistes, author, producer and all involved in the booking of this play, apart from the managements, are committed. I know that Sidney treasured the thought of playing the part of Henry, and was certainly prepared to lose the South Africa engagement, but I was fortunate enough in negotiating with the South African management to fit in with the dates that I believe we agreed. Sidney has had vast publicity in the South African territory of his forthcoming visit and a great deal of money has already been invested in many directions, and it would be fatal if Sidney were unable to fulfil his engagement there.

'In other words, Sidney has found himself in an impossible position and I am sure you will be the first to agree that your dates are always respected and considered to be the first call in any year, but I must ask you to help us this time, and try to give us the leeway of that week. Obviously the blame is at nobody's feet, but under the circumstances you are the only one who can give us the remedy.'

The following day Thomas dispatched a speedy response. 'As far as our end is concerned,' he wrote, 'we have always understood that Sidney would be back here on 11 October to start work on the 12th. This in itself has always been a very tight schedule as it literally gives us only two and a half hours on the morning of 7 September to equip him with clothes, wigs and beard for the very exacting part of Henry. However, by early preparation with our costume and make-up people, we have been able to cope with the situation. When you telephoned me yesterday and said that Sidney would be returning on a plane which did not get in till the early hours of the morning of the 12th and asked me if I could give him that day clear, I told you that I would make every effort to do so but may have to call upon his services in the afternoon of that day. When you subsequently telephoned me later in the afternoon and told me of the misunderstanding of the dates, I immediately contacted Peter [Rogers] and we discussed the situation fully as regards studio commitments, weather, location and other artistes' commitments which make it essential for us to complete the film by 27 November.'

'Therefore, unless Sidney can be available to us to start work no later than 13 October I am afraid we will reluctantly have to give the part of Henry to someone else. This would be a great pity as I think it is the best part we have yet offered him and also, being the 21st Carry On, it will receive a great deal more publicity than any of the others we have made. Sidney telephoned me last evening to discuss the dates with me and agreed that he had said he would be available on the 12th and that he would be talking to you later to discuss the matter. I hope you will be able to make Sidney available as, personally, I would hate making the film without him.'

'Gerald was very willing to accommodate the artistes,' reflected Peter Rogers, 'especially Sidney. I have always said that the star of the film is the name Carry On. I still stand by that. Gerald certainly looked upon Sidney as the star of the film. I can imagine his distress at having to recast. For me, quite frankly, I was seriously thinking of going back to my original idea and booking Harry Secombe for the part. He had just completed a film [*Doctor in Trouble*] for Betty [Box, Peter's wife]. Harry would have been fine. Sidney could have survived without the film and the film could have survived without Sidney.'

Thankfully, it didn't have to.

12

Man About the House

Carry On Henry proved to be, quite literally, Sid's crowning glory in the series. It was his most central part in the films. No self-contained sketches for Kenneth Williams and a chimp. No schoolgirl conspiracy for Barbara Windsor. And no unrequited love interest for Kenneth Connor. Just Sid. The King of the Castle. At the forefront of the action. With the tried and tested Carry On character actors bowing and scraping around him.

And, for only the third time in a Carry On, Sid became a father. In an edited ending to Carry On Henry, his son and heir are revealed as the result of a wrong-side-of-the-blanket tumble between his Queen, Joan Sims, and Cardinal Terry Scott. But still, domestic bliss beckoned.

It was an unintentional signposting of Sid's final change of public image. For once, at the age of 57, Sid would really be playing the role closest to himself. That of the contented husband and father.

With Two in Clover sustaining impressive viewing figures throughout its second run, Thames Television was quite happy to commission a third series. But Sid had other ideas.

Victor Spinetti explained: 'We did two lots of the show and then

Sid said to me, "We can't do another one, Vic." The powers that be certainly wanted more. There was serious talk of at least one more series to my knowledge. We had been blessed with colour for the second series and the ratings were even better than before. I mean, they were huge. It was Sid. They loved him. And there I was flying on his coat-tails. But Sid was adamant. He said, "Vic, I'm too old to go chasing the birds now. It's beginning to look unpleasant. The next thing I want to do is play someone married with a family."'

It is impossible to underestimate quite how big a gamble this was on Sid's part. He had been the undisputed champion of Thames comedy for many years. But by always playing the tried and tested Sid James type of character.

He had been the smooth-talking charmer George Russell in *George and the Dragon*. Working for crusty old Colonel John Le Mesurier as chauffeur and general dog's body in a county seat where the seat of any new parlourmaid wasn't safe from his wandering hands.

He had been the smooth-talking charmer Long Dick Silver in *Carry On Again Christmas*. Working alongside the goofy, hirsute bumbling of Bernard Bresslaw and desperately searching for the hidden treasure chest that lay beneath the worryingly masculine garb of Barbara Windsor.

And he had been the smooth-talking charmer Sid Turner in *Two in Clover*. Working alongside the grouchy self-efficiency of Victor Spinetti and trying to keep a country farm in operation with the dual distraction of little knowledge and a wandering eye for the local barmaid.

Writer Vince Powell remembers: 'We had a meeting with all the bigwigs from Thames. And Sid was there as well. The easy option, from our point of view, was to give them more of *Two in Clover* but I felt it was time for a change. Sid had been playing that sort of wheeler-dealer character for twenty years. At the meeting, everyone was suggesting characters and situations for Sid's new show. It was always the same. Sid the boxing promoter. Sid the publican. Sid the shady agent. He had done it all before. Anyway, I piped up and said, "I think we should have Sid married with a couple of kids!" The faces of the bigwigs from Thames just dropped. But before anybody could object Sid said, "I know Vince is right!" Not 'think he is right'. He said, "I know Vince is right." That was the start of *Bless This House*.'

Victor Spinetti concurs: 'Vince wrote the perfect pilot for him and that show kept Sid busy on television for the rest of his days. He was very canny like that, was Sid. He knew how long the public would accept him in that bird-chasing role. He never quite moved away from it. That would have been a disaster. But he was instinctively aware that the time had come to move on to something else. He apologised about turning down more episodes of *Two in Clover*, to me. He knew that we could have done more. And he knew I wanted to do more. But, there it is. No regrets. It was a pleasure to work with him and a pleasure to know him.'

Sid knew he owed a lot to Thames Television for keeping his small screen stardom sustained in the wake of the treatment from the BBC. 'He would do a lot of publicity for Thames,' recalls *Please, Sir!* actress, Penny Spencer. 'We were all flown over to Spain or Portugal or somewhere to promote our new series and Sid was there, enjoying the experience immensely. All I can recall is Sid having the time of his life and the wine flowing very freely. He clearly relished his position as Thames's King of Light Entertainment.' Moreover, Thames knew that the British public adored this actor. Any series in which he starred was that rare thing in entertainment: a certain hit.

In fact, *Bless This House* hadn't been Sid's first taste of domestic-based comedy. It would, however, be the lasting culmination of Sid's eagerness to deliver comedy from the heart of a family environment. Moving his cheerful cockney characterisation out of hobnailed boots and into carpet slippers.

For Christmas 1965, Sid had starred in the BBC Light Entertainment domestic situation comedy, *Sid and Dora*. This, in an attempt to avoid star billing favouritism, starred Dora Bryan and Sidney James. Recorded towards the end of November under the working title of *Round the Edges*, the show was produced by John Browell and propelled Sid towards the husband and wife situation that would inform the latter stage of his career.

Certainly in 1965, Sid's listening public at home wouldn't have expected him to be playing a husband with nothing more taxing on his brain than the problem of which Christmas party invitation to accept or not, as the case may be. As the *Radio Times* had it, the show presented the couple with 'a situation full of doubt and indecision: to go out or stay at home'.

The Christmas Day audiences obviously, in the main, stayed at home. And listened to *Sid and Dora*, for the reaction was positive enough for mooted ideas of a series to be seriously discussed in the spring.

In an internal memo under the banner 'Dora Bryan/Sid James', the Head of Light Entertainment commented: 'As you know, a gentleman's agreement exists that we should mount a series in the autumn with these artistes – but I am no gentleman – and the only kind of agreements I trust are the ones signed over sixpenny stamps. Do you think you could help me to draw the strands of this one more firmly together?

'Both artistes are willing and I think I can say enthusiastic, but here are my imponderables: will Dora sign on the line to start on a given date? Will Sid do likewise (provided, of course that the date is mutually agreeable)? Sid has agreed to scripts being written by Eric Merriman although preferring Hills and Green – but my spies tell me that Dora would rather wait for Hills and Green. Can this be sorted out? (Naturally, I have not approached a man of Merriman's calibre on a specific basis, but I am sure he would do it under his present conditions.)'

It was suggested that each artiste's agent be approached and to see what happened. The Booking Manager at Light Entertainment referred to the Booking Manager over at Drama Booking, believing: 'Frankly I would not think that this was exactly the right move . . . this intended series has some sort of tie-up with the "plot" we had when, if you remember, with your permission I myself spoke to Dora Bryan's agent and eventually agreement was reached over the fee (and a pleasant understanding over the question of billing).'

The Christmas Day offering had been scripted by Eddie Maguire and was, itself, something of a 'hotchpotch of discussion involving at one time Sheila Hancock (instead of Dora Bryan) and I also believe Messrs Green and Hills were at one time to be the writers.'

One can imagine the copy the partnership of Sid with another Hancock would have generated. But with his old writers back in harness, it would have shifted gear towards the more streetwise, domestic figure of *Citizen James*.

Again, internal discussions at the BBC proved that Eric Merriman was not even under 'some sort of mild commitment' to write the script. And that the producer, John Browell, was on sick leave and unavailable. It was suggested that Hills and Green be approached to ascertain their availability and 'at the same time Drama Booking Manager could perhaps sound out the agents of the two artistes to see what we are likely to learn from there. (I understand that Sid James' agent has told Head Light Entertainment-Sound that his client is ready and willing.) I understand that our requirements are nine programmes with an option of a further four – no transmission dates as yet but the recordings to take place during the autumn. It would seem that our first move should be a sounding out rather than any definitive commitment, then perhaps the whole thing will begin to fall into shape.'

Alas, it didn't!

For Sid, real domestic bliss was to be found in Bournemouth. At least during the summer season of 1966. He starred in Sam Cree's *Wedding Fever* for the first time and scored an instant hit. The farce was especially written for him and, following his heart-attack induced sabbatical from the show in 1967, Sid appeared in the Sam Cree-scripted domestic comedy for the following, consecutive four seasons in Torquay, Blackpool, Great Yarmouth and back to Torquay again.

It was a satisfying contrast for Sid from his more raucous big-screen image. But still, admirers of his films would not have been disappointed by the stage shenanigans they saw at the end of the pier. While family audiences would not have been shifting in their seats from humour considered too near the knuckle for the maiden aunt in her once-a-year flip-flops.

Sid was still Sid. He lived for the pleasures of life. But he was now a family man. With family responsibilities, a hide-and-seek obsession with a mouse and two young daughters. Under the assured direction of Eddie Fraser it was, as the *Blackpool Evening Gazette* reported: 'Well paced and excellently timed. This is a play that lives up to its description of "an uproarious family comedy". Even the youngest members of the packed house loved every minute.'

It was clearly the best of both worlds for Sid. Reassuringly cast as Sidney Jones, a 'sorely-tried family man', he could face the future as a grandfather with his sympathetic wife (played by Beryl Mason) in tow, while fending off fun and frolics from a former girlfriend, Maud. Parnell McGarry played the highly-sexed attraction: 'a buxom blonde who's a girl-and-a-half and a laugh-a-minute' according to the local rag. Which just goes to prove that you could take Sid out of the Carry Ons but you couldn't take the Carry On out of Sid!

Indeed, in the cinemas you could see Sid advertising huge

frankfurter hot dogs with a wicked invitation: 'Get your teeth into something this size, darling.' And in faraway Australia, he would don Lincoln green and plug cigars. At home and in the home, Sid's advertising image was much softer. In the 1960s he had done a newspaper campaign for double gazing. In the seventies, another print campaign for Global Travel Agencies.

Again, he was quite candid about the reasoning. The money was good. And, if you were clever, you could avoid life-long association with the product: 'I've already done one. For some bloke who makes beef suet,' he revealed in the early 1960s. 'It's a bit of a giggle, but they pay good money for that sort of thing. But they only get my voice, friend. Not my face. As soon as you show your face on a commercial you can kiss goodbye to your career as an actor.'

That attitude was changed forever when, in the mid-1960s, Tony Hancock agreed to star in a series of now classic commercials for eggs. Sid soon followed suit. Advertising apples and ice cream and milk on British television. He even recorded one of the legendary 'Look out, look out, there's a Humphrey about!' milk commercials in the mid-1970s.

Even by December 1967, Sid had established himself as the housewives' favourite, with homemakers in the Birmingham and Colchester area voting him their number one choice 'out of five famous men who have appeared in TV commercials'. Sid was selected as the perfect next door neighbour because he was perceived as being the 'most fun to be with'.

Terry Scott, who played the neighbour from hell in the film of *Bless This House*, might not have had a vote but the survey proved one thing beyond question: Sid was the encapsulation of the relaxed, neighbourly and friendly personality who had won the hearts of the nation.

Bless This House, broadcast on ITV from February 1971, was the ultimate proof. It quickly became the biggest personal success of his television career. And, from the very start, Sid had never been happier.

As with the Sam Cree stage farces, the familiar Sid elements were all in place. He still liked a pint or two down the Hare and Hounds. He still had an unfaltering eye for a short-skirted dolly bird. And he still had a passion for football – although his allegiance seemed to change from Arsenal to Spurs, to Chelsea and back again to keep the London crowd happy. But now he was at the centre of a domestic situation.

Indeed, he contrasted his latest film release, *Carry On Henry*, with his own domestic reality: 'With that many wives he was a nutcase, wasn't he?' he jokingly told the *TV Times*. 'I can just see myself behaving like that at home. I'd get shot. As for chucking chicken bones about, my wife would say, "I've just polished that floor," and my daughter would say, "Don't you know chicken bones are dangerous for the dog!" Slowly, Sid was moving away from screen lad to screen dad.

Sally Geeson, who played his screen daughter for six years, remembers: 'Sid was in his absolute element. He was always cheerful. Always loved the scripts. Always the most positive person to be around. He loved the audiences we had. He felt relaxed with his role. He relished this chance to play a domestic character. Sid really was like the Sidney character he played. And naturally it was a character that fitted Sid like a glove. But he was never complacent. I don't know where those stories about Sid being a trouble on set came from. You hear people today saying that he was always turning up with just minutes to spare before a recording, without attending rehearsals or anything. That is complete nonsense. I think to myself: "Who are you? You weren't there! I was! And I know!" Sid was never like that at all. Ever. He was a total professional and would insist on everybody knowing their lines as well as he knew his. It was a tremendously happy company.'

Discussing the first series, Sid told the *Daily Sketch* proudly, 'It's the first time I've ever been married with a wife and kids on the screen. Frankly it's the kind of role I've always tried to avoid in the past. I always reckoned I needed a funny man to bounce off. We're going to try to make each one warm, easily watchable, true to life and funny. Even if some laughs have to be scarified for reality, we'll do it.'

As the *TV Times* publicity blurb had it, Sid is a 'father, breadwinner and a representative for a stationery firm'. And that was that for *Bless This House*. Wallowing in generation gap comedy, household chords and protracted conflicts at work, Sid effortlessly slid through the situation and the comedy for six series. He could reflect on happy, rose-tinted memories of seduction and excess but he now had to relive it reflectively through the wild, long haired experiences of his son. Sid was facing the younger generation of pot and protest. Happily becoming the embodiment of the troubled father figure. Delighted when his son was getting some action, it was blind panic when his sexy teenage daughter was looking hot to trot.

Elements of pure Sid were added, of course: a sexy secretary could turn his head for three-quarters of an episode. Horse racing and beer were his cheerful weaknesses. And in the series three episode, 'Will the Real Sid Abbott Please Stand Up', a doppelgänger Sid roved free and easy through the domestic life of the real Sid Abbott. This allowed the actor to sharply contrast his old world Sid of *Hancock's Half Hour* with the new age, new man version of *Bless This House*.

Sid, the man, had previously been described as 'tough, but not hard. Human beings matter to him and it is seeing them pushed about or abused that angers him most. The only other hatred in his book is rudeness and woebetide the bumptious individual who tries to barge past Sid. People tend to imagine him as a kind of mechanical "life and soul of every party", perpetually wise-cracking and spending his entire life in a sizzle of flippancy. But most of Sid's spare time is spent away from people and quite uneventfully. He is a modern jazz fan and plays records or watches television with his wife most evenings. They like their own company and rarely invite friends home.'

The blurb that accompanied the release of *Carry On Cabby* in 1963 continued: 'Success is a surprise to Sid James and he accepts it with the same gusto that he greets the arrival of each day. There's nothing tired or bored about this man – he loves life and is very much alive.'

Now, if that real-life snapshot of Sid doesn't pre-date Sid's *Bless This House* performances by a decade, I don't know what does.

Still, that reassuringly domestic element had been hinted at before in Sid's Carry On legacy. He had seen his grim, fast imploding marriage rescued by the arrival of a baby in the self-same *Carry On Cabby*, for example. While his sitcom-styled marriage to *Till Death Us Do Part*'s Dandy Nichols in *Carry On Doctor*, brought with it the baggage of offspring gone bad. But now Sid wanted his work to reflect his reality. If he himself had to lay off the excessive booze and became a three-pipe a day man, then he would make three-pipe a day man films.

Bless This House paved the way. And certainly his performance in *Carry On At Your Convenience* – the first film to go into production following *Bless This House* being screened on television – was steeped in domestic situation: the dirty dishes and soggy washing; the generation-gap angst with his young daughter, played by Jacki Piper. And the erosion of working class values when she hooks up with the boss's son, played by Richard O'Callaghan. All would have been almost inconceivable before *Bless This House*.

'I'm convinced this is better than anything I've done on TV before, including the Hancock series,' Sid confidently told the press on the day of the first broadcast in February 1971. 'It's very funny, and we're playing it for real. I'm glad I now have a wife and family on TV. It's more natural than the permanent bachelordom of my other series.'

His faithful screen wife and co-star, Diana Coupland, agreed. 'In the series, Sid treats me just as my real husband does – as if I were an idiot,' she told the *Sun*. 'It's lovely. Most men regard their wives in this manner, but really we're more shrewd than they are. Sid's wife, Valerie, approves of me, too.'

And Coupland would suffer the usual fate of sitcom wives who become nationally popular: her own husband, James Bond composer Monty Norman, would be perceived as the 'other man' if the couple were spotted out together by the televisually intoxicated proletariat.

Indeed, such was the instant appeal of *Bless This House* that Philip Jones, Head of Light Entertainment at Thames Television, contacted producer Peter Rogers and director Gerald Thomas with a big screen idea. Following *Carry On At Your Convenience*'s blurring of the edges between Sid's film and television personality, Jones was keen to go the whole hog and invited the Carry On team to deliver a film spin-off version of *Bless This House*. Shot in the summer of 1972, in the wake of the second series for Thames and *Carry On Abroad* at Pinewood Studios, the film was a unique crossover for Sid. But not all of the cast would be recruited.

Sid and Diana Coupland were the domestic bedrocks, of course. And Sally Geeson had just proved her mettle on screen opposite Sid in *Carry On Abroad*. But Robin Stewart was out of the frame as the troublesome son.

Robin Askwith, who had auditioned for the role on television, had landed the part of Sally's boyfriend in the second series episode, 'Things That Go Bump in the Night'. 'I knew then that [Robin Stewart] was beginning to blow it,' remembers Askwith. 'During my episode [of *Bless This House*], he was very late for rehearsals for four days in a row which infuriated the rest of the cast. His excuse for the first day was that his wife, Jill, had sadly given birth prematurely to a stillborn child.' Sid, who had tragically gone through this, was rather suspicious: "I didn't know his wife was pregnant," he said.

'The next day [Robin] didn't turn up at all,' continues Askwith. Everyone put this down to poor Robin being distraught. But strange, no phone call. On the third day he arrived late yet again. "I'm so sorry about yesterday but Jill gave birth to another stillborn baby, she was having twins." He then burst into tears. His acting talent was never in question.

'On the fourth day, the cast and crew sat in stunned silence as he arrived two hours late, very distressed. "You're not going to believe this." "Triplets?" suggested Sid. The writing was on the wall.'

In the end, Robin Stewart did make it through the entire series of *Bless This House* on television. However, for the film version Sid's son was recast, with Robin Askwith playing the role. 'Sid, immediately, took me under his wing,' remembers Askwith. 'He encouraged me to use more facial expressions, which the likes of Lindsay Anderson [who had directed Askwith in *If*] had been opposed to. This, however, was a very different style of film. I learnt from Sid that "humour is a funny thing" and that everything had to be mapped out meticulously.'

Sid also saw the makings of himself in Robin. He advised the young actor: 'Just remember, Robin, son. One day, the public will treat you like they treat me. They'll want to buy you a drink, they'll want to tell you about their problems, they'll want to talk about girls, but above all they'll think they know you very well and they'll expect you to know them. I know you've got your head into Shakespeare at the moment but be prepared, it will all happen to you.'

Robin Askwith recalls: 'Sid taught me everything, from how to play serious poker to the secrets of film etiquette. He really *was* like a father.'

It was a natural gift with Sid, for Sally Geeson had already been made to feel like Sid's surrogate daughter. 'His daughter, Susan, would often visit Teddington Studios when we were recording the television episodes,' remembers Sally. 'We would joke that we were really sisters. And we really felt like sisters. Sid had two families. One at home. And us at the studios.

'When we were making the programme,' Sally continues, 'the four of us all had our dressing rooms at the top of Teddington studios. They were all in a row. And it really did become like art reflecting life, particularly with Sid and myself. Although I was a little older than the age I was playing, I was still like a daughter to Sid and I was always having boyfriend troubles. I vividly remember going to sit in Sid's room for a chat about things as a particular romantic crisis took over my life. Sid would sit there drinking whisky. Me drinking lemonade. And I would go on and on about so-and-so dropping me. Sid would listen patiently, nod and advise. He was a wonderful man.'

For Sid this was part of the job. He was the titular head of the 'family' of actors, the titular head of the on-screen family and the titular head of his real family at home. He loved Sally and Diana in a keen way. Almost as potently as he loved Sue and Valerie. At the peak of the success for *Bless This House*, it was almost as if Sid was Sid whether he was at home or in the studio. The lines had been almost completely wiped away. *Bless This House* became not just another acting job. It became his life.

'I learnt so much from Sid. I honestly did,' says Sally Geeson. 'And it wasn't simply lessons in how to conduct your life or the importance of being totally professional when at work. He was such a good teacher. He would show you the best way to read a line. The subtle ways to get the biggest laugh from just a pause. All those bemused looks and silent moments and reaction shots. He knew exactly what he was doing. He could play an audience like a symphony conductor. Gauging when to give a look or that wonderful laugh of his, maximising every single laugh from the lines and the situation. It was like a master class for me. Sid was in complete control of that show and that character.'

According to actress Patsy Rowlands, Sid was instrumental in landing her the job in the first place. 'I had made one or two Carry Ons with Sid at that time. We were out on location for a scene and I remember Sid was talking very animatedly and excitedly about this new telly thing he was working on. That turned out to be *Bless This House*. He had suggested the basic idea to the writers and he couldn't wait to get started. Of course, me being me, I said, "Ooh Sid, that does sound fun. Get me a part will you?" He stopped, looked at me for a moment and said, "You would be perfect!" I started laughing and said, "No, Sid. I'm only joking." But he said, "No. No, you would be great in this. Bad news though, you'll have to live next door to me for a couple of months!" "Lovely," I said. Those couple of months turned into years. I was in the film. And all the television series. Not every show. But I would pop in for a few lovely scenes with Diana and Sid. I had six of the most enjoyable years of my life on that show and I have to thank Sid totally for that. I'll be eternally grateful to him.'

Having quickly established an audience for this new domestic personality, Sid was keen to utilise his similar standing onstage as well. Sid had got a lot of useful mileage out of those Sam Cree farces. In fact, for Christmas 1971, Cree himself adapted *His Favourite Family* for an hour-long festive family romp for Yorkshire Television. Familiar stage co-star Beryl Mason reprised her role. Carry On co-star Kenneth Connor, replacing John Inman, added some eccentric energy to the fun. Produced under the working title of *Family Fever* (the original title of *His Favourite Family* and clearly revealing it as the sequel to *Wedding Fever* that it was), *All This – And Christmas Too!* was for all intents and purposes the Christmas special *Bless This House* never had. Even Juliet Kempson as Sid's daughter seems to have taken a crash course at the Sally Geeson School of Acting. Katie Allan, as Sid's other daughter, is even called Sally.

Following work on the *Bless This House* film and the third batch of television episodes, Sid premiered another stage romp in Australia. 'Funnily enough,' he told the press, 'that's in a bit of a domestic comedy too. It's called *The Mating Season*.' But this was no coincidence. As his producer William G. Stewart attests, 'Sid was a clever sod.' He knew that the new image should be enforced across the board. If he kept playing a loving husband and father he would be set for life.

The film version of *Bless This House* had opened at the start of 1973. Just as the third series was hitting the small screen, Robin Stewart was back in tandem. And so was Anthony Jackson who played Sid's best friend and neighbour and Patsy Rowlands' hard-done-by husband, Trevor. He had been replaced by Carry On stalwart Peter Butterworth in the film: 'I didn't mind too much,' reflected Jackson. 'Peter was a much bigger name than me, and the director didn't know me from Adam! He knew Peter could do the job. It was never discussed. We did the television series together. Sid went off to do a film. The film of the series as it turned out. And then he came back and we did another series on television together. It was the same thing, of course, but the television and the film were different jobs. I had no complaints. I was glad to be working.'

Both Anthony Jackson and Sid liked the variety of the series that the team of writers brought to the table: 'I could always tell when it was a Dave Freeman script or a Carla Lane script. I had a lot less to do in the Carla Lane ones!' laughed Jackson. 'Dave was an earthier comedy writer. And he wrote to Sid's real strengths. His old strengths. That of the blokeish comedian. The Carla Lane scripts probably stretched Sid more. He had to really act those. But I got the impression he enjoyed the Dave Freeman scripts better. It was basically me and him, down the pub, chatting about the three Bs: Birds. Betting. And Booze! Sid could play those scenes with his eyes shut. He had been playing them for twenty years. But he was always professional. Always perfect.'

Sid clearly saw *Bless This House* as both his pension plan and the realisation of an ambition to finally domesticate his image. So determined was he to continue with the show that he struggled with excruciating back pain during work on the fourth series at the end of 1973. And we are not talking the odd twinge here and there. But agonising pain. A Thames props man at the time told the press, 'There were days when the pain was so bad that lesser men would have limped into a quiet corner.' Sid would certainly have rather have kept that quiet.

He may have hit the age of 60 but he wanted to keep working. And he never wanted to let anyone down, particularly himself. At the peak of the success of *Bless This House* his press blurb proudly claimed that thanks to filming at Pinewood Studios, stage work at the Victoria Palace and television commitments at Teddington, Sid could often be working an 18-hour day. 'At that sort of pace, Sid obviously needs the relaxation of his own family life – and not the sort of hilarious goings-on in the Abbott television household.'

Victor Spinetti wondered why he worked so hard. 'He certainly didn't need the money. But, then again, he would have done if it hadn't been for Val. I sincerely believe he was working so hard to keep his gambling habit up. That extra money he got from public appearances or backhanders from stage managers and television producers would give him that gambling fix he craved. It was all part of the image he had. Even that character in *Bless This House* was more Sid James than anything else. No one else could have played that role. It was pure Sid.'

Again the edges were being blurred between fact and fiction. But only slightly. There was certainly no chance of his audience tiring of this series. As they would never tire of Sid himself.

'I wrote about five or six [*Bless This House*] scripts a year for about five or six years. Right up until Sid died,' recalled Dave Freeman. 'The character had changed over the years. William G.

Stewart, the producer, wanted a more domestic feel to Sid. He was a family man now, after all. But I do remember him saying to me that he liked the old Sid to shine through occasionally. So that's what I wrote. I wrote *Bless This House* as if the gambling, drinking, bird-chasing Sid of Hancock and the Carry Ons had found the woman of his dreams and settled down. It was the same Sid. Only a little bit tamed. Just like Sid himself, I suppose.'

The character would always have an eye for the ladies and retain the cheeky chappie personality that had made him a star but it was this comfortable, pullover and pipe image that made Sid a beloved member of the family. At 60 years of age it was fitting that he had mellowed. A mellowing that hadn't affected his adoration from the beer and chips, working class audiences of the past.

He had never been more popular. In fact, thanks entirely to the success of *Bless This House*, Sid was voted the Funniest Man on Television for 1974.

13

Barbara

Barbara Windsor, Britain's most accessible blonde bombshell, first bounced into Sid's professional life as he lay in a hospital bed recovering from a heart attack. Years later, Terry Johnson, directing the television version of his celebrated play *Cleo, Camping, Emmanuelle and Dick*, eagerly embraced this moment. Who can blame him? It was at the very epicentre of his drama-fantasy's belief that art imitated life and that life went right ahead and imitated art. The fact was, of course, that that first meeting of Sid and Barbara had nothing to do with the perks of stardom, cheeky sexual awakening or the National Health providing eye candy for its patients. No. That first accentuated waddle through a hospital ward was, in reality, on Pinewood Studios' sound stage C.

Sid's heart attack had been real, of course, but caused by overwork rather than over-strenuous extra-marital activity. But the on-screen chemistry of Sid and Babs had certainly reacted and overflowed the Bunsen burner immediately the two first appeared on that big screen together: Barbara in her fetching pink and white nurse's outfit which, ever since, every red-blooded schoolboy believes all nurses wear. And Sid, resplendent in blue and white pyjamas, with an air of hospital contempt pouring from every fibre. Struck dumb by this vision of a Florence Nightingale from the imagination of Max Miller.

Clearly Terry Johnson is laudably immersed in the pitfalls, peccadilloes and platinum blonde obsession of Alfred Hitchcock and dead comedians. Just like Hitchcock, Sid tended to treat every job as 'just another movie'. Both Hitchcock and Sid were also equally healthy admirers of the young ladies with the fairer hair. Unquestionably, Sid's career was surrounded by them. Not surprisingly. The 1950s had been the blonde decade. Every starlet worth her salt seemed to be getting her hair colour from a little bottle and Hollywood turned most of them into stars: Marilyn Monroe, Jayne Mansfield, Sheree North and Mamie Van Doren. And Sid's world of salt beef sandwiches and laundrettes had its own appealing batch: Vera Day, Liz Fraser, Sheree Winton and Barbara Windsor.

But Sid was still everybody's mate. Even if you happened to be petite, talk in a high voice and know how to perfectly fill a tight sweater.

Vera Day explains: 'There was never any chance of me falling for Sid. We always just laughed and joked on the set. Once I had got out of my husband's clutches I could enjoy the company of my fellow actors without worrying. But nothing ever happened between Sid and I. However, our relationship did get deeper when we did *The Chigwell Chicken* on television. I was having a terrible time with Arthur [Mason – her husband] at that time and, on the day of working on this live television, I came into work with a black eye. It wasn't really talked about in those days but it was Sid who took me aside. I was young and stupid but Sid realised that love has to be part of the mix, even in a violent relationship. Sid was absolutely wonderful. He said, "Come on babe. What happened? I know for a fact you didn't bump into a door." He had this wonderful way about him. He put you at your ease and you could talk about your troubles. He said, "Was he *schiker*?" Meaning was he drunk, in Yiddish. He was very non-judgemental. He didn't blame Arthur. He blamed the drink. He was very sweet about it. We had long talks about jealousy and drinking and what it can do to you and how it can destroy your marriage. So he was very, very supportive. I had actually moved out and away from Arthur by that stage and I was living in the Cumberland Hotel. But I know for a fact that Sid took Arthur aside one day and gave him a gentle talking to on how to treat ladies with respect. And Arthur was a big man, with a fiery reputation. But he greatly admired Sid. And he listened to him.'

Of course, it wasn't just on the film set or in television studios that Sid mingled with the great and good and glamorous of British film. He saw his involvement in charities as an important part of his success and would happily cavort and pose for photographs at various Variety Club events.

It was at these socials and not in *Carry On Doctor* that Sid and Barbara Windsor first appeared on screen together. In the very guise that, now, everybody seems to know them in. As themselves. There is Sid and Barbara having a frolic in a pedal-boat at Battersea Fun Fair. And Sid dressed up as Father Christmas helping Barbara dish out gifts to underprivileged children. They were in the same social circle for some time. For, although their paths didn't actually cross in the Carry Ons until near the end of the 1960s, Barbara's chirpy, cockney sparrow personality was a familiar one in the industry.

She had been an increasingly budding chorus girl since the mid-1950s. She'd wowed audiences on the London and New York stage. Scored a small screen hit with the BBC situation comedy *The Rag Trade* and, finally, joined the team at Pinewood for *Carry On Spying* in 1964. She was also an East End girl. Sid's natural habitat. The two were seen as the perfect comic couple in the eyes of the nation.

'Benny Hill once said he didn't know why my boobs got such laughs; they weren't funny at all,' Barbara told Maureen Cleave of the *Evening Standard* as the Carry Ons were set for a relaunch in 1992. 'What was funny was Sid James saying, "Ooh!" It was his reaction to them, the knock-on effect. I never minded a few laughs; I knew they weren't employing me for my feet. I've always thought my figure was a bit of a joke.'

And it was a joke the nation adored.

But it wasn't just an on-screen partnership that gelled. There was true affection between Sid and Barbara. And it was just that. Affection, rather than love.

It is beautifully revealed in the memories of Lilly Payne, whose family owned a shop on the Hammersmith Bridge in the 1960s and 1970s. It was frequented by countless stars, from the flamboyant world of James Bond to the cosy environs of the Carry Ons. 'Sid used to pop in a lot,' she recalls. 'Usually for fags, tobacco and a paper. Sid and our family actually got quite close. Sid was a lovely man. He was always so kind and caring. Fussing over the kids. And once he even bought my son, Martin, a comic when he was poorly! Sid was really a darling man.

'My husband used to like a bet, he was always in the bookies,' continues Lilly. 'That's how Sid and he got talking one morning. He came in one day, singing and shouting and laughing. "I've won! I've won!" he was saying. Sid was in the shop at the time and he said, "What have you won, Alf?" And he told him he had won a few hundred on the horses! Sid was amazed and said, "I have been betting for years and never won!" And Sid asked him to give him tips! So off Alf and Sid trotted to the bookies! After that, Sid always came in for a chat and often went to the pub with the males of our family.'

This instant bond was rock solid as far as Sid was concerned. If he met a down-to-earth bloke he could talk to, it was a lasting and meaningful friendship. Whoever you were. If Sid liked you, you stayed liked.

'Sid was so kind and caring,' says Lilly. 'It was obvious why he was so popular. He always got on well with fans and colleagues. I remember once he came in and bought a box of chocolates. I said, "Who's ill?" And he said, "It's for one of the youngsters on set. They were ill so I thought it would cheer them up!"'

This parental affection enveloped his most famous co-star. 'Once Sid and Barbara Windsor came in. Babs was very cold. She had been filming something with very little on! Of course, all the males in the shop were all looking on with tongues out! And Sid, bless him, pulled her under his coat to keep her warm. With Babs being so tiny I didn't see her in there and thought Sid had got fat! I exclaimed, "Ooh Sid. What have you done to yourself!" which caused Sid and Babs to cry with laughter.'

It was this playful and protective, fun-loving quality of Sid's that made him so popular with both his audience and his work cohorts. He was the mother hen. Particularly where young ladies were concerned. He was deeply aware that in the film industry, beauty can be lured into corruption. And he was determined to look after people in the films he was working on.

He would give his favourite people pet names. Liz Fraser became Lizzle. Carol Hawkins was Carolle. While Sally Geeson was Salary.

He was the gentleman . . . with a natural eye for the ladies, of course. He was Sid James, after all. The onscreen role wasn't a complete act. And the Carry On series did employ some of the most interesting, attractive and downright sexy actresses in the business.

Those 'appalling, insular, hilarious movies' as Benedict Nightingale dubbed them in *The Times* in 1998, were Sid's domain. He was the King well before *Carry On Henry*. But that was the film that finally cemented the major on-screen appeal of Sid and Barbara.

In *Carry On Doctor* it had been a mere medical flirtation. A blown kiss making Sid reach boiling point. In *Carry On Camping* it was a mid-life crisis over a saucy schoolgirl who, after days of teasing, hitches up with a group of hippies and leaves him in the lurch. She's a pantomime servant at Sid's mercy in *Carry On Christmas*. Somebody else's girl in *Carry On Again, Doctor*. And even in *Carry On Henry*, it's a brief, unconsummated faux marriage that ends in frustration for Sid. Throughout this era, he is denied the pleasure. It's as if Barbara is the ultimate Carry On fantasy. And if Sid bedded her, the joke would wither and die.

The trend continued. Sid is more interested in the treasure than what the map is tattooed upon in *Carry On Again Christmas*. Barbara ends up marrying Sid's son in *Carry On Matron*. And regresses even further to play a forward, fully developed 13-year-old schoolgirl sat on Santa's lap for the *Carry On Christmas* presentation of 1973.

By this stage, Sid had entered his third and final Carry On phase. If not quite the dirty old man, he had become the mature chap who gets his oats. His last three Carry On films team him, almost constantly, with Barbara. The two became closer than ever before. These films see Sid at his most lusty: falling for Barbara the cheeky much-married home-wrecker, Barbara the beauty contestant and, finally, Barbara the serving maid. Moreover, as Sid aged and Barbara matured on screen, the blurring between art and life became almost imperceptible.

'Sid wasn't my type,' says Vera Day, 'but he was an attractive man, in that he listened and he was supportive. And, of course, when Barbara Windsor was going through her difficult emotional time I can quite understand Sid being his usual supportive self. And if that went to the next level of a relationship, as it can do, then that's what happened. It's a real source of comfort when someone actually sits down and talks things through with you. That problem can vanish. One thing can lead to another and that's that. Sid was fun, friendly and happy. And everyone is attracted to a happy person.'

Barbara's emotional marriage to East End criminal, Ronnie

Knight, had cast her in the role she never wanted to play: that of a gangster's moll. But Sid commanded real respect from the underworld of London. He might not have been able to go as far as he wanted but he was revered. Even to the extent of a burglary at his home being reported at the end of November 1966: clothing and cameras worth between three and four thousand pounds being taken from his Buckinghamshire home. However, once the criminal underworld had been alerted to the fact that the goods were the property of Sid James, they were returned to the front of the house without a whimper. Now that is clout. A trick not repeated when, after the Barbara situation became fairly common knowledge, £1,000 worth of silver was lifted from Sid's home in August 1974.

It was clear. Sid and Barbara had a connection. They were cut from the same cloth. And, as far as the audience was concerned, there were together. The Carry Ons had a lot of clout as well.

Robin Askwith remembers filming *Bless This House* on location on Windsor High Street. 'Sid was constantly hounded by the general public. "'Ello, Sid mate." "All right Sid, how's it going then?" "How's that Barbara Windsor then?" "Give us an autograph for me wife, Sid mate." Sid took me aside. "Do you know, Robin son, I don't think anyone has ever said, 'Excuse me, Mr James' in my whole career, they think they know me. Well, I'm paid well. It's just part of the job. Remember that." I took great notice of this advice given to me right outside the castle that day, and I hope I haven't let Sid down.'

Barbara herself remembered 'walking for a cup of tea with Sid when we were doing a show at the Victoria Palace and a taxi driver shouted that it was lovely to see us together. I said to Sid that no one would remember but he said, "Don't you believe it." I bet he's looking down at us now and saying, "See, I told you so."'

The show was *Carry On London!*. They were doing it twice nightly, live onstage, and the public loved it. And Sid knew his public. He knew the magic that he and Barbara could create on screen. And he was delighted to recreate it onstage. It was so overpowering that it might as well be real.

According to Barbara, en route to Brighton for the first day of location filming for *Carry On Girls*, it was Sid who finally encouraged her to take on the stage assignment. 'Sid said: "This show. I've only just heard you won't do it." "That's true. It's not right for me." "Why's that, then?" "Well, I'm doing OK as I am," I said. "I'm doing films, theatre, a bit of telly. I don't want to do the Carry On girl onstage. The theatre's too special to me to play that character there."'

By the end of the journey, Sid had convinced Barbara that it was the right thing to do. She had promised to contact her agent, Richard Stone, and commit to the run. It wouldn't be the happiest of productions. And illness would keep Barbara out of some of the performances. But it was a comparative success.

It was launched at a London press junket in July 1973. Sid was still on tour in New Zealand with *The Mating Season* but promoted the show down the phone while Barbara, singer Trudi Van Doorn and Carry On team members Bernard Bresslaw and Jack Douglas were there in person.

Upon his return, Sid made his way to an upstairs room at the Palladium. 'When we all met up for the first day's rehearsal,' remembers Barbara. 'He breezed in straight from London Airport and greeted everybody warmly with his familiar chuckle. I sensed there was something missing – he had no enthusiasm, and didn't seem to care – but I put it down to jet lag.'

That and the fact that he had already seen the script. Before long the rest of the cast joined him under the cloud.

'I wrote a couple of bits for the show,' said Dave Freeman, 'and Sid and I had got very friendly over the years. I confided in him that it wasn't all going as swimmingly as we had hoped. I actually went to Birmingham where they were trying it out. Bill Roberton [brother of star Jack Douglas] was producing the show, and I have clear memories of sitting up with him for half the night, desperately trying to do something with the opening sketch. It just didn't work. We cut it when the show opened in London. But it wasn't the happiest show I ever worked on. There was an undercurrent of squabbling over the material. I heard it lost money but the management kept it on because they had nothing else to put on until the autumn. The main fault was that the Carry On fans thought they would see two hours of comedy when in fact what they saw was a series of variety acts with a few Carry On sketches at long intervals.'

Jack Douglas remembered: 'At that first rehearsal we all felt a little let down. Sid and I were with the same agent so we bonded over it. I said, "Come on, gang. We can make this work." And Sid agreed. He knew how popular the Carry Ons were. "We can't let them down, Jackson. We can't let them down." He kept saying that to me. He meant the audience. And none of us wanted to let them down. Bernie Bresslaw complained that the script made us all "glorified compères". But then again he was an actor. I was a comedian. I could see the potential. Sid was very much an actor as well, of course, but he saw that we could do something with it. We had to do something with it as far as he was concerned.'

Jack Douglas also held himself responsible, albeit partially, for the romance that flourished between Sid and Barbara Windsor. 'That was my fault!' he claimed. 'Well . . . sort of! We later learned that something had been going on when we had been down in Brighton [filming *Carry On Girls*]. But during the stage show we were all invited to appear on *Open House* [a radio magazine programme] and be interviewed by Pete Murray. We were told it would be a live broadcast, from the stage of the Victoria Palace. We were on air at 9.30 in the morning. I protested to Peter Rogers that some of us had a long way to travel in for such an early start. In the end we were all put up in a hotel and Sid and Barbara were thrown together.'

In fact, Sid had already secured a flat off Dolphin Square. 'He'd already had one coronary,' said Valerie James, 'and I didn't want him to have the long journey home every night. I said, "Let's get you a flat in town," which we arranged. I got his dresser to cook for him and do his washing and ironing. I arranged for a car to take him to and from the theatre every night. I thought it was perfect. Of course, I laid it on a plate for him, didn't I?'

'Sid was a great actor,' Valerie continued, 'the most wonderful performer, but he hated ad-libbing.'

Jack Douglas 'couldn't believe this, but it was true. We had done a silly game show for ATV called *Jokers Wild*. I chaired that at times. And cracked jokes. That was the idea. A load of comedians telling jokes on a given subject. But Sid wasn't a comedian. Even if the gag was written down in front of him, he couldn't deliver it. But the public loved him. He really could do no wrong. He struggled through it. Got a laugh. Laughed himself when he fluffed a line. Got another huge laugh. Finally admitted defeat and handed it to me to finish. Got another huge laugh. He got three laughs out of one joke and didn't even deliver the punchline! That was the power of Sid.

'During *Carry On London!*, the audience were lapping it up. I would ad-lib stuff with Kenneth Connor and Peter Butterworth. They were both wonderful at that. If something happened we could milk it and milk it for several minutes. The audience would love it. One night, I went off on a tangent when I was in a sketch with Sid. He just stared back at me blankly and froze. I quickly got it back on track. Anyway, once we were off he said, "Look Jackson. Never do that again!" "What?" "Ad-lib!" I said, "You're joking." But he wasn't. "I know my lines," he said. "I can give you the exact same performance every time, but if you throw me something I don't know, I'm finished." I never did it again.'

'Everyone in that show ad-libbed,' remembered Valerie, 'which threw Sid. He was unhappy and Barbara supported him a lot. He felt she was his crutch to lean on. A lot of their relationship started from that.'

Sid and Barbara were birds of a feather. And spending all day at the studio and all evening in the theatre together, the friendship became stronger and stronger. They were both people of the theatre, first and foremost. Barbara delighted in telling Sid that she had seen him onstage in the most prized role of his career.

'*Guys and Dolls* is a part I always wanted to do ever since I was fourteen and in a show called *Love from Judy* on Shaftesbury Avenue,' she remembered when she toured in a revival in 1998. 'We'd get tickets for other shows through Equity and at the Coliseum was a musical called *Guys and Dolls*. I used to go to nearly every matinee because we did ours on Wednesdays and they did theirs on Thursdays. It's funny how your life comes round in circles because a year later the show cast changed and Nathan Detroit was played by Sid James. Years later when I told him I'd seen him do it he didn't believe I'd been born then!'

Sid and Barbara's relationship became common knowledge in the industry but was never confirmed in the press. However, by the end of 1973 with *Carry On London!* in full swing, rumours started to appear. Sid was quick to quash them, telling the *Sun* journalist Kenneth Eastaugh, 'It's the most stupid thing I've heard. Barbara and I have known each other for years. We're old workmates. If something was going to happen it would have happened years ago, wouldn't it? I mean, I'm only flesh and blood. Anything can happen to anybody. But ask yourself: Why should it suddenly happen now, after all this time?'

It seemed convincing to Fleet Street. Although not to Ronnie Knight. 'He came up to me once, ranting in my face about Sid,' remembered Dave Freeman. 'I did my best to calm him down. He wasn't the sort of person you wanted to be angry around you. I said, "Come off it. I mean, Sid! Look at him!" But we all knew about it.

And Sid was a lovely fellow. We all loved him. Just not as much as Barbara did!'

Jack Douglas concurs. 'He was a very attractive man. All the young girls would scream and shout for Sid at the stage door after the show. And, personally, I think he was at that awkward age for a man. He had just hit sixty. He was fairly vulnerable. When a bright young thing like Barbara shows you some encouragement then you are flattered. And tempted. I really don't think Sid was obsessed with her as some of the stories would have us believe. He had a brief fling and that was that. He went back to Val and the kids.'

'You don't get to know anybody much in films,' said Barbara. 'I had a lot of scenes with Sid. We did our scenes and went home. But when you're rehearsing a stage show, you're brought into closer contact. You're rehearsing in some dirty old hall, doing the same bit of dialogue or business together over and over again. You're making each other coffee. In the breaks there's nowhere to go, so you talk to each other. Besides this, Sid saw me doing things like singing and dancing that he didn't know I could do. All he'd seen me at until now was wiggling my bottom and my boobs around a Carry On set! Now he started to admire me professionally. I used to see him standing at the side of the stage watching me with amazement and admiration all over his face.

'Sid used to call me Tiger,' Barbara continued. 'He said one day, "The thing I like about you, Tiger, is that you're kind, but you don't knuckle under." I said, "I'm kind to everybody lower than me in the show because I know what it's like down there."'

So did Sid. But affection for colleagues and pet names were the norm with him. It didn't mean a passionate obsession. He had given nicknames to many of his favourite female co-stars. And even Arthur Mullard! But, for Barbara, this was a true romance.

'He used to send me a dozen red roses every week and write nice little notes,' she remembered.

'I was absolutely shocked when I heard about Sid and Barbara,' says Vera Day. 'First and foremost I would never have thought that Barbara would have been his type. Sid liked the classy sort of lady. He quite fancied Diana Dors. She wasn't exactly a classy lady but classier! Barbara was like a little caricature. But obviously something clicked. Having been married to a gangster, Barbara would have been very liberal, I suppose. So she would have said, "Yes, go and gamble or do whatever, as long as you don't shoot someone that's fine by me!" But, as far as I was concerned, Sid always seemed so thrilled with his classy, attractive, triumph wife that no one else could have come close.'

For Victor Spinetti, who was part of the influential Joan Littlewood East End Theatre Workshop troupe with Barbara from the late 1950s, 'Sid was the common man. By that rationale, he and Barbara were perfect. They were the working class, comedy couple that the nation would have taken to their hearts. Unfortunately,' he continues, 'it was all too late. As far as Barbara told me, it was just a case of getting the sex out of the way and moving on. Sid went on and on and on about it and she thought, "Oh, why not?" But of course Val was the one who kept his life together. Without her, Sid would have been far less secure. But would he have been happier? Who can tell? He would have undoubtedly been penniless at the end of his life if it hadn't had been for Val.'

'If he had run off with someone like Barbara and married her – and they were a wonderfully raucous pair – they may both have ended up broke. But they would have had a bloody good time.'

'I've known Barbara an awfully long time,' asserts Spinetti, 'and, in a way, Sid was like John Lennon. Barbara could have been his Yoko. It could have happened. But Barbara didn't want to play that part. John was always saying to me: "Is this it, Vic, you know? I've got the wife. There's food on the table. The kid's in school. The fucking privet hedge around the house. Is this it?" And then Yoko poked her head over the privet hedge and called "Hello". That could have been Barbara for Sid. If Barbara had been a slightly different woman they might have gone off together. The domestic situation kept Sid going, but the free-spirited relationship with Barbara was like a new world opening up for him. Like all of us, Sid wanted to share a life with someone but not have that tight reign of "What have you been doing?" or "Who have you been sleeping with?" I'm a great believer that if you want something you give it away. You want love. Give it. You want freedom. Give it. Sid wanted love and freedom. And he gave it.'

However, the affair was over by the time the stage show came to an end. In a letter of tongue-in-cheek apology to Louis Benjamin at the Victoria Palace, Peter Rogers acknowledged formally that he had received notice of the production's termination: 'Sad but necessary,' he wrote on 12 October 1974. 'I don't think I realised until lunchtime yesterday just how much your sense of professionalism has been hurt by the behaviour of certain of my "children" . . . I can assure you that they will never have the chance to do it again.'

Reading between the lines, this bad behaviour has to cast Sid and Barbara as the 'children'. Whether their relationship aided and abetted the declining fortunes of *Carry On London!* is impossible to ascertain but, clearly, the impresarios at the heart of the revue were not happy about it.

Moreover, Sid's continued back problems had plagued the run at the Victoria Palace and led to a holiday in Marbella with his agent, Michael Sullivan. It also gave Sid the perfect break from home and the opportunity to weigh up the situation. After seven days Sid telephoned Valerie. She caught the first available flight to Marbella and was met at the airport by Sid.

'We had a week together and we tried to get back to normality,' she remembered. 'Obviously it wasn't one hundred per cent for a while. He had to make another Carry On film with Barbara and then he was due to go to Australia [for *The Mating Season* tour]. He said, "I promise you that when we leave for Australia, it will all be over. But we've got to wait until then because I've got to work with her.'"

The film, *Carry On Dick*, proved to be Sid's last. And it was shot when six of the principals were still pedalling innuendo onstage at the Victoria Palace. Naturally, the relationship put both Sid and Barbara under enormous pressure. But, in his heart, it was over for Sid. Typically, the Carry On threw the two together in their most touching and affectionate relationship on screen. If anything, it is Barbara who is the temptress here. And Sid the kindly, good-natured gentleman who is bemused and flattered by the attention. Was this the real situation as Sid saw it shining through?

Barbara felt they were becoming too close and that it was affecting her work. 'Before this film it didn't bother me to do all that wiggling in front of Sid, but I had a scene where I had to seduce him – and I just couldn't do it. I couldn't shake everything about in front of him. The change in our relationship had put a wall between us when it came to doing things like that in a scene. Sid said, "What's the matter with you? You're acting like I've got leprosy. Come on, let's get on with the scene." But I couldn't. I broke down and wept.'

For Valerie it was purgatory living through that period. 'But I wanted my man back, so I went along with everything he wanted to do. I didn't provoke him or make him feel uncomfortable or guilty. He and Barbara made the film together and at the end I said, "Is it now over between you?" He said, "No, I'm going to let her know on the phone tonight." I really did feel sorry for her.'

Finally, Sid admitted that he had to talk to Barbara. 'That evening he went into our bedroom and rang her,' says Valerie. 'They were on the phone for what seemed like an eternity. Then he came and said, "Barbara wants to talk to you." I got on the phone and she was very upset and crying. She said, "We love each other. I want him, he wants me." I said, "It's Sid's decision, he's standing in the room." He looked petrified. I handed him the phone and said, "Darling, it's up to you."

'I went downstairs and waited for him. Finally, he came down looking like a bird let loose. He said, "I'm doing exactly what you suggested, I'm meeting Barbara at the Dorchester tomorrow but it's over."

'In the end he was scared of her. She was pushy and Sid was frightened of her and of her husband [Ronnie Knight]. He felt so guilty and scared.'

For Barbara, Sid's 'jealousy and obsessive behaviour were not controllable'. And whether or not his marriage was happy, it was certainly a strong one that it would be difficult, if not impossible, for him to leave.

'The only way I could see it ending was by making sure we didn't work together. So when Sid and I were offered *Carry On Laughing*, a series of half-hour Carry Ons for TV, I turned it down. Gerald Thomas [who was producing the series] told Sid, who rang me immediately. "You can't do that," he said.'

According to Barbara, Gerald was very understanding. 'I do realise you're the only one who can end the affair – Sid won't.'

'I had not bargained for how determined Sid would be,' says Barbara. In the end, with a promise of friendship and a three-fold increase in her fee, Barbara was on the show. 'I was thrilled . . . the scripts were great . . . I'd be getting a fortune . . . but the minute I walked into the ATV studios at Elstree on the first Monday morning and Sid saw me, I knew I had made a mega mistake. "A round of applause for our beautiful Miss Windsor," he said loudly. "Doesn't she look wonderful?" I smiled, of course, but inside I was cringing. By the end of the day, he was demanding to see me. "You made me a promise, Sid," I said, furiously. "You promised that if I did the show, we'd just be friends. Right?"

'Sid didn't say anything. He just looked at me adoringly, and I knew it was hopeless.'

Jack Douglas, who was almost constantly involved with Sid and Barbara on every facet of the Carry On empire at this time, is adamant that 'Sid was not a broken man. But we certainly knew what had been going on. I was very fond of Sid. And I was very fond of Barbara. I know our director, Gerald Thomas, was aware of what was happening. He had to be, of course. But it never affected Sid's performance on screen. He was his usual happy, laid-back self as far as I was concerned. If he was going through mental and physical problems at the time, he must have been a far, far better actor than anyone has ever given him credit for. He would do the lines. Have a quick drink and a chat. And go home to his family.'

Producer Peter Rogers agrees: 'Sid was as professional as he always was. He certainly wasn't the lovesick, drunken wreck of the newspaper articles and reports that have been published after his death. He would give the make-up girl a peck on the cheek when he arrived and that was all. At the end of filming he would pop his head round the door at the Pinewood bar and say "Cheerio" to Gerald, myself, Joan Sims and anybody else who was having a drink, and happily go home. He worked for me for something like twenty years and he was always the same. Always the most professional of men. There was a real sense of assurance when we had Sid in the cast. He was the head of the Carry On family of actors and enjoyed his position. I have nothing but fond memories of him.'

Indeed, it was only after Sid's death that the stories started to emerge. Before Sid's death Barbara would chuckle and recall: 'Me two beauties . . . I nearly died laughing doing a slow sensual strip for one scene in *Carry On Henry*. Sid was marvellous. He would always close his eyes whenever I showed my boobs or bottom!'

Even during the writing of Kenneth Eastaugh's pioneering volume *The Carry-On Book* in 1977, rumours of the affair were denied by Barbara. When Sid had died she explained, 'Sid was my best friend and in show business they are hard to find. We were great mates. He was always the perfect gentleman. Off-screen, he was a very quiet man with lovely manners and very protective with women. He wouldn't allow any foul language and he always stood up and opened doors for women. I loved him dearly.'

However, four years later in December 1980, when she sold her story to the *Daily Mail*, she revealed that Sid had told her, 'If I can't have you, I want to die,' while painting the affair as 'the classic case of an old man's unrequited love'. At the time, Valerie said, 'My husband and I were continuously and happily married for twenty-four years until his untimely death and his love for me and our children was undiminished and total to the end.'

Valerie later explained, 'I'm certain that Barbara wanted him very much. But thank God it was with me that he ended his days.

'He loved his home and me and his children. No one's going to take that away from us. I loved him with my life and he adored me. We merely had a little hiccup. When I knew about the affair he said, "I don't want you to get into any slanging match with Barbara." I said, "I'd never descend to her level."'

In Barbara's mind, the situation was never resolved. 'It makes me so sad. We never made it right, at the end. I just wish I had picked up that phone before he died,' she told journalist Nigel Dempster.

The closure for Barbara came with Terry Johnson, his National Theatre play *Cleo, Camping, Emmanuelle and Dick*, and the television adaptation of the same, *Cor, Blimey!*. Samantha Spiro played Barbara and the character in the TV version even morphed into the real Barbara at the very end of the film. It was an endorsement from the only source left alive and willing to discuss it.

For Barbara, the play was a fantasy based on their lives, 'but one in which a remarkable amount rings true'. Many have now taken the fact, figures and fatigue within the play as the gospel truth. There may be many elements that are correct. There are even more elements that are tailor-made from Barbara's view of the events. She is, after all, the last 'man' standing of the principal characters in the piece. As far as Valerie was concerned: 'I just want Sid to be at peace because I'm sure he's been disturbed by all of this. He would have been devastated by the play.'

Liz Fraser was equally outraged. 'I would have sued the playwright,' she says. 'I simply didn't recognise the person that was being depicted onstage. That was not Sid James. Sid was great fun and a very warm person. I knew him for many years and that character of Sid was a million miles from the real, lovable person I knew.'

In truth, the play – both onstage and television – was a beautifully acted reproduction of a madcap world of innuendo. Barbara Windsor was right. It is a 'fantasy'. One that should be taken with an enormous mouthful of salt-beef sandwich.

Sid and Barbara had an affair. And it ended. That was the reality. The cheeky, kiss-me-quick world of Carry On is not reality. It's something rather better. Where no one gets upset for long. Nothing goes so wrong that it can't be fixed with a drink on a stick. And young ladies lose their skirts at the merest hint of an embarrassing situation. They were, according to Sid, 'a bizarre series of humorous events strung together by happy accident'.

Joan Sims may have been as versatile as a buxom Swiss army knife but there's simply no denying Barbara Windsor's place as the Queen of Carry On. And forget that nonsensical, oft-repeated claim – as often as not from Babs herself – that she only did a handful of them, darling. She made just one film without his presence and, most importantly, in a series collaboration with Sid that was sometimes up, sometimes down, sometimes close, sometimes distance but always earthy, funny and true, she became the definitive female signifier for the essence of Carry On comedy. Eight omnipresent feature films. Four slap-dash and misunder-stood situation comedies. Three energetically butchered cut and paste clip shows. Three whisky-soaked and chestnut-stuffed Christmas spectaculars. And a near legendary, long-running revue that as often as not allowed them to do their thing twice nightly. That's an awful lot of shared knob-jokes. This is their combined legacy. It's certainly more than enough to make Sid and Barbara the ultimate Carry On couple then, now and forever.

Newspaper libraries are packed to the gills with fascinating unpublished photographs. But newspapers themselves are usually fairly lazy creatures. When the world of Carry On needs to be summoned up in four paragraphs and a single image they tend to settle on that one of Sid and Barbara in *Carry On Abroad*. You know the one. They are Vic and Sadie holidaying on the Mediterranean island of Els Bels. In actual fact it's Sid and Barbara slumming it at Pinewood Studios. Barbara is caught in a frozen moment of panic and embarrassment as those most over-exposed and, frankly, underdeveloped breasts in British comedy history are clasped out of sight with her rigid fingers of iron. Sid, on the other hand, has the retrieved and detached bikini top in his grip. But he's not looking at the goods. Those oh so tantalisingly close objects of delight, very nearly on full display. Oh no. He, rather sheepish and otherworldly, is looking away into the eyes, off-camera, of his wife. He's been caught.

For me it captures that mixture of respect, naughtiness, fun, energy and sheer affectionate camaraderie that makes the two of them the perfect figureheads of Carry On. And that's how it should be.

14

Ever Decreasing Circles

For the last five years of his life Sid James happily trod water. He was under no illusion about his career. He had reached as far as he ever wanted to. He was a star on film, on the stage and on television. Three spheres that were dominated by three different pieces of work: the Carry Ons, *The Mating Season* and *Bless This House*.

He could happily coast through these hugely enjoyable, extremely lucrative bodies of work until he decided to call it a day. For, as throughout his long career, he worked for one simple thing. The money. If he could have a great time while he was earning it then so much the better.

His series of films had, beyond all expectations, became a national treasure. 'It is not beyond the bounds of possibility that the National Film Theatre will one day mount a season of Carry On films,' wrote Derek Malcolm in the *Radio Times* in 1974. 'The thought is no longer absurd. The Carry Ons are not exactly cinematic art. But they are exceedingly artful in their way, and have become both a phenomenon and an institution. They are, in fact, easily the most successful and longest running of all British film comedy series. Even the splendid and more memorable

Ealing comedies can't compete either in terms of longevity or box-office success. Yet critics have seldom given the Carry Ons more than a cursory nod. They are almost taken for granted, regarded in the trade as an eccentric law unto themselves – films which succeed with the public as sure as night follows day.'

Although Sid was occasionally vocal about their quality or lack thereof, he was delighted to be involved in such a sure-fire hit.

'Sid got paid five thousand pounds a film, and the rest of us got between three and four, which paid the mortgage, dear,' says Barbara Windsor. 'It was rather like being back at school. They never spent any money on locations, and if we were shooting in November, a mile from the studio in a muddy field they'd painted green because it was supposed to be summer, we'd have to schlep it to the studio and back on foot in the lunch hour. It was lovely though. We were all actors, not comics. If someone had a line that was good for you, they gave it to you.'

The debate that has raged for many a year with regards to the moral dilemma of the producer and director getting rich on the work of actors whose contracts did not include a residual for television screenings and other exploitation, was never an issue with Sid. Unlike Williams and Windsor, and others who have taken the series to task, Sid died in harness. Not for him years of television repeats and compilations and constant requests for funny anecdotes and home video and, now, DVD sales. All of which passed the actors by financially. Barbara Windsor maintains: 'If Sid were alive he wouldn't have stood for it. He would have got us some money. He loved money.' But it was never an issue with him. For the simple reason that at the time of his death the Carry Ons were still a going concern. He never once threatened to turn his back on the franchise. He may not have been in the film currently on release at the time of his death but he certainly hadn't put a return to the series out of his mind. Sid enjoyed the company of his fellow team members and enjoyed the sizeable wedge that each Carry On assignment brought. Unlike many, he never once complained about the poor payment. He was satisfied. He earned what he thought the films and his starring role in them deserved.

As Gerald Thomas commented, 'They weren't living in hovels!' During Sid's lifetime, it was a constant source of employment. How many other actors could sit back reasonably safe in the knowledge of work on one or two films a year – with a salary that could buy you a nice little house for each – was on the cards?

No, Sid was not embittered about his treatment. As Jim Dale says, 'I spread my wings and came over here to America but do I blame Sid for staying where he was? Certainly not. He had one heck of a career behind him. If he chose to spend five or ten weeks out of his professional year filming Carry Ons and laughing all day long, then why not. He was secure in those films.'

Director Roy Ward Baker is equally convinced. 'I'm sure from Sidney's point of view, the Carry Ons were just another acting job, much as the films we had made together in the late 1940s were just acting jobs. The Carry Ons really aren't my kind of thing. I've only ever seen a handful of them. All of them starring Sidney. However, it is far too easy to dismiss them as junk. They certainly aren't junk. Those performances of Sidney take a great deal of skill. Broad comedy, at that level, is very hard to maintain and he makes it look effortless. If anything, the hurry-scurry nature of the Carry Ons made it even more difficult for him. But his personality always shone through. And he was always professional.'

Although Sid's last professional association with them was in January 1975 when the last of his four appearances in the television *Carry On Laughing* episodes was broadcast, it was never Sid's intention to opt out of the series.

Talking to the *TV Times* on the set of the television series at Elstree Studios, Sid reflected that several members of the cast were concerned that this new venture would spell the end of the films.

'But,' he said, 'we hear we're doing yet another film some time in 1975 so we're carrying on just as before. Sometimes I think we'll carry on until we drop, but it will have been a giggle – for everybody.'

Writer Dave Freeman confirms that the role of Fred the Butcher in *Carry On Behind*, the film the team did indeed reunite for just before Sid's 62nd, and last, birthday, in April 1975, 'was written very much with Sid in mind. The only change I probably would have made was to call the character Sid instead of Fred. But the lines would have been much the same. It was Sid. The bird-chasing rogue. In the end Windsor Davies did a very fine job. That was the beauty of the Carry Ons. If people weren't available, then the role was recast. No fuss. No disrespect. Just necessary to keep the films rolling along. Sid was first choice, of course, but he wasn't even in the country.'

Indeed, Sid had left for Australia on 28 December 1974, immediately after completing work on the *Carry On Laughing* shows. The play was the same. *The Mating Season* had given him the perfect combination of domestic situation comedy and knowing, leering comedy. It was Carry On meets *Bless This House*.

He may have been missing the 27th film at Pinewood Studios but halfway around the world Sid was still waving the flag for the Carry Ons. These hugely popular, award-winning Australian dates were emblazoned with frantic publicity: 'Here is your chance to see Britain's favourite comedian carrying on in the funniest comedy for years!'

And it wasn't just in the Commonwealth. On a trip back home after the Australian leg of *The Mating Season* tour, Sid stopped off in Phnom Penh, Cambodia. He met a rich businessman who took him to dinner and then offered to take him to a cinema. A reluctant Sid agreed, only to discover that his new-found friend was the owner. And that his cinema ran nothing but Carry On films. Twenty-four hours a day!

'And it was packed,' said Sid. 'As for me, I was greeted like the second coming. Since doing the Carry Ons there is nowhere in the world I can go for a rest. All round me, everywhere, in a million different lingos, people are saying, 'Carry On, Carry On!' Whenever I arrive somewhere fresh I think, "Maybe here I won't be recognised?" You've got to be kidding!'

Sid returned home at the end of 1975 to start work on the sixth and final series of *Bless This House*.

Talking to the *TV Times* when the series was broadcast from January 1976, Sid was cheerful about the show: 'After six years and nearly seventy episodes, you'd think the cast might be a bit stale,' he pondered. 'But in fact we've matured together, and I think this latest series – it's also the last – is the best by miles.'

Dave Freeman, who penned three of the programmes that year, recalled, 'There certainly was talk in the air that we were going to call it a day after that batch. Sid wasn't that well during the recordings. He had had continued back trouble for several years. Painful but nothing serious. His heart seemed up to the job.'

Indeed, for Sid's last film, *Carry On Dick*, the insurance documentation indicated that Sid was back to full strength. Hattie Jacques's contract had a clause concerning her cardiovascular system and it was noted that 'there was a similar exclusion for some years for Sidney James'. But no longer.

'He was always laughing,' continued Freeman. 'He was a very happy man on that show. Maybe he felt he wanted to go out on a high.'

One of Freeman's scripts struck a particular chord with Sid: 'It was one about a second hand freezer that Sid acquires ['The Frozen Limit']. I was very proud when Sid told me it was his favourite show. Not just of the series. But of all of them. I was happy to gear up to write another twenty shows when I heard that! To please Sid with something that I had written was the nicest reward of all. He was always very grateful to the writer. Few comedians were that understanding.'

Sally Geeson said, 'There was a huge gap in my life when the series finished.' However, her screen mother, Diana Coupland, sensed that the series may not be coming to a close after all. 'Sid and I had discussed this and we had decided that as long as we were both alive the show would continue,' she said.

'I don't think Sid would have ever completely retired,' comments Jack Douglas. 'He loved this business too much. And he was clever. He had lots of things that interested him away from the business. That's essential. You have to keep life in perspective. I love this business but you need to be away from it at times. Sid had his family. His hobbies. He had been a fine athlete and sportsman in his day. That was very important to him. He loved to look good. He was always a snappy dresser. In his Cyril Castle suits. He loved fine food and wine. Sid was someone who wanted the best things in life. A bit like me really! And he loved the fame and the fortune that came with it. We saw a lot of each other. Away from the studios. Socially. He was always a dedicated man in everything he did.'

'If you look at the series *Bless This House*,' comments Harry Fowler, 'that was another facet of Sid's character. In a way it's the same Sid from Hancock and from the Ealing films but he became this perfect straight man. I always saw a lot of Ted Ray in his performance there. He retained that dignity and he kept that show together. It was a brilliant, straight performance in a comedy. The perfect straight man. He brings this self-contained temperament to the role. It's a joy to watch. But, of course, by that stage he had this bag of handy tools that he could bring out, adapt and use. He had this subtle quality that was marvellous. It's so subtle that often audiences now don't spot it. People tend to underestimate what a great actor he was. Even in his broadest work, he would bring out this bag of acting tools and use them. Without anybody noticing. And you can't get much broader than the Carry Ons he was doing at the same time. But still, there's a subtlety to what he's doing. *Carry On Dick* is a perfect example.'

Indeed, while the lusty Sid persona is at the forefront in *Carry On Dick* and, arguably, that glorious Sid laugh is overused for the only time, there is also a sincere, restrained performance at the heart of the film. The juggling act between comic icon and respected actor is perfectly meshed together. Again, as with the 1949 film *The Man in Black*, Sid is given two roles. Not two characters this time, but two aspects of the same character: the highwayman Dick Turpin, the light-hearted, mask-wearing rogue. And the gentle, reserved clergyman. His 25-year film career almost comes full circle in *Carry On Dick*. And it's played on Sid's own energetic terms.

Clearly, Sid's bag of tools was still in perfect working order and his popularity was at a peak as the viewing figures for *Bless This House* proved, week in and week out. Towards the end of February, Sid himself hinted that this might not be the last series after all. Perhaps the audience appreciation had made him change his mind from the decision a week or so earlier. Perhaps, one or two more series might be squeezed in before his ultimate decision to bow out gracefully. 'I want to retire at sixty-five, like every other sane person,' he said. 'Put my feet up, and take it easy. It will be the first time in my life that I've been able to. When it happens it will be for good. Completely. I'll spend my days fishing.'

Indeed, this life of Riley wasn't an idyllic dream. It wasn't just a tired man pondering as he planned for his twilight days. Retirement from the business was always at the back of his mind. He wasn't 'one of those actors who would rather act than eat'. Sid was an actor who acted in order that he and his family could eat well. But even in his younger days he would pine for 'rough physical work' like that he left behind in South Africa. He had a dream: 'I'd buy a few good boats, and set up in business as a professional fisherman. Deep sea only.'

Co-star, friend and fellow angling devotee, Bernard Cribbins attests: 'Sid always loved fishing. It was a shared passion of ours.

Before our cricket match in Brighton in the fifties, we had driven down to the coast to enjoy a bit of mid-morning fishing. We got the lugworms out and had a pleasant hour or so. We didn't catch anything. But after a short time Sid was really being pestered by kids. So we had to call it a day. They loved him. And he loved fishing. It was his way of relaxing.'

Sid's home in Iver Health was perfect for his idea. Situated right on the banks of the River Colne he mused: 'I can fish all day if I want.' And he felt he had earned it: 'I've been working for nearly sixty years,' he explained.

Sid's luxury item back when he had recorded *Desert Island Discs* had been a double bed. Sixteen years on he felt he had more than earned the chance to take a lot more luxury lie-ins. But he still had something of a mission to fulfil. 'What I want to do between now and my retirement is earn enough money so that my wife, Val, and my eighteen-year-old daughter, Suzie, will be taken care of in the best possible way – financially,' he explained.

And it would not be a wrench to walk away from the limelight: 'I'll be able to give up show business without any trouble,' he said in February 1976. 'It's not a drug. Not for me. It's just a job. And it's bloody hard work.'

Looking at those final episodes of *Bless This House* you see a man in control and cheerful. Yes, he looks a little older. Perhaps a little fatter. Slightly out of condition. Without doubt he was working hard. Working too hard. His career was diverse, tireless and packed to the rafters. But that was Sid. He doesn't look like a man close to death. But he was.

The collapse came on a gloomy Monday evening in Sunderland. It wasn't the grandest theatre Sid had ever played but the Sunderland Empire was as good a venue as any to once again plod out the familiar Sid for a less than full auditorium.

The play still was not the thing. But it was the same play, *The Mating Season*, and it was Sid that the eager fans had paid to see.

75 pence for the cheaper seats. A full two pounds for the best in the house.

Under the promotional banner of Sydney James Productions (Jersey) Limited, a shrewd business associate of Michael Sullivan, this was a committed tour of long standing. Perfectly timed to coincide with the television run of *Bless This House*, the gruelling tour schedule embarked from the Grand Theatre, Wolverhampton on 8 March 1976. Sid gave eight performances a week as the tour made its steady way around the country: Wimbledon, Birmingham, Richmond and Sunderland.

He had got himself match fit for the show with 'weekend workouts in the gym' but, by this time, Sid was a weaker man. Extremely sick during the recent recording for the *Bless This House* television series, a relentless traipsing round the fun palaces of the British Isles was just what the doctor didn't order. David Jackley, the manager of the touring company, considered Sid's role 'a most strenuous part which involves being onstage practically all the time'.

But Sid was determined to keep working and keep earning. He had a plan in mind. And to stop now wasn't it. He would give the public what they wanted until the very end and what they wanted was the jovial, chuckling Sid they had long taken to their hearts.

To die with the sound of laughter in his ears was a romantic, stark end for a man who had been hearing that same sound for 30 years. But it was not the end Sid would have wanted.

When Bing Crosby died while playing the 18th hole on a Spanish golf course the following year, one can imagine that that was the ending he would have chosen. Dying in a Sunderland theatre would not have been Sid's. The screen Sid would, no doubt, have favoured slipping away with a smile on his face while a jealous husband thumped on his bedroom door. The real Sid, with a complete lack of innuendo-induced sniggering, would have been happiest to pass quietly away with his rod in his hand.

It was not to be.

'I used to drive Sid every Monday to whichever town he was playing,' said Valerie. 'I'd set up his dressing room and organise his wardrobe. On the first night I'd check the lighting and sound and watch his performance because he was a perfectionist. He'd give notes to the cast.

'On that Monday night [26 April 1976] I was watching up in the dress circle. Audrey Jeans was playing opposite Sid and there was a scene where she had to use an aerosol spray, saying, "I can't bear the smell of cats," referring to the perfume of another woman. That night she used the spray and it went under Sid's nose. I saw that he couldn't breathe. Suddenly, he collapsed. The audience were laughing, because they thought it was part of the play.'

Even the cast thought Sid was playing a trick. 'At first I thought it was a gag,' said Olga Lowe. 'In retrospect, it was a wonderful way to go.'

The *Sun* newspaper reported the tragic news to the people who loved Sid the most. His audience. The actor, it reported, 'died last night after collapsing onstage in front of a first-night audience. Stagehands ran to help as the craggy-faced star fell back on a settee, gasping for breath. David Jackley, manager of the company touring with the farce *The Mating Season*, tried to revive him with the kiss of life. A doctor in the audience went to help as Sid was carried off-stage at the Sunderland Empire, Wearside. The 62-year old actor was rushed away in an ambulance. But he was dead when he reached the town's Royal Infirmary. Mr Jackley said, "Sid was about twenty minutes into the first act when it happened. It was completely unexpected. We had had our usual half-hour chat in his dressing room before the show and there was nothing wrong with him. We had a laugh and a joke before he went on." A theatre spokesman said, "The audience thought it was a gag. But when he did not get up they realised something was wrong."'

Mel James, the stage manager, saw it happen. 'Sid delivered a line and then went to sit in an armchair,' he told the *Daily Mail*, 'but as he did so, he suddenly collapsed and fell back into the chair.'

Valerie, the paper continued, 'rushed downstairs and everyone was running around the stage. Finally they managed to get the curtains down. Then someone [Mel James] called out: "Is there a doctor in the house?" But Sid was dead.'

Audience member, Dorothy Parker, told the *Daily Express*: 'Mr James was there when the curtain rose and he seemed all right.' One can almost sense Sid's smile of irony that it would take his death for someone to call him Mr James!

Mrs Parker was seated in the stalls. 'Some lines of dialogue were spoken and then he sat down and he started to hold his chest and was obviously in some difficulty breathing. Olga Lowe must have realised something was wrong. She ad-libbed for a few minutes and then she seemed to indicate to bring the curtain down.'

Another member of the audience thought it was part of the act when he collapsed: 'It wasn't until the curtain was run down that we realised something terrible had happened.'

'When Sid collapsed, actress Olga Lowe who was onstage with him said, "Sid's been taken ill," the *Daily Mirror* reported. 'A doctor in the audience went onstage to try to help the comedian. An ambulance took Sid to hospital but he was already dead.' The Empire's assistant house manager, Judith Simpson, remembered that Sid had the audience laughing at his performance until the very end.

There was certainly nothing to laugh about backstage as, unbeknown to the audience out front, Valerie tenderly held the hand of the man she loved. The ambulance men swiftly arranged Sid's transportation to hospital and, as the *Daily Mirror* revealed: 'They tried to revive him in the ambulance, and then they worked on him at the hospital. Half an hour later they came and said, "There's nothing more we can do. He's gone."'

Theatre boss, Len Harper, said, 'Sid was irreplaceable. The show business tradition is that the show must go on. But this is one show that will not.' The 400-strong audience that fateful Monday evening all received their money back. The rest of the week's run in Sunderland, and the rest of *The Mating Season* tour was cancelled as a mark of respect to Sid.

Sid's Christmas commitment to film *The Mating Season* for ITV was fulfilled by Bruce Forsyth. A planned hour-long variety special and the final, final (maybe) series of *Bless This House* that had been on the cards since the start of 1976 was shelved.

How could it not be?

For Diana Coupland, Sid was 'one of the finest actors of comedy. Nobody can replace him – he was a marvellous man. We have been together for six years in the series. He was a magnificent actor. He never complained of feeling ill.'

For *George and the Dragon* co-star, Keith Marsh, Sid's death was equally shocking and surprising: 'You can lose touch with people in this business. You have a great time while you're working together. Then everybody goes off to do something else. That was the case with Sid and I. But, I noticed he was playing in Birmingham. This was just a week or so before his death. I went backstage to see him and he was the same as always. He was his usual cheerful self. His sudden death just days later came as a great shock.'

Hattie Jacques remembered Sid as 'the most unselfish of actors. Never deliberately upstaging anyone. To my mind he was a better comedian than Hancock; for whom in *Hancock's Half Hour* he was straight man, fall guy or whatever. Within the confines of the series, Sid was by turns a bored, respectable householder; the (noticeably) South African voice of conscience; a mere man overwhelmed by things like vacuum cleaners and paint pots; a shocked reader of the hairier Sunday papers. He was infinitely versatile.'

Hattie Jacques told the *Evening News* that, 'he belied his brash image and all the things he looked like. In fact he was a very kind man – yes, and chivalrous. That old-fashioned word really applied to him. He cared for all his friends and they cared very much for him.'

Vera Day remembers that, 'when I heard that Sid had died, it was this beautiful spring day. And I felt so very, very sad. Because he was such a happy, wonderful, lovely man. I felt really sad that my little boy had never met him. Keegan was two years old at the time and my little boy would have loved him. Sid would have been the perfect sort of uncle figure. Throwing him up in the air, rolling around on the floor and playing with him. And I remember I was upset that that would never happen and that I wouldn't see my old mate again.'

Jim Dale also found it hard to take in the news. 'I vividly recall receiving a telephone call from the television programme *Nationwide* within hours of Sid dying. They urgently asked me if I would go on the show that evening and talk in tribute to him. I very politely refused. Many of his colleagues and friends gave the same answer to the TV companies. The reason? It was too soon, and too much of a shock to talk to millions of people about Sid in the past tense.'

For Sid's audience was in total bewilderment. The last episode of *Bless This House* had aired a mere four days before Sid's death. On the Thursday evening at 8pm, Sid was laughing, dancing, reminiscing and desperately trying to get himself out of the doghouse for the umpteenth time onscreen. On the Monday evening he was dead. Part of the nation's identity had gone.

'Sid James was a rare bird,' said writer and comedy guru, Frank Muir. 'He wasn't much of a comedian and he wasn't much of an actor. He was something much more. He always spoke directly to the audience and whatever he did gave a kind of deep feeling to the people watching him.'

Writing in the *TV Times*, on behalf of everybody involved with *Bless This House*, producer William G. Stewart said, 'Apart from expressing our personal loss, so many people have asked: "What was Sid like to work with?" It is six years since Philip Jones, Head of Light Entertainment at Thames television, took Sid and I to lunch and later launched *Bless This House*. In those six years Sid's own family and our "family" at Thames became one much larger family and the whole thing revolved around Sid. He had a quiet, totally professional approach to his work and recognised that everyone on the series, from the company executives to the stage crew, mattered. What we personally will miss were his sense of humour, his quiet kindnesses to us all, his generosity over other people's talents, the wonderful hospitality that he and his wife, Val, showed us at his lovely home and, especially, the thousands of occasions when work stopped and he just talked to us. We shall all have our personal memories of Sid. Two of mine will be arriving early at rehearsal to see him sitting in a corner with Betty Crowe and John Lynton, our stage managers, going through his lines – and the number of times I personally had a problem on the set and he would quietly come up and say: "Can I help?" His family know of our affection for Sid. Quite simply he was a very special person and we all loved him dearly.'

The funeral ceremony at the Golders Green Crematorium, held at the end of April, was attended by 200 mourners. His *Bless This House* family, Diana Coupland and Sally Geeson, joined his real family.

Bernard Bresslaw and Jack Douglas represented the Carry On team.

'I shall certainly miss him deeply,' said Bresslaw. 'I am very, very shocked and very upset. I have some of my fondest memories in the business of working with Sid. I first worked with him about eighteen or nineteen years ago [on *Too Many Crooks*]. He was a marvellous person to work with and a marvellous person to be with. His will be a big loss. I am one of many, many people who will miss him'

Jack Douglas explained: 'Many of the Carry On people are working in the provinces and could not be here. Others were just too upset to come.'

Liz Fraser was touring in a production of *One of the Family* with Stephen Lewis and familiar old co-star of Sid's, Irene Handl. 'I remember hearing the news of Sid's death and I said to Irene, "You really have to look after yourself." She was in her seventies and she was doing theatre. Films. Television. Writing books. Rushing here, there and everywhere. I said, "You have to take things easy. Look what has happened to Sid."

'Anyway, we are just about to go on. The night after Sid's death. I was the first onstage. Playing Irene's daughter. I take my first step on to stage and Irene whispers, "Oh Liz. Liz!" And she clutches her heart. I don't know what to do. I'm onstage. She's off in the wings. Stephen came on. I tried to catch his eye. Desperately trying to keep it together. Anyway, Irene makes her entrance. On cue. Word perfect. Nothing the matter with her! I like to think Sid had a laugh over that!'

Barbara Windsor, the person that everyone expected to be there except the immediate family and friends, was 'supposed to be rehearsing [the role of Maria in William Shakespeare's *Twelfth Night* at the Chichester Festival] but I just can't face it. I'm too upset. He was wonderful to work with. He *was* the Carry On films.'

Barbara may have protested a touch too much when she added, 'He was like a father to me, so good, so nice. He understood how shy I was. He knew I wasn't the kind of girl I portrayed on the screen. I can't believe I'll never see my darling Sid again.'

'The films will carry on without Sid,' continued Jack Douglas, 'but it will never be quite the same.'

Indeed, Jack was set to start filming a new one the following week. Louis Benjamin, who had faced the ups and downs of *Carry*

On London! at the Victoria Palace, speaking at the service, said that Sid's attitude would be to 'Carry on living! Sid provided the world with laughter and happiness.'

Producer Peter Rogers told the *Sun*: 'Sid became synonymous with the Carry Ons. It is a chip of the machinery gone. I have known him for twenty-five years as friend and professional – we shall all miss him very much. He was not going to be in the next Carry On simply because he wasn't available, but he was always planned for them when we could get him.'

'To lose any close friend is a dreadful feeling,' continued Rogers, 'but Sid was comparatively young and seemingly quite fit. He wasn't going to be in *Carry On England* because he was booked up with *The Mating Season* for much of the summer. People have accused me of being heartless and uncaring. But what could I do? *Carry On England* was budgeted, the studio was booked, the actors were ready to start work. I couldn't abandon the project and, in many ways, I don't think Sid would have wanted me to do that. But, as part of the Carry On team, he really was irreplaceable.'

Director Gerald Thomas said of Sid: 'He was a super person to get on with, he had great comedy timing, and he was a very generous actor. He always encouraged young people. He never upstaged anyone. We've lost a fine comedy talent, and I have lost a great friend.'

Terry Scott felt anger alongside the sadness: 'Sid was going to retire next year', he said. 'I am furious that he didn't ease up a long time ago. Sid shouldn't have gone on working so hard, but then he was probably a compulsive worker.'

Philip Jones, Controller of Light Entertainment at Thames Television, 'felt it a special loss but the wave of sympathy and affection from the public was quite unique and outstanding. I suppose it was the fact that Sid was "the nice bloke next door" to taxi drivers and bank managers alike that prompted so many letters, phone calls and messages of affection for a friend departed. There have been many tributes to his career in films, on the stage and on television and to all who knew him he was a true professional. And such was the warmth of his personality that there are few people who cannot instantly see in the mind's eye that expressive wrinkled face and hear that mischievous laugh. Alas, they remain now in image and recording only.'

For Harry Fowler, that recorded image is enough to keep Sid among the true comic originals: 'Those sort of people don't die,' he says. 'You know, Sid is in with the immortals like Tommy Cooper and Eric Morecambe and Max Miller. You know, the average person in the street dies and, apart from the close family, they are forgotten about. Not people like Sid. As long as there is videotape and film and machines to play them on he will live forever. Sid is always here.'

His widow, Valerie, who was naturally 'devastated and couldn't imagine living without him', took one grain of comfort. 'Sid died making people laugh. I suppose, for him, it was the perfect way to go,' she said.

Epilogue

SO HAUNT ME

Sid James was gone. But forgotten? Hardly. Film co-star Lance Percival believes: 'Sid's name is almost as alive today as it was in the 1950s, 60s and 70s. Everyone remembers the lived-in face and that chuckle.'

'There is a simple test,' Percival continues. 'Show a photo of Sid to some kids in the street and see how many of them know who it is. All of them will recognise him and over half will know his name.'

Indeed, over 30 years after that fateful day in Sunderland, Sid's swaggering screen image remains a potent influence on comedy and everyday living. His ultimate achievement was the creation of a timeless character. The ageless encapsulation of base, carnivalesque pleasures. As long as people drink and smoke, and bet and screw, and gorge and laugh, then Sid will be the benchmark besides which all good-time fellows are judged. He's the leader of the pack and King of the Hill. The ultimate lad. The cockney rebel.

Not that the Carry Ons could carry on for long without him. Despite the best-laid plans of Peter Rogers, Gerald Thomas and Jack Douglas, it was clear that the production of *Carry On England* was overshadowed by Sid's death. 'We got on and did the job,' remembers Jack, 'but Sid was in all of our thoughts. Particularly the old-timers like me.'

'Of course, we all miss him terribly,' commented another loyal, old-timer, Kenneth Connor, on the set of *Carry On Emmannuelle* in 1978. 'But that's another great thing about life – you come to accept these things. What happened to Sid, I mean the fact that he died, is something we all know is going to happen to us one day and, as they say, there is so much of it about that you have to become accustomed to it. But it was a shock to us all to lose him like that.'

Even Jim Dale, Carry On's great white hope from Broadway's *Great White Way* for the 1992 revival, was thinking about Sid: 'It was Cole Porter who, when informed of the death of George Gershwin, commented, "You can tell me he's dead but I don't have to believe it if I don't want to." That's exactly how I felt about Sid. It was strange. Being here in America I could reassure myself that all my friends from the Carry Ons were still Carrying On in England without me. It was a nice dream.

'Of course, I was rudely awakened when I agreed to take on the leading role in *Carry On Columbus*. With that film I was taking over the mantle of Sid. That's how I felt. And I wanted to give it my very best, if only in loving memory of all those wonderful films in which I had played second banana to Sid himself. In the old days there's no question Sid would have played Columbus and that's how I played it. Of course, when you turn up for the first day of filming at Pinewood and there's nobody left from the old gang but you it's quite a shock. It was my responsibility to keep the flag flying for Sid.'

And the clout of Sid refused to dim. The films and television shows he made, oh so many years ago, remain best sellers on DVD. Everything that survives from his pioneering radio work with Tony Hancock has been digitised and lapped up by old and new admirers. Television – on one channel or another - repeats one of his films on a weekly basis. Sid's likeness appeared on boxer shorts and T-shirts. On phonecards and mugs. On ashtrays and lighters. On toilet seats. And even, when the poster for *Carry On Dick* was skilfully utilised, on condoms!

Some were official. Some not. But it was Sid who became the face of laddish comedy. Through the years of political correctness on to the age of post-modern irony, Sid was the representative for good times had by all.

As Victor Lewis-Smith wrote in the *Evening Standard* when Channel 4's *Without Walls* documentary celebrated the star in 1993: 'In those happy, nonchalant sexist days, Sid was a national institution and, post-feminism, he is again being hailed as a comedic hero by a generation of New Lads.'

There were documentaries. Blue plaques on his home and places of work. National Film Theatre retrospectives. The National Theatre resurrection of infidelities. And university theses on the great and good of lowbrow British comedy. 'It's not quite as silly as it sounds,' critic Charles Spencer observed. 'The [Carry On] films provide a real insight into British popular culture and character, and in particular our peculiar, embarrassed attitude to sex, brilliantly identified by George Orwell in his essay on saucy seaside postcards, of which the Carry On films are a direct descendant.'

Even the National Theatre players were forced to admit that those corny old films and the corny old actors that enlivened them had something special and interesting to offer. Geoffrey Hutchings, cast as Sid, says: 'I can't say I was an admirer [of the Carry Ons]. I was at the Royal Shakespeare Company when they were coming out and I suppose I was too grand for them. But there was something about Sid that made him a bit of a hero. People say he wasn't a great actor or a great comedian. I'm not so sure. He played the persona he developed and did it very professionally. He perfected his craft.'

And his spirit, it seems, refused to leave the site of his final performance. Comic droll par excellence, Les Dawson, said he had had the most shocking experience of his life in the dressing room that Sid had used at the Sunderland Empire. Just months before his own death in 1993, Les refused to appear at the theatre.

Victor Spinetti remembers: 'The last time I came across Sid was after he had gone. I was playing the narrator in a tour of *The Rocky Horror Show*,' he explains. 'I wasn't feeling very well. As it turned out I had a very bad chest infection. I remember leaning against this radiator in the dressing room. I wasn't feeling very well at all and a guy came up to me and said, "Oh, this is the dressing room Sid James died in!" That was the Sunderland Empire. I was struck down. I only did one night of the show. Just like Sid only did one night of his show at the Empire. And the rest of the week I was in my hotel room, desperately ill. I'm convinced it was the curse of Sid and that dressing room. He didn't like it and I think he made sure I wouldn't like it either!'

And another good friend from the business, Bernard Cribbins, recalls 'many, many happy memories of the times me and Sid spent together. Strangely, the coda to all those happy times was years and years after Sid's death. I was doing a performance of *The Snowman*. I was all dressed up to go on. In my dickie bow and dress suit. The members of the orchestra were taking their places. At that moment the manager of the theatre came over to me and said, "Have you played the Sunderland Empire before?" "No," I said, "this is my first time." With that he pointed to where the harp was positioned. "You see that harp? That's the spot where Sid James died!" And I was on. As I walked to the podium I said a little prayer for Sid and started "Good evening, ladies and gentlemen . . . " But I know for a fact that Sid was certainly with me that evening.'

For many of us he still is. And that's more than enough. He is one of the boys. An ever-present joy giver. The personification of the true pro. And, yes, Sid, a star. 'Stars come and go,' he once said, 'good character actors stick around forever. I am just a jobber, nobody could ever think of me as a star. I just act myself. People can either take me or leave me.'

Millions still consider him a star. A hero. And a friend.

As Harry Fowler says: 'Every time I hear Ethel Merman singing "There's No Business Like Show Business", I see Sid sat in the front row.'

Appendix I

AN ACTOR'S LIFE FOR ME

From 1913
Performer on the South African vaudeville circuit.
Clown with Boswell's Touring Circus.

1929
Prince Charming in *Sleeping Beauty*.

1938
February: *Double Error*, Johannesburg Repertory Players.
Radio presentation of *Double Error* for the South African
Broadcasting Corporation.
They Walk Alone, Johannesburg Repertory Players.
The Corn is Green, Johannesburg Repertory Players.

1939
A children's programme for the South African
Broadcasting Corporation.

1940
Sid staged and appeared in the charity revue *Hoopla* at the
Jewish Guild Memorial Hall.
From 5 to 13 April: George in *Of Mice and Men*, the Library Theatre.
The Importance of Being Earnest, Johannesburg Repertory Players.

1941
From 21 March, staging and performing with the Defence Force Entertainment Unit group 'The Amuseliers'.

1945
From 12 to 27 October, Tomasino the fisherman in *A Bell For Adano*, Johannesburg Repertory Players, the Library theatre.
The Wind of Heaven, Gwen Ffrangcon-Davies Theatre Company, Rhodesia.
George Pepper in *The Red Peppers*, the Gwen Ffrangcon-Davies Theatre Company, Rhodesia.

1947
Eddie Clinton in *Black Memory*, Bushey Studios.
Dancing with Kay Kimber at the London Hippodrome.
From 14 April: Ralph Marshall's revue, *Get In*: 'A Pleasure Cruise of Laughter', Wood Green Empire.
Nationwide tour in Jack Hylton's revue, *Burlesque*.
Passer-by in *The October Man*, Denham Studios.
From 4 September to 9 October, Bill Stewart in six instalments of *The Fabulous Miss Dangerfield* for the BBC Light Programme, producer Cleland Finn, recorded 1 to 19 September.
8 December: 'Interlude at Augusta' an episode of *Paul Temple and the Sullivan Mystery* for BBC Radio. As Mr Constantine, producer Martyn C. Webster

1948
Shakey Morrison in *Kid Flanagan*, BBC Television, live performance 1 August. Second performance 5 August. Alexandra Palace. Producer Joel O'Brien.
Hildy Johnson in *The Front Page*, BBC Television, live performance 15 August. Second performance 19 August. Alexandra Palace. Producer Joel O'Brien.

No Orchids for Miss Blandish, Alliance-Tudor/Renown.
Night-Life Nixon in *Night Beat*, London Film Studios.
Rowton in *Once a Jolly Swagman*, Pinewood Studios.
Knucksie the punch-drunk barman in *The Small Back Room*,
London Films Studios.
Burlesque transferred to the West End venue, the Princes
Theatre.
Men Without Shadows, the Lyric Hammersmith.
Kiss Me Kate, the Coliseum.
They Walk Alone and *The Corn is Green* for the South African
Broadcasting Corporation.

1949

American film director in *Family Affairs*, BBC Television.
22 February: *Across the Line*, English section of the Overseas
Service.
Freddie Evans in *Paper Orchid*, Garnesh/Columbia.
Henry Clavering and Hodson in *The Man in Black*, Hammer
Films/Exclusive, Oakley Court.
Mundin in *Give Us This Day*, Plantagenet/General Film
Distributors.
High Button Shoes, opening at the Manchester Opera House,
touring and taking the London Hippodrome in May.
Touch and Go.

1950

11 February: *Family Affairs*. Alexandra Palace. Producer
Michael Mills.
6 April: interviewed on *Film Time*, Home Service, transmitted 4
May.
29 July: 'They Knew What They Wanted', part of the BBC
Light Programme series *Saturday Night Theatre*. Producer
Cleland Finn.

Joe Clarence in *Last Holiday*, Watergate/Associated British
Picture Corporation, Welwyn Studios.
Carlo the Italian club owner in *The Lady Craved Excitement*,
Hammer Films/Exclusive, Bray Studios.

1951
6 January: *Here's Television*, BBC Television. Lime Grove
Shepherd's Bush.
6 June, recorded 31 May: *Curtain Up – 1066 and All That*.
Producer Archie Campbell.
Kiss Me Kate, the Coliseum.
John C. Moody in *Talk of a Million*, Associated British.
Lou in *Lady Godiva Rides Again*, British Lion, Shepperton
Studios.
Lackery Wood in *The Lavender Hill Mob*, Ealing Studios.
Army Sergeant in *The Magic Box*, Associated British Picture
Corporation, Borehamwood.
Bookie in *The Galloping Major*, Group 3.
13 November: *For Art's Sake*, BBC Home Service. Producer
Vernon Harris.

1952
Sergeant Body in *I Believe in You*, Ealing Studios.
Danny Marks in *Emergency Call*, Butchers Films,
Nettlefold Studios.
Ned Hardy in *Gift Horse*, Molton/Independent Film
Distributors, Isleworth Studios.
Police sergeant in *Cosh Boy*, Independent Films, Riverside
Studios.
Sidney in *Miss Robin Hood*, Group 3, Associated British Films,
Southall Studios.
Eric Hace in *Time Gentlemen, Please!*, Group 3 Films,
Southall Studios.

Taxi driver in *Father's Doing Fine*, Marble Arch/Associated
British Pictures-Pathe, Elstree Studios.
Bernardo in *Venetian Bird*, Pinewood Studios.
The Tall Headlines, Grand National Films.
Barrow boy in *The Yellow Balloon*, Associated British-Pathe,
Elstree Studios.
22 October, recorded 21 October: *Curtain Up – The Troubled
Air*. Producer Cleland Finn.

1953

8 and 12 February: *The Passing Show 'Our Marie'*. Three small
parts in two performances. Producer Michael Mills.
Finnimore Hunt in *The Wedding of Lilli Marlene*, Monarch
Films, Southall Studios.
Gino Rossi in *Escape by Night*, Southall Studios.
Hawkins in *The Titfield Thunderbolt*, Ealing Studios.
Mr Adams in *The Square Ring*, Ealing Studios.
Mr Hobson in *Will Any Gentleman . . . ?*, Associated British,
Elstree Studios.
Syd Baden in *The Weak and the Wicked*, Associated British,
Elstree Studios.
Superintendant Williams in *Park Plaza 605*, Eros Films.
Sharkey in *The Flanagan Boy*, Hammer Films/Exclusive, Bray
Studios.
Hank Hamilton in *Is Your Honeymoon Really Necessary?*,
Advance, Adelphi.
25 February, recorded 23 January: *The Stars in Their Choices
'Golden Boy'*, the BBC Light Programme. Producer Donald
McWhinnie.
From 28 May, Nathan Detroit in a tour of London theatres in
Guys and Dolls.

1954

January, *Guys and Dolls* transfers to the Coliseum. A Columbia recording is released alongside a single of Sid singing 'Brush Up Your Shakespeare'.

1 February: *20th Century Theatre* 'Another Part of the Forest'. The BBC Home Service. Producer Peter Watts.

Harry in *The Rainbow Jacket*, Ealing Studios.

Beverley Forrest in *The House Across the Lake*, Hammer Films/Exclusive, Bray Studios.

Charlie Badger in *Seagulls Over Sorrento*.

Store Watchman in *The Crowded Day*, Advance, Adelphi.

Ed Weggermeyer in *Orders are Orders*, Group 3 Films, Beaconsfield Studios.

Honest Sid in *Aunt Clara*, British Lion.

The Foreman in *For Better, For Worse*, Associated British Films, Elstree Studios.

Benny in *The Belles of St Trinian's*, London Films, Shepperton Studios.

Parkinson in *Father Brown*, Facet Films, Riverside Studios.

From 2 November to 15 February 1955: Sidney Balmoral James in 16 episodes of *Hancock's Half Hour*, BBC Light Programme. Producer Dennis Main Wilson.

From 13 December, 'The Wreck' in Jack Hylton's *Wonderful Town*, Oxford. Then six weeks in Manchester. Then the Princes Theatre, London.

1955

Henry the airport trickster in *Out of the Clouds*, Ealing Studios.

Banky in *Joe Macbeth*, Columbia.

Man in *The Deep Blue Sea*, London Films.

Ice-Berg in *A Kid for Two Farthings*, London Films, Shepperton Studios.

Tony Lewis in *The Glass Cage*, Hammer Films/Exclusive, Bray Studios.

The nightclub manager in *A Yank in Ermine*, Monarch Films, Beaconsfield Studios.

Harry Mason in *It's a Great Day*, Grove Film Productions/Butchers, Shepperton Studios.

Arthur Pritchett in *John and Julie*, Group 3/British Lion, Beaconsfield Studios.

19 April to 5 July: *Hancock's Half Hour* series two, 12 episodes for the BBC Light Programme.

9 May: *Wonderful Town* opens in the West End at the Princes theatre.

September, *Sixpenny Corner*, ITV.

19 October to 29 February 1956: *Hancock's Half Hour* series three, 20 episodes for the BBC Light Programme.

1956

Black Jake in *Ramsbottom Rides Again*, Jack Hylton Film Productions/British Lion, Beaconsfield Studios.

Barney West in *The Extra Day*, British Lion, Shepperton Studios.

Frank Allen in *Wicked As They Come*, Columbia.

Boris in *The Iron Petticoat*, Remus Pictures, Pinewood Studios.

Flash Harry in *Dry Rot*, Remus/Independent Films, Shepperton Studios.

Harry the snakeman in *Trapeze*, Susan Productions.

21 April, recorded 11 April: *Saturday Night Theatre*, 'The Volunteer', the BBC Home Service. Producer Michael Bakewell.

10 May: *Double Cross*. Producer Ernest Maxin.

4 July to 29 August: Sid in *Finkel's Café*, seven episodes for the BBC Light Programme. Producer Pat Dixon.

6 July to 14 September: *Hancock's Half Hour* series one, six episodes for BBC Television.

14 October to 24 February 1957: *Hancock's Half Hour* series four, 20 episodes for the BBC Light Programme. Producer Duncan Wood.

8, 5, 22 and 29 December: Abbie in parts 2 to 6 of *The Crime of the Century*, Riverside Studios. Producer Andrew Caborn.

17 December: *The Adventures of Robin Hood*, 'Outlaw Money', Sapphire Films for ITC Granada Television, Twickenham Studios.

19 December: Chantey Jack in *The Buccaneers*, 'The Hand of the Hawk', Sapphire Films for ITC Granada Television, Twickenham Studios.

1957

Jimmy Hall in *Quatermass* 2, Hammer Films, Bray Studios.

Joe in *Interpol*, Warwick Films, Columbia.

Mr Hogg in *The Smallest Show on Earth*, British Lion, Shepperton Studios.

Luke in *The Shiralee*, Ealing Studios.

Dusty in *Hell Drivers*, Rank, Pinewood Studios.

Jimmy in *Campbell's Kingdom*, Rank, Pinewood Studios.

Johnson in *A King in New York*, Attica Film Company, Shepperton Studios.

Joe Ryan in *The Story of Esther Costello*, Romulus.

29 April to 10 June: *Hancock's Half Hour* series two, four episodes for BBC Television.

28 September: *These Are the Shows* with Tony Hancock, BBC Television. Producer Francis Essex.

30 September to 16 December: *Hancock's Half Hour* series three, 11 episodes for BBC Television.

18 November: Filmed introduction to *Hancock's Half Hour* series two, episode one. BBC Television repeat.

17 December: The Genie and Friar Tuck in *Pantomania* presents 'The Babes in the Wood', BBC Television. Producer Graeme Muir.

23 December: *Hancock's 43 Minutes – The East Cheam Repertory Company*, BBC Television.

1958

21 January to 3 June: *Hancock's Half Hour* series five, 20 episodes for the BBC Light Programme.

4 February to 11 March: *East End-West End*, ITV.

15 April: *Educated Evans*, Riverside Studios Hammersmith for BBC Television. Producer Eric Fawcett.

12 May: Interviewed about *Another Time, Another Place* for Picture Parade, BBC Television. Producer Alan Sleath.

3 August: *Welcome to London*, with Tony Hancock and Bill Kerr. The BBC Light Programme. Producer Tom Ronald.

6 September, recorded 31 August: *Holiday Playhouse*, the Playhouse theatre for the BBC Light Programme. Producer Alastair Scott-Johnston.

29 September: *William Tell 'Secret Death'*, Sapphire Films for ITC Granada Television, Twickenham Studios.

26 December to 27 March 1959: *Hancock's Half Hour* series four, 13 episodes for BBC Television.

Chief Petty Officer Thorpe in *The Silent Enemy*, Independent Films, Shepperton Studios.

Jake Klein in *Another Time, Another Place*, MGM Studios, Borehamwood.

Albert the cabin steward in *Next to No Time*, British Lion, Shepperton Studios.

Franklin in *The Man Inside*, Warwick Films, Columbia.

Porter at the YMCA in *I Was Monty's Double*, Associated British, Walton Studios.

Stagecoach drunk in *The Sheriff of Fractured Jaw*, 20th Century Fox, Pinewood Studios.

25 December: Christmas special of *Hancock's Half Hour* for the BBC Light Programme.

1959

4 to 25 January: four *Hancock's Half Hour* remakes for the Transcription Services.

21 February, recorded 17 February: *In Town Tonight*, BBC radio. Producer Charles Chilton.

7 March, recorded 5 March: *Saturday Night on the Light – Stump the Storyteller*. Producer John Bridges.

Sid in *Too Many Crooks*, Rank, Pinewood Studios.

Sid Gibson in *Make Mine a Million*, British Lion, Shepperton Studios.

Percy Baker in *The Thirty-Nine Steps*, Rank, Pinewood Studios.

Police Constable Edwards in *Upstairs and Downstairs*, Rank, Pinewood Studios.

25 September to 27 November: *Hancock's Half Hour* series five, 10 episodes for BBC Television.

29 September to 29 December: *Hancock's Half Hour* series six, 14 episodes for the BBC Light Programme.

18 October: *What's My Line*, BBC Television. Producer Ronald Marsh.

23 November: Introduction for *Tommy the Toreador* on *Picture Parade*, Riverside Studios, BBC Television. Producer Chris Doll.

24 December: *Merry with Medwin*, Associated-Rediffusion. Director Peter Croft.

Cadena in *Tommy the Toreador*, Associated British, Elstree Studios. An EP featuring 'Watch the Birdie' was released.

Fings Ain't Wot They Used To Be: LP record.

Bert in *Desert Mice*, Welbeck Films, National Studios Borehamwood.

Herbie the agent in *Idle on Parade*, Warwick Films, Columbia.

30 December 1959 to 17 February 1960: Tutor in *Educating Archie*, eight episodes for the BBC Light Programme. Producer Geoffrey Owen.

1960

13 February, recorded 6 February: *Peter Calls the Tune*, the Paris studio for BBC radio.

Sergeant Frank Wilkins in *Carry On, Constable*, Anglo Amalgamated, Pinewood Studios.

Look at Life 'Flea Circus'. Narrator.

4 March to 6 May: *Hancock's Half Hour* series six, 10 episodes for BBC Television.

4 April, recorded 24 March: Castaway 486 on *Desert Island Discs*.

9 July: *The Sidney James Show*, BBC Radio. Producer Tom Ronald.

23 July, recorded 13 July: Interview for *In Town Tonight*.

16 July: *Juke Box Jury*, BBC Television.

17 September: *The Billy Cotton Band Show*, BBC Television. Producer Bill Cotton Jnr.

Chief Petty Officer Mundy in *Watch Your Stern*, Anglo Amalgamated, Pinewood Studios.

Commercial for beef suet.

Sammy Gatt in *And the Same To You*, Monarch/Eros, Walton Studios.

Alphonse in *The Pure Hell of St Trinian's*, British Lion, Shepperton Studios.

This is Hancock, LP record.

Pieces of Hancock, LP record.

19 November: *Juke Box Jury*, BBC Television. Producer Stewart Morris.

24 November to 29 December: Sidney Balmoral James in *Citizen James* series one, six episodes for BBC Television. Producer Duncan Wood.

25 December: *Citizen James* sketch with Bill Kerr, Liz Fraser and Sydney Tafler for *Christmas Night with the Stars*. Riverside studios, for BBC Television. Producer Graeme Muir.

1961

11 February: *Juke Box Jury*, BBC Television. Producer Stewart Morris.

4 March, recorded 3 March. Interview for *In Town Tonight*.

9 March to 1 June: Sid in *It's a Deal*, for the BBC Light Programme. Producer Tom Ronald.

11 March: *The Sid James Show*, ATV.

8 July: *The Sid James Show*, ATV.

17 September: *The Billy Cotton Band Show*, BBC Television.

2 October to 25 December: *Citizen James* series two, 13 episodes for BBC Television.

10 October: Guest celebrity on *Play Your Hunch*, BBC Television. Producer Stewart Morris.

11 September and 11 November. *Juke Box Jury*, BBC Television. Producer Johnnie Stewart.

Sid Randall in *Double Bunk*, Bryanston/British Lion, Twickenham Studios.

'Double Bunk' and 'The Ooter Song' issued on Decca Records.

Café patron in *A Weekend with Lulu*, Hammer Films/Columbia, Bray Studios.

Richie Launder in *The Green Helmet*, MGM Studios, Borehamwood.

Honest Syd Butler in *What a Carve Up*, New World Pictures, Twickenham Studios.

Sid in *Raising the Wind*, Anglo Amalgamated, Pinewood Studios.

30 December: *Juke Box Jury*, BBC Television. Producer Harry Carlisle.

Harry in *What A Whopper*, Regal/Viscount, Pinewood Studios.

Presenter of *Laughter and Life* for Gilbert Gunn.

Bert Handy in *Carry On Regardless*, Anglo Amalgamated, Pinewood Studios.

1962

12 January: *Let's Imagine – A World Without*, BBC Television.

Features an extract from *Citizen James*.

Captain Wellington Crowther in *Carry On Cruising*, Anglo Amalgamated, Pinewood Studios.

14 April, recorded 7 April: *Juke Box Jury*, BBC Television. Producer Johnnie Stewart.

14 July: *Twist*, BBC Television. Producer Johnnie Stewart.

31 August to 23 November: *Citizen James* series three, 13 episodes for BBC Television.

19 November, recorded 18 November: *What's My Line*, BBC Television. Producer Richard Evans.

1, 8, 15 and 22 October: four editions of *What's My Line*, BBC Television.

The dance instructor in *We Joined the Navy*, Associated British, Elstree Studios.

Puss in Boots, the Coventry Theatre.

25 December, recorded 23 November: *Juke Box Jury* panel for *Christmas Night with the Stars* with Sydney Tafler. BBC Television. Script by John Chapman. Producer David Croft.

1963

15 March, recorded 10 February: Interview *Let's Imagine – Being Beautiful*, Lime Grove Studios for BBC Television.

16 March, recorded 9 March: *Juke Box Jury*, BBC Television. Producer Neville Wortman.

28 April, recorded 22 April: *The Cliff Richard Show*, BBC Television. Producer Neville Wortman.

10 July to 28 September: Sid Stone in *Taxi!* series one, 13 episodes for BBC Television: 'It's Lonely Up Front', 'Barricades in Bailey Street', 'Everybody's In – Goodnight', 'The Outing', 'The Villain', 'The Runaway', 'A Long Way to Go', 'The Accident', 'The Benefit of the Doubt', 'Who's Taking Who for a Ride?', 'Ten Years Hard', 'Can't You Drive a Little Faster?', 'Don't Do As I Do'. Producer Michael Mills.

25 September: Interview about *Carry On Cabby* for *Scotland at*

Six, BBC Radio. Producer John McGregor.

16 November: trailer for *Juke Box Jury*, Riverside studios for BBC
Television. Producer Tom Fry.

Charlie Hawkins in *Carry On Cabby*, Anglo Amalgamated,
Pinewood Studios.

1964

January: 'Wing Commander Hancock – Test Pilot' and 'The
Threatening Letters', Pye single.

15 March: *Star Story*. Reading of 'The Understudy' by W.W.
Jacobs for BBC Television. Producer Michael Geliot.

4 April to 27 June: *Taxi!* series two, 13 episodes for BBC
Television: 'Get Me to the Church', 'The Scousers', 'Two Little
Ducks', 'It's a Long Way Home', 'The Price of Smoked
Salmon', 'Sunday Mornings are for Sleeping', 'Three Bags Full
Sir', 'Christmas in May', 'Will You Marry Face?', 'We've Got to
Live in the Winter', 'Two-Five-Two', 'It's a Mug's Game'.

Beauty contest judge in *The Beauty Jungle*, Rank, Pinewood Studios.
Cinema advertisement for frankfurters.

'Birdy' the blind man in *Tokoloshe, the Evil Spirit*, Lonehill Studios.

Mark Antony in *Carry On Cleo*, Anglo Amalgamated, Pinewood
Studios.

11 April, recorded 4 April: *Juke Box Jury*, BBC Television.
Producer Neville Wortman.

A *Tribute to Tony Hancock*, Pye World Record Club.

24 October, recorded 17 October: *Juke Box Jury*, BBC
Television. Producer Neville Wortman.

November: *It's Hancock*, Decca Records.

Robber in *Babes in the Wood*, the Granada, East Ham.

1965

From 4 May: Edward L. McKeever in *The Solid Gold Cadillac*,
Saville Theatre.

Sid Marks in *Three Hats for Lisa*, Seven Hills/Anglo

Amalgamated, Pinewood Studios.

8 May: Interview for *Late Night Saturday*, the BBC Light
Programme.

30 May: Interviewed about *Three Hats for Lisa* on *Movie-Go-Round*, BBC Radio.

26 June, recorded 20 June: *Light Up the Night*, Camden
Theatre for the BBC Light Programme. Producer John Browell.

9 July: Interview for *Late Night Extra*, BBC Radio.

George Brain in *The Big Job*, Anglo Amalgamated/Warner-Pathe, Pinewood Studios.

Johnny Finger, the Rumpo Kid in *Carry On Cowboy*, Anglo
Amalgamated, Pinewood Studios.

28 November: Guest on 'The New London Palladium Show',
patter and song and dance routine with host Jimmy Tarbuck.

Robber in *Babes in the Wood*, London Palladium.

25 December, recorded 21 November: Sid in *Sid and Dora*, the
BBC Light Programme. Producer John Browell.

1966

27 March, interviewed about *Carry On Cowboy* on *Movie-Go-Round*, BBC Radio.

9 April: *Armchair Theatre*: 'Don't Utter a Note', ABC Television.
The Mortician in *Where the Bullets Fly*, Golden Era Films.

From 28 May: Sidney Jones in *Wedding Fever*, the Pier Theatre,
Bournemouth.

Sir Rodney Ffing, the Black Fingernail in *Don't Lose Your Head*,
Rank, Pinewood Studios.

19 November to 24 December: George Russell in *George and the
Dragon* series one, six episodes for ATV Producer Alan Tarrant.
Robinson Crusoe, the Golders Green Hippodrome.

1967

26 March: Interviewed about *Don't Lose Your Head* on *Movie-Go-Round*, BBC Radio.

3 April, recorded 20 March: *The Dick Emery Show*, BBC
Television. Producer Ernest Maxim.

20 May to 1 July: *George and the Dragon* series two, seven
episodes for ATV.

8 October, recorded 5 October: *The David Jacobs Show*, BBC
Radio 1 and 2.

Charlie Roper in *Carry On Doctor*, Rank, Pinewood Studios.

1968

6 January to 17 February: *George and the Dragon* series three,
seven episodes for ATV Producer Jack Williams.

From 18 June: *Wedding Fever*, the Torquay Pavilion.

Sir Sidney Ruff-Diamond in *Carry On . . . Up the Khyber*, Rank,
Pinewood Studios.

1 September: Interviewed on location about *Carry On . . . Up
the Khyber* on *Movie-Go-Round*, BBC Radio.

26 September to 31 October: *George and the Dragon* series four,
six episodes for ATV.

18 December: *The Mike and Bernie Winters Show*, Thames
Television.

1969

12 January: Interviewed about *Carry On . . . Up the Khyber* and
Carry On Camping on *Movie-Go-Round*, BBC Radio.

20 January, recorded 10 December 1968: *Commentary for
Private Lives*: 'The Starling', BBC Television. Producer Jeffrey
Boswell.

18 February to 1 April: Sid Turner in *Two in Clover* series one,
seven episodes for Thames Television. Producer Alan Tarrant.

Sid Boggle in *Carry On Camping*, Rank, Pinewood Studios.

18 June and 25 June: *The Bruce Forsyth Show*, Thames
Television. Producer Gordon Reece.

Sid Jones in *His Favourite Family*, the Windmill Theatre, Great

Yarmouth, then the Grand Theatre, Blackpool.

Stop Exchange, in South Africa.

Gladstone Screwer in *Carry On Again, Doctor*, Rank, Pinewood Studios.

5 November: Interviewed about *Carry On Up the Jungle* on *Line Up – Film Night*, BBC Television. Producer Barry Brown.

24 December: Ebenezer Scrooge in *Carry On Christmas*, Thames Television. Producer Peter Eton.

25 December: *Two in Clover* sketch for *All-Star Comedy Carnival*, ITV.

1970

10 February to 17 March: *Two in Clover* series two, six episodes for Thames Television.

Bill Boosey in *Carry On Up the Jungle*, Rank, Pinewood Studios.

17 May: *The Roy Castle Show*, BBC1.

Sixteen week tour in *Wedding Fever* started in Great Yarmouth, transferring to South Africa and playing Cape Town and then the Johannesburg Civic Centre, from 23 September to 3 October.

Sidney Bliss in *Carry On Loving*, Rank, Pinewood Studios.

24 December: Long Dick Silver in *Carry On Again Christmas*, Thames Television. Producer Peter Eton.

1971

3 January: *The Val Doonican Show*, BBC Radio 2. Producer John Browell.

King Henry VIII in *Carry On Henry*, Rank, Pinewood Studios.

2 February: Interview on *What Happened to Hancock?*, BBC Radio 4. Producer Michell Raper.

2 February to 21 April: Sidney Abbott in *Bless This House* series one, 12 episodes for Thames Television: 'The Generation Gap', 'Mum's the Word', 'Father's Day', 'Be It Ever So Humble',

'Another Fine Mess', 'For Whom the Bell Tolls', 'A Woman's Place', 'The Day of Rest', 'Make Love . . . Not War!', 'Charity Begins at Home', 'If the Dog Collar Fits . . . Wear It!', 'The Morning After the Night Before'. Thames Television. Producer William G. Stewart.

4 February: Interview about *Bless This House* for *Late Night Extra Live*, BBC Radio 1 and 2.

20 February: *Cilla*, BBC 1.

19 May: *Jokers Wild*, Yorkshire Television.

From 4 June to 4 September, *Wedding Fever*, Pavilion Theatre, Torquay.

9 June: *Jokers Wild*, Yorkshire Television.

The Golden Shot, London Weekend Television.

The Mating Season, summer season in Torquay.

24 October, recorded 20 October: Interview about *Carry On Matron* for *Down Your Way*, BBC Radio. Producer Phyllis Robinson.

13 November: *Cilla*, BBC 1.

24 December: Sid Jones in *All This – And Christmas Too!*, Yorkshire Television. Producer Bill Hitchcock.

Sid Plummer in *Carry On At Your Convenience*, Rank, Pinewood Studios.

1972

21 February to 15 May, *Bless This House* series two, 12 episodes for Thames Television: 'Two Heads Are Better Than One', 'Love Me Love My Tree', 'It's All in the Mind', 'Another Lost Weekend', 'Parents Should Be Seen and Not Heard', 'Strangers in the Night', 'Get Me to the Match On Time', 'Wives and Lovers', 'Never Again On Sunday', 'People in Glass Houses', 'A Rolls By Any Other Name', 'A Touch of the Unknown'.

Sid Carter in *Carry On Matron*, Rank, Pinewood Studios.

From 3 September: Sidney Gillespie in *The Mating Season* at

Melbourne's Comedy theatre and subsequent Australian tour.
16 October: *Show of the Week*, 'Sacha's in Town', BBC 2.
Vic Flange in *Carry On Abroad*, Rank, Pinewood Studios.
Bless This House, Rank, Pinewood Studios.
13 December: *The Val Doonican Half Hour*, BBC Radio.
The BBC Presents Fifty Years of Radio Comedy, features
Hancock's Half Hour extract, BBC Records.
The Storyteller and Chamberlain Victor in *David Frost Presents
Sleeping Beauty*, Starline/EMI Records.

1973
22 January to 28 May: *Bless This House* series three, 12 episodes
for Thames Television: 'It Comes to Us All in the End', 'Tea for
Tea and Four for Tea', 'To Tell or Not to Tell', 'Blood is Thicker
Than Water', 'One Good Turn Deserves Another', 'The
Loneliness of the Short Distance Walker', 'Watch the Birdie',
''Will the Real Sid Abbott Please Stand Up', 'Atishoo! Atishoo!
We All Fall Down', 'Entente Not So Cordial', ''I'm Not Jealous,
I'll Kill Him', 'A Girl's Worst Friend is her Father'.
Sidney Fiddler in *Carry On Girls*, Rank, Pinewood Studios.
May: *The Mating Season*, New Zealand tour.
Carry On Sid, Network Seven, Australia.
The Sid James Show, Network Seven, Australia.
Australian television cigar commercial.
Carry On London! preview at the Birmingham Hippodrome.
From 4 October: *Carry On London!* at the Victoria Palace.
'Our House' and 'She's Gone', Pye Records.
4 October: *What A Carry On!*, ATV Producer Alan Tarrant.
Interview on *Open House*, BBC Radio.
Unique Hancock, BBC Records.
24 December: *Carry On Christmas*, Thames Television.
Producer Gerald Thomas.

1974

20 February to 10 April: *Bless This House* series four, six episodes for Thames Television: 'Money is the Root of . . . ', 'And They Will Come Home . . . ', 'Who's Minding the Baby?', 'A Beef in his Bonnet', 'The Bells are Ringing', 'The First 25 Years are the Worst'.
Dick Turpin in *Carry On Dick*, Rank, Pinewood Studios.
The Golden Hour of Tony Hancock, Golden Hour records.
Comedy. Four-record collection included a reissue of *The Golden Hour of Tony Hancock*.
14 October to 16 December: *Bless This House* series five, 10 episodes for Thames Television: 'They Don't Write Songs Like That Any More', 'The Gipsy's Warning', 'The Biggest Woodworm in the World', 'Home Tweet Home', 'You're Never Too Old To Be Young', 'The Policeman, the Paint and the Pirates', 'Happy Birthday, Sid', 'Freedom Is', 'Mr Chairman . . . ', ' . . . And Afterwards At . . . '.
From 28 December: *The Mating Season*, Australian tour.

1975

4 to 25 January, *Carry On Laughing* series one, four episodes for ATV. Prince Rupert and Arnold Basket in 'The Prisoner of Spenda', Baron Hubert Fitz-Bovine de Outlook in 'The Baron Outlook', Lovelace in 'The Sobbing Cavalier', Sir Francis Drake in 'Orgy and Bess'. Producer Gerald Thomas.
From 20 June: *The Mating Season* at the Winter Gardens, Blackpool.
The World of British Comedy, includes *Hancock's Half Hour* extract, Decca Records.
The World of Tony Hancock, Decca Records.
From 30 September: *The Mating Season*, Melbourne's Comedy Theatre.
Interview on 3XY Melbourne radio.

1976

29 January to 22 April, *Bless This House* series six, 13 episodes for Thames Television: 'The Frozen Limit', 'Beautiful Dreamer', 'Fish with Everything', 'The Naked Paperhanger', 'Remember Me?', 'Something of Value', 'Men of Consequence', 'Skin Deep', 'Friends & Neighbours', 'Well, Well, Well . . . ', 'The Phantom Pools Winner', 'A Matter of Principle', 'Some Enchanted Evening'.

Television commercial for the Milk Marketing Board.

8 March to 26 April: *The Mating Season*, United Kingdom tour. Cardiff New Theatre. Grand Theatre, Wolverhampton. Wimbledon Theatre. Richmond Theatre. Sunderland Empire.

Appendix II

HOME JAMES!

1946: 3 Queen's Gate Mews.
1947: I Canning Place.
1947: Allan House, Kensington.
1952: Roland House, Roland Gardens, off Brompton Road.
1954: 21 Lymington Road, Hampstead.
1956-1963: 35 Gunnersbury Avenue, Ealing.
March 1961: 42 Malvern Court, Knightsbridge.
April 1961: 31 Compayne Gardens, Hampstead.
1964-1976: 'Delavel Park', Iver Lane, Iver, Buckinghamshire.
1966: Dolphin Square, off Vauxhall Bridge Road.
1974: Flat in the South of France.

Appendix III

OFF THE WALL

2 October 1992: Sir Harry Secombe unveils a British Comedy Society blue plaque on Gunnersbury Avenue, W5; stolen in 1998 and replaced.

11 May 1997: William G. Stewart unveils a Comic Heritage blue plaque at Teddington Studios.

26 April 1998: Jack Douglas unveils a British Comedy Society blue plaque in the Hall of Fame, Pinewood Studios.

8 September 2002: Valerie James unveils a Comic Heritage blue plaque on the ground floor of Broadcasting House; subsequently moved to the BBC Radio Theatre, W1.

Bibliography

PAGING YOU

All of Me: My Extraordinary Life, Barbara Windsor (Headline, 2000)

Barbara: The Laughter and Tears of a Cockney Sparrow, Barbara Windsor (Random Century, 1990)

The Confessions of Robin Askwith, Robin Askwith (Ebury Press, 1999)

High Spirits, Joan Sims (Partridge, 2000)

Just Williams: An Autobiography, Kenneth Williams (JM Dent, 1985)

Oh, Yus, It's Arthur Mullard: His Own Moving, Funny Life Story, Arthur Mullard (Everest Books, 1977)

There's No People Like Show People: Confessions of a Showbiz Agent, Michael Sullivan (Quadrant Books, 1984)

Index